Your

KITCHEN GARDEN

Andrew Bicknell

Your

KITCHEN GARDEN

Andrew Bicknell

Illustrations by
Will Giles & Sandra Pond

First published 1990

This edition published in 1995 by
Tiger Books International PLC, Twickenham
ISBN 1-85501-691-5

10 9 8 7 6 5 4 3 2 1

Filmset in Britain by SX Composing, Essex

Originated in Hong Kong by Regent Publishing Services

Printed in Italy by G. Canale and C. SpA, Turin

A CIP catalogue record for this book is available from the British Library

Andrew Bicknell is one of the most professional and, at forty, one of the youngest gardening writers in Britain. He is the author of *Dr Greenfingers' Guide to Healthy Houseplants* (1980) and *The Houseplant Troubleshooter* (1986), and, with George Seddon, of *The Essential Guide to Perfect Houseplants* (1984), *The Complete Guide to Conservatory Gardening* (1986), and *Plants Plus* (1987).

CONTENTS

	Page
Introduction	7
Salad Plants	18
Sprouting Seeds	30
Brassicas	34
Spinach and Other Leaves	42
Stalks and Shoots	46
Pods and Seeds	58
Tubers	70
Root Crops	74
Onions	90
Vegetable Fruits	94
Oriental Vegetables	106
Herbs	118
Soft Fruit	134
Top Fruit	146
Nuts	166
Index	168
Acknowledgements	176

INTRODUCTION

*T*he modern kitchen garden need no longer be just a source of fruit and vegetables for the inhabitants of the adjoining house. It has the potential, increasingly, to be an interesting place in its own right; one where the gardener can gain a lasting sense of pleasure and achievement through experimenting with new and improved varieties.

Recent years of research and experimentation by plant breeders have been primarily for the benefit of commercial growers; but there have been useful spin-offs for the home grower, too. Home-grown fruit and vegetables have always tasted freshest, but the latest developments mean that the gardener can now choose better-flavoured varieties, which may be larger or smaller, depending on which is most desirable. You can now choose to grow tiny sweet-flavoured tomatoes, for example, for eating in salads or spiking on a kebab; or extra-large potatoes, specifically bred for their soft texture and good flavour when baked in their jackets.

Perhaps even more important, today's fruit and vegetables are far more pest- and disease-resistant. This takes much of the element of chance out of kitchen gardening and means that the crops are more reliable than they used to be.

Few of us nowadays have gardens spacious enough to devote large areas to the growing of fruit and vegetables. Today's families have different needs and if we are lucky enough to have a good-sized garden, the chances are that it will need to accommodate not only lawns, shrubs and flower beds, but also a climbing frame or a swing. Fortunately, this need not be a deterrent. New varieties of fruit and vegetables are often bred specifically for their space-saving qualities and new techniques that involve growing plants much closer together can now provide substantial crops in quite limited areas.

In fact, even the tiniest of gardens can now boast its own home-grown crops since many vegetables and fruits can now be grown in containers, giving the gardener a great deal of satisfaction for remarkably little work.

Another exciting recent development for the kitchen gardener is the introduction of new varieties of Chinese vegetables. Whilst it is always a pleasure to experiment with different varieties of familiar crops, it is even more interesting to try growing something completely different – and these vegetables introduce new and subtle Eastern flavours into our Western cuisine.

Whether you are an experienced gardener or a complete novice, there is no doubt that there has never been a better time to try your hand at kitchen gardening. The new kitchen garden is easier, more convenient, more reliable and offers even greater rewards than the garden of the past. But the greatest reward of all has existed since kitchen gardening began: the enjoyment of tasting your own delicious home-grown fruit and vegetables – and sharing that taste with family and friends.

SEASONAL CONVERSION TABLE

Throughout the book the months have been converted to seasons that are applicable to both Northern and Southern hemispheres.

Northern hemisphere			Southern hemisphere
March	*early*	**Spring**	August
April		**Spring**	September
May	*late*	**Spring**	October
June	*early*	**Summer**	November
July		**Summer**	December
August	*late*	**Summer**	January
September	*early*	**Autumn**	February
October		**Autumn**	March
November	*late*	**Autumn**	April
December	*early*	**Winter**	May
January		**Winter**	June
February	*late*	**Winter**	July

SOILS

How well your fruit and vegetables grow depends in the first place on whether they are at home in the soil in your garden. Many plants are fortunately not too fussy about the soils in which they are planted and will flourish regardless; but others have distinct preferences. It is obviously not practicable for gardeners to change the basic composition of one type of soil into another – clay into sandy soil, for example – but they can modify it, to grow a wider range of plants. The starting point is to consider what type of soil you have and what can be done to improve it, if necessary.

The five main types of soil are sand, clay, loam, chalk/limestone and peat. Each has its virtues, but some create more problems for gardeners than others.

Identifying soil types

Knowing that there are different types of soil is all well and good. What every gardener wants to know is the type of soil to be found in his or her own garden. This can be found out in two stages – first by looking at it and then by feeling it.

Testing for soil acidity and alkalinity

If you want to grow vegetables and fruit that don't like lime or prefer slightly acid conditions, it is essential to know beforehand that the soil is not alkaline – containing calcium in the form of chalk or lime. The calcium content of soil is measured on a pH scale (short for 'potential of hydrogen' scale). The practical application is simple.

The scale runs from 0 to 14. A reading of 7 given by the soil-testing kit indicates that the soil is neutral, neither acid nor alkaline. Between 7 and 14, soil is acid in varying degree but readings above 8 are not usual. Between 7 and 0, soil is alkaline in varying degree, but readings below 4 are unusual.

A soil-testing kit consists of a test-tube, a chemical reagent and a colour chart. Some dry soil is added to the reagent in the test-tube, shaken well and the colour to which the solution changes is matched against the same colour on the chart. The different coloured shadings correspond to levels on the pH scale. If the soil is excessively alkaline, it can be made less so by digging in large amounts of manure, compost or peat. To counteract acid soil add lime, but don't overdo it.

SAND

Look
If soil has a high sand content, water drains away very quickly. Removing a spadeful of this soil a short time after a shower will reveal a barely dampened soil that will soon dry out completely.

Feel
If a handful of sandy soil is squeezed, it will crumble into small particles and run through the fingers.

Sand soil
More than three-quarters of this soil are sand particles, and fairly large ones. This makes it very free-draining, and liable to dry out quickly – especially in warm weather – and the vital nutrients in the soil (such as calcium, nitrogen, phosphorus and potassium) are soon washed out of it. The plus side is that sandy soil is easily worked and warms up early in spring, giving vegetables in particular a head start.

The most effective way of preventing this soil from drying out too quickly is to dig in plenty of animal manure in autumn or winter. Micro-organisms in the soil break down this raw manure into moisture-holding humus, which is usually lacking in sandy soil. If manure is not available, use well-matured garden compost. Failing that, dig in peat.

CLAY

Look
Half an hour after a heavy shower of rain look at the state of the ground. If the water has not drained away from the surface but lies in puddles it indicates a clay soil. The longer the puddles remain the higher the clay content. Conversely when there is a drought, the soil dries out solid and is totally unworkable.

Feel
A handful of clay soil, if tightly squeezed, will hold together.

Clay soil
More than three-quarters of this soil are clay and silt particles. These are minute, much smaller than the particles of sandy soil, so instead of being free-draining clay soil holds water, and nutrients are not so easily washed away. But wet soil is cold soil, taking a relatively long time to warm up in spring and preventing early sowing or planting. Also, when clay soil is wet, it is sticky and hard to work. In very dry weather it can be equally unworkable, setting hard, like concrete.

To make it a little more free-draining, as well as more fertile and easier to work, dig in manure, if available, or compost and peat, to build up humus, which loosens the texture. Liming also produces a more crumbly soil, as well as reducing levels of acidity, often high in such soils.

Scatter calcium carbonate or calcium hydroxide on the surface of the soil in autumn. Use 5½oz per sq yd/165g per sq m, to increase the pH level by about 0.5 on sandy soils, double that quantity on loam soils, and triple on clay soils.

Don't manure or fertilize the soil for two months before liming or for two months after. Increase the level of liming slowly, testing regularly, until the required pH reading is reached. It is better to be over-cautious than to over-lime and then have to take action to reverse what has been done.

Minerals in the soil

Soil contains minerals that are essential for the healthy growth of vegetables and fruit. The amounts vary, but deficiencies of one mineral or another are spotted fairly easily. The most important of these minerals are nitrogen, phosphorus, and potassium.

Nitrogen contributes to the growth of leaves and stems. If growth is stunted and leaves turn yellow, a deficiency is indicated.

CHALK/LIMESTONE

Look

Chalk/limestone soil usually drains well after rain, but remains moist for hours afterwards. There may also be white or grey deposits on the soil surface, especially in dry weather. This indicates a soil with a very high chalk/limestone content – the degree can be checked with a soil-testing kit that indicates the level of alkalinity and acidity in the soil, as explained later.

Chalk/limestone soil

The problem with soil in chalk and limestone areas is that it is too alkaline for a number of vegetables. This is because calcium carbonate, which is responsible for the alkalinity, reacts with some minerals in the soil, depriving the plants of nutrients essential for their good health. On the plus side, chalky soil drains well and is easy to work. While some vegetables prefer a chalk or limestone soil, it can be too alkaline.

To counteract excessive alkalinity, add generous amounts of manure, compost or peat. Some plants are lime haters, blueberries among them. Others, such as currants, gooseberries and raspberries prefer a slightly acid soil. To meet their needs, dig holes 18-24 in sq/45-60 cm sq and 18in/45cm deep where they are to be planted and fill them with well-rotted manure, compost and peat and only a little of the original soil.

PEAT

Look

Very few gardeners would find themselves with a peat bog for a garden, but it would be instantly recognizable – waterlogged and spongy. Raw peat can in time be broken down into a rich soil that is light, crumbly, moisture-retentive and easily worked.

Peat soil

Only an eccentric would try to cultivate a garden on a peat moor or in a peat bog. Although these are potentially fertile because they are made up largely of organic matter, making the fertility usable would be a daunting task. But soils that over a long time have been created in peaty areas are a different matter. In this case, the raw peat, which once had few available nutrients, has been broken down into a humus-rich soil, easy to work and able to hold moisture.

Though good soil for lime-hating plants, some peaty soils may be too acid for many vegetables. The solution is to lime to achieve a balance – neither too acid nor too alkaline.

LOAM

Look

On loam soil water drains away quite quickly, but because there is a balance of humus, sand and clay it will hold moisture. Remove a spadeful of soil and it will be damp, not sodden, and remain so for a day or two.

Feel

A handful of loam soil, if tightly squeezed, will crumble into large pieces when released.

Loam soil

There are seldom problems with this soil. It is a mixture of humus, sand and clay particles (sand predominating). The sand gives efficient drainage while the clay holds the nutrients in the soil. It warms up quite quickly in the spring and is easy to work. Loam is the gardener's ideal soil.

Phosphorus is essential for strong root growth and the development of a plant's seeds and fruits. If phosphorus is lacking, growth will be stunted and fruiting and seeding will be poor.

Potassium helps in the overall growth of plants, particularly in the process of photosynthesis, the conversion of absorbed sunlight into food. Potassium also builds up a plant's resistance against disease. Lack of potassium will show in scorched leaf edges, mottled and curled leaves.

Soil-testing kits are available for measuring the level in the soil of these important minerals.

Other trace elements in the soil, but in much smaller quantities, include magnesium, sulphur, iron, copper and zinc, all helping to keep plant growth sturdy and healthy.

Fertilizing the soil

What you get out of the soil in terms of healthy vegetables and fruit depends to a large degree on what you put into it. That means fertilizing the soil in some way. There are many artificial or inorganic fertilizers that add minerals to the soil and produce abundant growth over the short term. A long-term approach is necessary in order to build up the fertility of the soil in a natural way for years to come. And that leads you into organic gardening, not something to be taken lightly.

The committed organic gardener will not use any artificial fertilizers or chemicals. Instead, he will build up richness in the soil by adding compost or well-rotted manure, regularly and in large quantities,

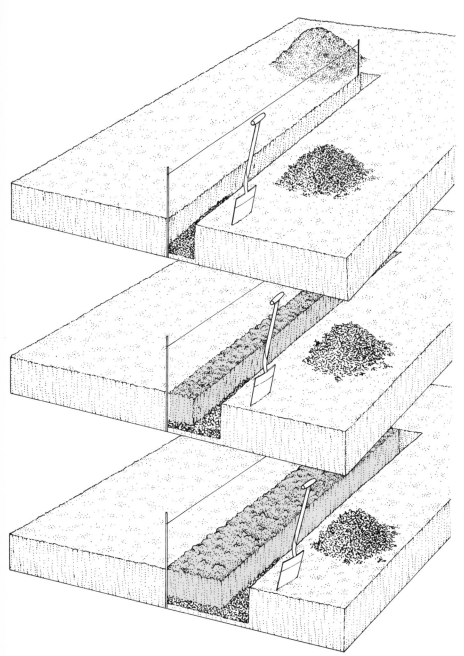

Dig in autumn. Divide the area to be dug down the middle along its length with string attached to stakes at each end.

Dig along the length of the plot to a spade's depth, removing the soil from that trench to the head of the adjacent undug side of the plot.

Work manure or compost into the bottom of the trench.

Working backwards along the plot, dig another trench, moving the soil from this trench into the previous one and so on to the end of the plot.

Move over to the other half of the plot and dig trenches, working forwards, until the end of that half is reached.

The final trench is then filled with the soil removed from the first.

Except, perhaps, when creating a vegetable garden or improving especially poor soil, double digging is for those who like punishment. The same principles are followed, but the trenches have to be wider. When the soil has been removed from the first trench, the soil at the bottom of the trench is broken up by a fork, to the depth of the fork, and manure and compost is worked in.
After autumn digging, the soil is left to the frost to work on. In spring, it should need only a light raking over.

not just for a year or two but every year. In the early stages of building up fertility, compost or manure will have to be supplemented by fertilizers, and if you are following the fully organic path, you will buy organic fertilizers and not chemical ones.

The best organic fertilizers are fish meal, bone meal, blood meal, and hoof and horn meal. These are expensive but they have a long-lasting effect, contributing to the health of the soil for the future (and for the plants grown in it) rather than forcing growth for a single season.

Regular manuring of the soil will add to its fertility, improve its texture and supply minerals. Soil to which manure is fre-

quently added has a more open structure, making it much easier to work, while helping it to retain moisture. One valuable type of manure, if available, is well-rotted animal manure (fresh manure, especially chicken manure, is over-rich in nitrogen, producing soft, disease prone leaf and stem growth). Spent mushroom compost

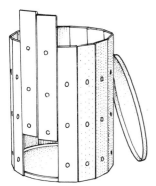

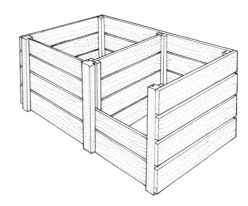

and seaweed can also be used.

Garden compost can be a good source of minerals. However, the average garden compost heap will not yield anywhere near the amount of compost needed for a whole garden. Instead, it may be used as a mulch around particular plants.

Eventually – and it can take anything up to 20 years – you will achieve a harmonious balance where the soil is rich and fertile and pests and diseases should not be a major problem, if they are a problem at all. In the meantime, what do you do to control pests and diseases?

The first principle is to practise good garden hygiene, removing and burning any dead vegetation that may harbour pests and diseases. Don't put it on the compost heap, or you may return pests and diseases straight back to the soil, making matters even worse. Diseased plants should be lifted and burned.

Pests are usually controlled by sprays, either based on chemicals or derived from plants. Derris and pyrethrum, derived from plants, are favoured by the organic gardener, but they do kill beneficial insects, such as bees and ladybirds, the gardener's helpmates, whereas there are chemical sprays that don't kill these insects.

An alternative is a solution of soft soaps, which is the nearest you can get to an organic pesticide and certainly helps to keep pests in check. It is based on potassium salts of fatty acids with other constituents and diluted with soft or rain water.

The latest product in the fight against pests is a spray based on a combination of naturally occurring fatty-acid soaps. It is harmless to most beneficial insects and – equally important – is non-persistent. The insecticide sprays cope with aphids, scale insects, mealybugs and whitefly. There is also a spray against rust and powdery mildew.

There is just one snag: none of the fatty-acid or soft-soap sprays should be used anywhere near fish.

Cultivating the soil

Arguments rage among gardeners about whether to dig or not to dig the soil. Instead of turning over the soil the non-diggers spread a generous layer of compost over it. This is converted into humus by bacteria in the soil. Worms do the rest, working the humus into the soil, and aerating it at the same time. The system works well and produces a fertile and (thanks to the worms) a well-draining soil, but only if there are ample supplies of compost to provide a deep enough mulch over the surface of the soil to smother the weeds. Many gardens may not provide enough compost and the alternative is to buy in some mulching material, such as shredded bark, not particularly attractive to look at, or peat.

Serious digging, except when creating a new garden, is therefore most likely to be restricted to the vegetable garden. Single digging, to the depth of a spade, is easier than double digging, and is usually adequate.

Mulching

Where permanent fruit trees and canes are planted a yearly mulch is the answer. Garden compost, leaf mould and peat can be used as mulches applied round the base of plants to a minimum depth of 2in/5cm, but twice that depth is more effective in keeping down weeds. Leave the mulch there for worms to take down into the soil, or it can later be forked into the surface of the soil. Mulches should be applied on moist soil in late spring when the soil has warmed up.

Making compost

Every gardener should find a corner for a compost heap. Kitchen and garden waste (as long as it is not diseased) is there for free and will turn into valuable compost to add fertility to the soil.

A container is not even required; the waste can be piled up in layers and covered with a sheet of black polythene while bacteria get to work on it. This method does not generate the high temperatures reached in enclosed structures, so the process takes longer and the compost will not be ready to use for about a year, or longer. Even if the matter has not rotted completely, it can still be dug into the soil.

Wooden or metal bins are more efficient for breaking down the waste and the resulting compost is ready to use earlier. During spring and summer, it will be ready in about three months. In autumn, waste will take until the following spring to decompose.

If two bins are constructed side by side, one can be filled and the waste left to rot down while the other is being filled with waste as it becomes available. There should be adequate ventilation in the bins as air is needed to help break down the waste. Layers of vegetable waste, about 6in/15cm thick, can be alternated with layers of manure, if it is available. The nitrogen in the manure will help to decompose the matter more quickly. Water each layer as it is added and when the bin is almost full, cover the top layer with a 1in/2.5cm layer of soil.

GARDEN MANAGEMENT: GROWING UNDER GLASS

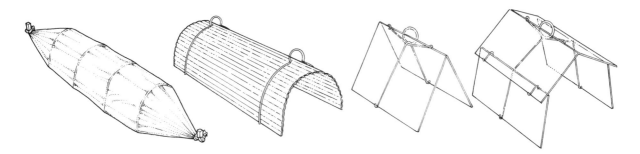

The idea of growing for the kitchen garden under glass might conjure up images of great glasshouses looked after by a large staff of dedicated gardeners, but this is certainly no longer the case. The changes in growing under glass have been as great as the revolution in the rest of the garden. It is now both simpler and cheaper, largely because gardeners realize what they can do without whilst still getting good results.

A heated greenhouse is a great asset if you want to start sowing early, but the warmth inside a house can be used instead. Seed can be sown in trays and placed in a heated or unheated propagator in a warm, light place indoors to create the best possible conditions for germination. Even simpler and cheaper is to enclose the trays in plastic bags instead of using a propagator.

A greenhouse owner will often transfer his seedlings, when they are growing well, to a garden frame, but even that is not essential. Trays of plants can be placed either in an unheated propagator with the vents left open or in plastic bags with holes punched in them. However, it is essential to bring them in each evening. After a week or two, the seedlings will be hardened off ready to be transplanted to the garden.

Greenhouses, propagators and frames are thus not essential for successful plant raising – they just make the job easier and more efficient.

Cloches

When it comes to investing in growing under glass, cloches are the cheapest choice, especially as the 'glass' is now made of sheet plastic. The first use for cloches in the gardening year is when they are placed in position a week or so before sowing to warm up the soil a little. At the end of the season they will be in position to extend the life of some vegetables into autumn or even winter. At all times they will allow the more exotic vegetables to be grown in cooler areas.

The cheapest but not necessarily the most efficient type of cloche is the polythene tunnel. This consists of hoops of wire pushed into the ground and covered with thin polythene. This is held in place by another row of hoops on top of it. The polythene at each end of the tunnel is knotted round stakes pushed firmly into the ground. (These ends must always be securely fixed, because if they come adrift the tunnel will turn into a wind tunnel which will play havoc with the plants.) In winter, the edges of the plastic can be pushed into the ground along the length of the tunnel to keep out the cold, but in summer heat can build up rapidly under the cloches, so the edges should not be tucked in. This allows some ventilation.

The wire supports will last for several years, but the polythene will have to be renewed every year or two. If you buy a thicker-gauge polythene you will get more wear out of it.

The next step up in the range is the rigid plastic cloche. One type is made of corrugated plastic to make a semicircular tunnel, secured by wire hoops. Another type is moulded in straight-sided sections to form an almost square tunnel, perhaps with ventilation panels. Don't forget to cover each end of the cloche with a sheet of plastic or glass to avoid a wind tunnel.

The most effective, and expensive,

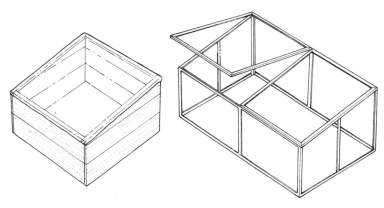

cloches are made of glass, providing greater light and warmth than those made of plastic. The simplest form is a tent cloche – two pieces of glass secured in a tent shape by a wire frame or clips. Barn cloches are more elaborate, with four pieces of glass held together by a frame, two to form the walls and two the sloping roof. For tall crops, the glass structure can be elevated on a wire frame. Here again sheets of glass or plastic must be fixed at both ends of the cloche run.

Frames

The cheapest garden frame is the one you make yourself. Make a square wooden frame, 3ft/90cm by 3ft/90cm, with the back wall slightly higher than the front. For the cover, make a square frame from 2in sq/5cm sq timber. Stretch heavy-duty polythene over it, securing it firmly around the edge.

The most efficient frame to buy is all in wood, with either hinged or sliding glass panels. This type will warm up more quickly and, more important, conserve heat. There are also all-glass frames with a

metal framework. These lose heat more quickly than wooden frames but are more easily moved. If you install heating in the frame, plant raising becomes more reliable, and it may eliminate the need for buying a greenhouse. Soil-heating cables can be laid under the soil or air-warming cables fixed on an inside wall.

Greenhouses

A cheap version is available, though it is unlikely to improve the appearance of the garden. Horticultural polythene is stretched over a framework of metal hoops in a typical greenhouse shape. This type must be properly ventilated or the build-up of high humidity encourages many types of pests and diseases. The disadvantage of polythene is that it does not retain heat as efficiently as glass and it will need replacing every three or four years.

Permanent greenhouse structures are made from metal or wood frames glazed down to the ground or built on a 2-3ft/60-90cm base of brick or wood. This base makes the greenhouse warmer, but excludes a lot of light. To get the maximum

winter sunlight, site the greenhouse east to west and away from buildings or trees that overshadow it.

Make sure the greenhouse is adequately ventilated and if you can afford it, install some form of heating. Tubular greenhouse heaters are a permanent fixture, or fan heaters can be taken into the greenhouse as required.

Propagators

If you want to use a greenhouse to raise plants but don't want the expense of heating the whole structure, heated propagators are the economical answer. They consist of a base tray with an enclosed network of heating cables. The tray is filled with a layer of dampened sand on which the pots and seed trays are placed, covered by a plastic dome.

Choose a propagator with a thermostat so that the temperature can be controlled, and with a ventilator so that humidity may be reduced when necessary.

To raise plants indoors, an unheated propagator with a base tray and plastic dome can be used.

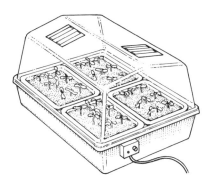

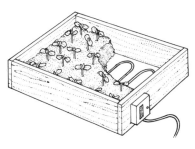

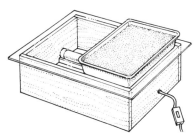

GARDEN MANAGEMENT: GROWING IN CONTAINERS

Growing fruit and vegetables in containers is not just for those who have small gardens and want to make the most of what space they have. Container plants can play their part in any garden, imaginatively arranged on patios or dotted around among plants on the ground.

There are also practical reasons for growing plants in containers. Pots of herbs near the kitchen door are great time savers, and can be taken indoors into the kitchen when winter comes. A bay tree virtually demands a tub near the house so that it can be easily moved under cover to protect it from sharp frosts. Some vegetables and fruits need a different type of soil to that in your garden – perhaps rather more acid – and their needs are most easily met by being grown in containers.

Choosing a container

A container will probably outlive the plants growing in it so the choice is important. The cheapest are made of plastic. They may be circular or square tubs, or pots and window-boxes in all sizes. The best way of avoiding a hotchpotch is to choose containers in one discreet colour. Plastic containers have the advantage that the compost in them dries out less quickly and the roots are somewhat warmer.

Terracotta containers are more attractive, but they are also more expensive and heavy to lift. The compost dries out quickly and the roots are cooler. The drying out can be slowed down by lining the

Containers should suit surroundings.

terracotta containers with thick plastic sheeting with holes cut into it to allow excess water to drain away.

Vegetables can also be raised in growing bags. These are tough plastic bags filled with the growing medium. The bags are laid on a flat surface – a patio, say – and holes are made in the top through which the plants grow. They are an unlovely sight, but very practical for growing tomatoes.

Planting containers

Tubs, pots and window-boxes are prepared for planting in a similar way. Make sure that there are enough drainage holes in the bottom of the container for water to drain away quickly. This is most important for window-boxes and they should have holes along the whole length. Spread a 1in/2.5cm layer of crocks or pebbles along the bottom, and on top of it a 1in/2.5cm layer of peat. The crocks will ensure good drainage and the peat will help to retain moisture. Fill the container with loam-based potting compost to within 1-2in/2.5-5cm of the top; the gap will make watering easier.

Use loam potting compost for preference, especially for fruit trees, as the heavier compost will give stability in the wind. Peat potting compost can be used for annual vegetables but loam is better as long as it is a quality type. All too often loam composts dry solid like concrete, preventing air and water from getting to the roots.

Potting compost contains nutrients, but these are used by plants within a few weeks. After that, regular feeding is needed during the growing period if the plants are to remain healthy and vigorous. The compost for vegetables should be renewed every year. In containers with permanent plants, such as fruit trees, remove the top 3-4in/7.5-10cm of compost every spring and replace with fresh.

Unfortunately, compost in containers dries out quickly. Get into a routine of checking the compost every day, sticking your finger into it to feel whether it is damp below the surface. In spells of continuing warm weather, do this twice a day and don't be surprised if you have to water the plants on each occasion.

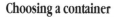

'Little Gem' five weeks after sowing.

SOWING

All annual vegetables are easily raised from seed. Seed is cheap, certainly far cheaper than buying established seedlings. So for a comparatively small sum it is possible to be self-sufficient in vegetables for most of the year if your garden is big enough. There is also the satisfaction of nurturing seeds, through seedlings to mature plants, with the reward of something to eat at the end of it.

Sowing seed indoors or under glass

The earliest time that seed can be sown outdoors is usually early spring or spring after the soil has had time to warm up. A much earlier start can be made by sowing indoors in winter or late winter so that the small plants are ready to plant out when frosts are over.

If you are sowing for a large number of seedlings, use seed trays, or pots for smaller quantities. Fill the tray or pot with loam seed compost and level it off at the rim with a piece of wood. Then press down the compost to just below the rim with a flat piece of wood, to get a firm surface.

Sow large seed individually, about 1in/2.5cm apart and cover with a light sifting of compost. If the seed is small, shake some of it from the packet into the palm of one hand and take a pinch of it between the finger and thumb of the other hand. Scatter the seeds as evenly as possible and press them gently into the compost: don't cover them with compost. As soon as you have sown each pot or tray, label it clearly – seedlings are very hard to identify when they first emerge.

The compost has to be watered after sowing, either from above, using a fine rose, or from below, which is slower but better because it causes less disturbance to the seeds. Stand the container in a sink of tepid water that reaches about 1in/2.5cm below the rim. Let the water soak up through the compost until you can see beads of moisture on the surface. Remove the container from the water and let it drain thoroughly.

Cover the tray or pot with a sheet of glass, or enclose it in a plastic bag or place it in a propagator. Keep the container in a warm place in the light, but out of direct sunlight. Once the seeds have germinated, remove the glass or plastic and keep the seedlings in the light, but again away from direct sunlight. Make sure that the compost is always moist, but not sodden.

When the first true leaves have devel-

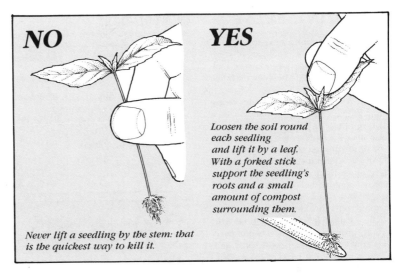

NO

Never lift a seedling by the stem: that is the quickest way to kill it.

YES

Loosen the soil round each seedling and lift it by a leaf. With a forked stick support the seedling's roots and a small amount of compost surrounding them.

oped, the seedlings are pricked out to another container of loam compost. Loosen the soil round each seedling and lift them by a leaf. Never lift a seedling by the stem: that is the quickest way to kill it. Support the seedling's roots and a small amount of compost surrounding them with a forked stick. Lower the seedling into a hole made with a dibbler and carefully firm the compost round it. Keep the seedlings well watered and place them in a warm spot.

When after a few days they have settled down after the change, start hardening them off before planting them outside. If you have a cold frame, put them in there with the frame totally closed at first. When the weather warms up, wedge open the lights of the frame a little during the day, but close them at night. Alternatively, containers of seedlings can be placed in a propagator outdoors during the day, with the vents open. Bring the propagator indoors at night until the seedlings are hardened off and the weather is warmer. Another method is to enclose the container in a plastic bag with holes punched in it. Use sticks or a wire frame to hold up the plastic so that it does not touch the seedlings. Later, transplant the seedlings into the open ground: the recommended distances are given under each vegetable entry.

Seed can also be sown individually in peat pots or blocks, causing far less disturbance when transplanting.

Instructions about sowing seed directly into the ground are given under each vegetable.

There is one technique worth trying – fluid sowing – which involves mixing the seed with commercial wallpaper paste. The method spaces small seeds more evenly, speeds up germination, cuts out overcrowding of seedlings, and makes thinning much easier.

Before sowing, the seed has to be sprouted. Spread several layers of paper tissues in the bottom of a plastic box. Dampen them and pour off any excess water. Cover with a single sheet of kitchen paper. Dampen that and spread the seed thinly over it. Put the lid on the box and keep it in a warm place, but not more than 70°F/21°C, so an airing cupboard would be too warm. (If the seed needs light to germinate, as some does, leave off the lid, but it is essential to ensure that the paper does not dry out.)

As soon as the seed has germinated, go on to the next stage. Make a wallpaper paste, of a brand free of fungicide or the seed will not germinate. Mix the paste to half the strength recommended for wallpapering.

Rinse the germinated seeds gently from the kitchen paper into a fine sieve. Add them to the paste, stirring gently so that they are not damaged. The paste with the seeds in it is then squeezed out along drills in the soil using an icing bag with a ¼in/0.6cm nozzle. An icing bag can be improvised by cutting off the corner of a plastic bag and fitting a nozzle.

Pour the paste into the bag, securing the top with string. Take out drills in the soil slightly deeper than those for sowing untreated seed. Water the drills thoroughly and then squeeze the paste along them evenly. Cover with soil before the paste begins to dry out. Once the seedlings have started to grow, keep them well watered.

CROP MANAGEMENT

There are various procedures to follow in order to improve the efficiency of your growing programme and to ensure that crops remain healthy. These are outlined below.

Crop rotation, which prevents crops being grown in the same ground for two years running, has been practised in some form since the Middle Ages. In those days, part of the ground was left fallow every third year so that it could recover its fertility. Since then, the main part of crop management has become the rotation of crops, and this has been refined and adapted to today's kitchen garden.

The rotation is generally a three-year cycle of growing three different groups of vegetables – brassicas, roots, peas and beans – in different parts of the garden, and providing them with the different levels of soil fertility and the range of nutrients they need. This is a far more economical system than keeping land fallow and it still has the great virtue of discouraging the build-up of pests and diseases.

The current development of raised-bed cultivation in the kitchen garden can also be traced back to the strip farming of the Middle Ages. This has also received much refinement with the passage of time.

On the other hand, close-block planting – growing plants not in rows, but in groups of equidistant spacing – is new to today's kitchen garden.

Crop rotation

This is an absolute must for two reasons. One is that if the same crops are grown in the same piece of ground year in year out, there will be an inevitable build-up of pests and diseases in the soil. For example, brassicas encourage the appearance of club-root and onions will attract eel-worm. The second reason is that different crops have different needs. Some vegetables, such as peas and beans, require a rich soil; root crops do better in a less rich soil; brassicas need a lime-rich soil. To meet these different needs, the kitchen garden is divided into three basic parts that will receive different treatment according to the crops to be grown there. These change each year – the rotation of crops – to avoid the build-up of disease and to establish an appropriate cycle of manuring and cultivation as the crops move round the garden.

(There is also a non-rotating part of the

CROP ROTATION
Move the crops round in a three-year cycle.

Group 1
Peas, beans, leeks, all types of onions, and all salad plants. Group 1 vegetables are the heaviest feeders and their ground needs plenty of manure or compost.

Group 2
The brassicas – cauliflowers, cabbages, Brussels sprouts, spinach, kale, broccoli and the Oriental vegetable brassicas. Group 2 crops need a well-limed soil to keep such diseases as club-root at bay.

Group 3
The roots – potatoes, celery, parsnips, turnips, swedes, celeriac, scorzonera and salsify. Group 3 crops don't need such a rich soil as the brassicas. If manure or compost is in short supply, they will grow well enough with an application of general fertilizer.

At the end of the first growing year,

Move peas and beans to the area where roots (Group 3) were growing

Move the brassicas (Group 2) to where the peas and beans (Group 1) were growing. The soil should be quite rich in nitrogen after these crops, and an application of general fertilizer should be all that is needed.

The roots (Group 3) move on to the former brassica (Group 2) bed.
At the end of years two and three, move the crops through the same sequence, so that all are back in their original position at the beginning of year four.

garden where the more permanent crops are grown, from rhubarb, asparagus and herbs, to cane and top fruits.)

Preparing raised beds

Site the beds north/south along their length so that they can get the maximum amount of sun. The maximum width of a bed should be 4ft/1.2m, so that all parts can be reached easily. A convenient length is no more than 10ft/3m. Allow about 18in/45cm for the path so that you can walk with ease between the beds. (The paths could be constructed of bricks or covered with bark chippings.)

To prepare the ground initially, single or double dig it (see page 00). Double digging is hard work but for raised beds is worth the effort. After digging, rake the ground to form a shallow mound with a gently sloping camber, as on a road.

Dig the bed every year, preferably in autumn before the growing season gets under way the following year. This will give time for frost to break down lumps in the soil, needing only a light raking in late winter or early spring before sowing begins.

Raised beds and block planting

Close planting of vegetables in narrow raised beds makes more economical use of space. The beds are usually about 4ft/1.2m wide. A narrow path divides one bed from the next so that crops can be reached from either side without having to trample on the bed itself, as happens in conventional gardening, compacting the soil and making it difficult to work. Weeding is also cut down because the closely planted crops smother most of the weeds. Ground divided into a series of narrow beds also makes crop rotation easier to arrange.

Block planting

There are many advantages in this method of vegetable gardening. It makes more economical use of space, allowing intensive cropping. Experiments over recent years have shown that closer planting does not reduce overall yield; indeed in general, crops have been heavier though individual vegetables smaller. The performance of cabbages clearly demonstrates the effect of close planting; adjust the spacing between plants and you can get large or small heads. This practice has been adopted by commercial growers with great success and there is no reason why the home grower should not follow their example.

Plants grown in rows at wide distances apart develop irregularly because each plant is competing for the limited sunlight where not overshadowed by neighbouring plants. Grow plants in block formation and this problem is resolved. Weeds are also kept to a minimum. The most efficient form of block planting is where plants are grown at equal distances apart in a series of hexagonal formations.

A square formation is slightly less effective: a block will contain fewer plants.

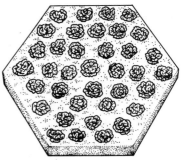

Hexagonal block planting is most efficient because plants are equidistant.

Intercropping

Intercropping allows a greater range of vegetables to be grown, by making the best use of the space available. Quick-growing crops can be planted between slower-growing plants. The quicker plants will be ready for harvesting as the slower are beginning to mature and need the extra space that has been freed. This method works where vegetables are grown in rows not in blocks, since block planting has already pared down the distance between plants to the minimum for optimum results.

Quick-maturing salad crops such as lettuce, salad onions, corn salad, radishes and some of the Oriental vegetables grown to the seedling stage can be planted between winter brassicas or carrots. Inter-cropping should not be practised too intensively or it will interfere too much with the development of the main crop. It is best to use the method to grow just a few salad crops rather than to be too ambitious and have a disappointing main crop.

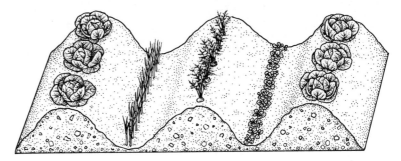

Intercropping increases the range of vegetables grown simultaneously in one area.

Catch cropping

Catch cropping is another way of getting two crops from the same piece of ground in a year. However, with this process you first grow quick-maturing crops and then clear the ground to make way for late main crops. For example, the early sowings might be of small carrots and beetroots, Oriental vegetables and salad crops. As these crops are eaten the ground is freed for transplanting Brussels sprouts in early summer; sowing winter cauliflowers in early summer; and sowing spring cabbage in late summer.

Applying these techniques makes the most productive use of limited space and increases the range of crops that can be grown.

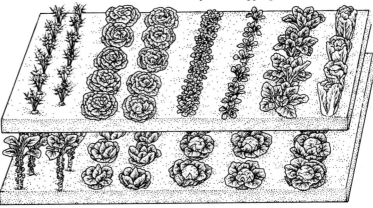

Raising two crops successively on the same piece of ground is the principle of catch cropping.

Mixed salad

SALAD PLANTS

*T*he modern cut-and-grow-again technique for salad plants achieves several pickings of small, tender but crisp leaves made from a single sowing. Lettuce varieties that grow in loose-leaved formation are particularly suited to this technique. With regular cutting, American cress, watercress, corn salad, chicory and endive will also produce new tender growth.

Do consider the less common salads: Italian chicory, usually known as radicchio, is now available in supermarkets, expensively packaged. It is far cheaper to grow yourself. Its red or red-and-white variegated leaves add bright colour contrast in leaf salads. The young tender leaves of dandelions give a different, sharp taste to mixed green salads. Celtuce, with small lettuce-like leaves and stems, can be eaten raw or cooked, like celery.

Crispness is the secret of delectable salad plants; grow them at home so that you can eat them in peak condition straight after cooking.

All these leaves have distinctive flavours and it is a pity to drown them in dressings; a little oil, or simply salt and black pepper is often all that is needed.

AMERICAN CRESS
(Barbarea praecox)

American or land cress looks and tastes like watercress but is less fussy about growing conditions: it will crop outdoors all year round, and given protection in winter will do even better. It can be spaced evenly in a block to form a close-knit bed of green leaves. Like watercress, it can also be grown in containers.

Varieties

Seed catalogues will identify it either as American cress or as land cress.

The plant's needs

Grow American cress in rich moist soil in a shaded part of the garden. Prepare the soil before sowing, digging in plenty of well-rotted manure or compost.

Sowing seed

In spring, take out drills ½in/1.25cm deep and 6in/15cm apart. Sow seed thinly and

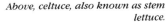

Above, celtuce, also known as stem lettuce.

American cress, less fussy than watercress.

CELTUCE
(*Lactuca sativa* var. *angustana*)

As its name suggests, celtuce is something of a novelty: a combination of celery and lettuce. The stems, though they don't taste much of celery, are pleasant to eat but, like celery, can be eaten raw or lightly braised. The small young leaves are a rich source of vitamin C.

Varieties

Usually referred to in seed catalogues simply as celtuce.

The plant's needs

Celtuce requires a rich fertile soil, so plenty of well-rotted manure or compost must be dug in before sowing. It is a very thirsty plant, needing frequent watering, especially in warm weather. The stems become tough, stringy and inedible if the plants are allowed to dry out.

Sowing seed

In spring, take out drills ½in/1.25cm deep and 12in/30cm apart. Sow thinly and cover the seed with a fine sifting of soil. Thin out seedlings to 10in/25cm. Keep well watered all the time. Cut off the leaves when they are still small for eating raw. Pull up the plants for the stems no more than three months after sowing. Young and small should mean tender.

level. This is a cut-and-grow-again salad plant, like watercress, and new growth will soon appear.

Successional sowings can be made through to early autumn. The later sowings will provide leaves for winter and spring. Give some winter protection by surrounding the plants with straw or covering with a cloche.

Growing in containers

A few plants could be grown in an 8in/20cm plant pot filled with loam potting compost. Sow about eight seeds and thin to the four strongest. A box 12in/30cm wide, about 2ft/60cm long, and at least 6in/15cm deep would be more satisfactory. Make three rows 4in/10cm apart in the compost, starting about 2in/6cm from the box edge. Sow the seed thinly and cover with soil. Thin plants to 4in/10cm apart when they can be handled easily. Container-grown plants must be kept well watered at all times. To extend the crop into winter, improvise a cloche over the box, supporting plastic sheeting on hoops of wire.

cover with a light sifting of soil. Thin seedlings to form a block of plants, 6in/15cm apart each way. Keep well watered especially during periods of warm weather, when twice daily watering may be necessary. Remove any flowering stems. The first leaves should be ready for cutting in about eight weeks. Take individual leaves or whole heads, cutting just above the soil

CORN SALAD
Valerianella locusta

Once the seed has been sown, corn salad can be left to its own devices. It is a cut-and-grow-again salad plant that can be cropped all year round, removing leaves or whole plants as needed. It comes into its own in winter when salad plants are scarce in the garden: though corn salad is hardy, plants will thrive better if protected by cloches during winter. Plants can be grown close together in blocks in the ground or in containers.

Varieties

For spring or summer sowings, Large-Leaved Italian is ideal. Cavallo and Vert de Cambrai produce hardier plants for winter growing.

The plant's needs

Corn salad will grow in all types of soil. Choose a sunny sheltered part of the garden. Soil should be well draining with manure or compost dug in beforehand. If grown on poor ground, the results will be disappointing.

Sowing seed

In spring or late spring, take out drills 1in/1.25cm deep, 4in/10cm apart. Sow seed thinly and cover with a sifting of soil. When seedlings are about 2in/5cm tall, thin to 4in/10cm apart. A block 12in/30cm by 24in/60cm will contain 28 plants.

In 10 to 12 weeks leaves should be ready for cutting. Take a few leaves from each plant; that way new growth should keep on appearing. Winter plants will grow better if covered with cloches. Failing that, place generous bundles of straw around the plants.

The cut-and-grow-again technique with seedling plants

Sow seed by broadcasting and cover lightly with soil. Thin seedlings to 2in/5cm. When leaves are about 3in/7.5cm tall, cut individual leaves or whole heads, leaving about 1in/2.5cm of the stems to grow again. After a few cuttings it will be obvious when plants are exhausted. Pull them up and sow fresh seed.

Container growing

The container should be about 10in/25cm wide, 24in/60cm long, and at least 6in/15cm deep. Fill it with quality loam compost. Sow seed for the mature crop as already described, spacing rows 4in/10cm apart, starting at about 2in/5cm from the edge of the container. Thin seedlings to 4in/10cm apart.

The cut-and-grow-again technique is ideal for container growing. Broadcast sow the seed as already described and start cutting when leaves are about 3in/7.5cm tall. Make successional sowings when the plants are becoming unproductive. All container-grown plants must be kept well watered; twice a day may be necessary in warm weather.

USING CORN SALAD

Corn salad is rich in minerals and vitamins. Small seedling leaves can be dressed whole in a vinaigrette dressing. Mature leaves make an excellent substitute for lettuce in winter. They can also be used in green salads (shredding the larger leaves) to add contrasting flavour and darker colouring. The larger leaves can also be stir-fried briefly in a little oil, with salt.

DANDELION
(Taraxacum officinale)

The young tender leaves of dandelions have a distinctive if somewhat bitter taste. Much of the bitterness can be removed by blanching them in the dark, creating an interesting addition to a green salad. They can also be stir-fried.

Varieties

You will not come across dandelion seed in many catalogues, the plant's popularity being far from universal. But if you can, it is far better to buy seed rather than dig up plants growing in the wild to transplant to your own garden. Seed specifically bred for salad eating usually produces larger, more tender leaves. The French are masters at growing dandelions, and two varieties that may be found are Pissenlit and A Coeur Plein. They are worth searching for.

The plant's needs

Dandelions are not fussy about the type of soil they grow in as long as it drains well; they should not be grown on permanently wet ground. The most succulent leaves will be produced from fertile, well-manured or composted soil.

Sowing seed

In spring, take out drills ½in/1.25cm deep and 6in/15cm apart. Sow seed thinly and cover with a sifting of soil. Thin out seedlings to 6in/15cm apart. Seed can also be sown in a box for transplanting, and this has the advantage that the transplanted seedlings can be arranged in convenient groups for blanching. It may be possible to blanch a few plants in winter in the first year but it is wiser to allow the plants to become more established and to start blanching in the following spring. Always remove flower-heads as they appear.

Growing in containers

Containers should be about 12in/30cm wide, up to 24in/60cm long and at least 6in/15cm deep. Circular containers make blanching easier. Sow seed as already described and thin to 4in/10cm.

Blanching outdoors

As soon as the leaves start to show in spring, cover the plants with a bucket or box. They should be ready for picking in

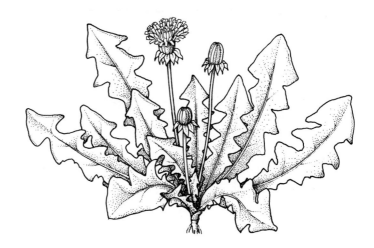

10 to 14 days. Cover other groups of plants in succession for continuing supplies. Blanching should stop in early summer so that plants can build up strength for the following year's growth.

Plants growing in containers can be blanched in the same way, under a bucket or box, but there is an alternative way of blanching a few at a time. Tie the spreading leaves of a plant together to form a head. This method will blanch only the inner concealed leaves.

Forcing and blanching indoors

Mature plants can be lifted for forcing and blanching indoors from late autumn to early winter. Cut off any leaves near their base and plant the crowns about 4in/10cm apart in boxes of loam potting compost. Water well, cover with another box and place in a cupboard or cellar. Keep at a minimum temperature of 50°F/10°C. Roots should be ready to cut in four to six weeks. To ensure a continuing supply throughout the winter, roots can be stored in sand in a cool place and planted for forcing as required.

USING DANDELION LEAVES

Only small tender leaves should be eaten raw. Chop them and toss them in vinaigrette, or mix them with other green salad leaves. To stir-fry, shred the leaves finely so that they will cook quickly, then stir them in hot oil and a little salt for about three minutes. Add some finely chopped spring onion for contrasting flavour.

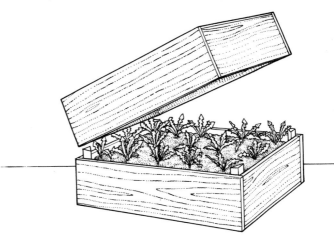

CHICORY
(Cichorium intybus)

Chicory, in its various forms, has always been popular in Mediterranean climates such as southern Europe, but some of the varieties are hardly known or grown in cool, temperate climates. They are well worth trying.

Radicchio is a loose-leaved type long established in Italy, but until recently largely unfamiliar elsewhere. The leaves are green in summer and turn red, or variegated red-and-white when the weather turns colder. When shredded they add dramatic colour to green salads. Radicchio can be cultivated as a cut-and-grow-again salad.

Sugar Loaf, similar in appearance to cos lettuce, produces tight heads of green leaves, concealing inner blanched yellow leaves. Like radicchio, this can be a cut-and-grow-again salad, cutting leaves here and there over several weeks. Plants can then be thinned out to provide larger-hearted plants at the end of the growing season.

Witloof (or Belgian) is probably the most familiar form of chicory. Over the winter months it is forced and blanched to produce tight conical heads of leaves; new F_1 hybrids make blanching easier.

Grumolo, a recent introduction from Italy, is welcome because of its hardiness, not needing any protection during the winter months. Over winter the plants develop small rosettes of bright-green leaves ready for cutting in spring.

Sugar Loaf chicory.

Varieties

Varieties of loose-leaved green chicory that turn red include Rossa di Treviso (Red Treviso), Rossa di Verona (Red Verona), and Variegata di Chioggia (Variegated Chioggia) with attractive variegated red-and-white leaves.

Sugar Loaf may only be described as such, but there are named varieties, including Bianca di Milano and Crystal Head.

Witloof may also only be described as such, but look out for the new F_1 hybrids Zoom or Normato. Their great virtue is that they don't need to have the soil piled around them when forcing and blanching .

The rosette-shaped Grumolo is offered as Grumolo Verde.

The plant's needs

All types of chicory will do better if they are grown in rich fertile soil that retains moisture. During the growing season the plants need to be moist, but there may be problems if the plants are overwintered and not adequately protected. Then prolonged damp is likely to rot the plants.

In winter, prepare the ground ready for sowing by digging in plenty of well-rotted manure or compost. Chicory has long roots, so the soil should be prepared to a depth of at least 9-12in/22.5-30cm.

Sowing seed for cut-and-grow-again crops

Don't sow seed too early in the year or the plants are likely to bolt - flowering and running to seed rather than producing leaves. Sow seed of red-leaved and sugar loaf chicory in late spring or early summer, either in drills ½in/1.25cm deep and 3in/7.5cm apart, or by broadcasting it. Keep well watered. When leaves are 2-3in/5-7.5cm tall, cut them to just about ground level, taking a few leaves from each plant. New growth will appear.

In late summer or early autumn, thin the plants to 6in/15cm apart and leave them to develop into mature, hearted plants. As the weather gets colder the red-leaved chicory will start to take on its red colouring. To extend the crop into winter, cover it with cloches.

Growing in containers

Containers should be 12in/30cm or more wide, 8-10in/20-25cm deep, and about 2ft/60cm long. Sow in rows or broadcast it (as already described) and use as cut-and-grow-again leaves throughout the summer and into autumn. If hearted chicory is required, thin the seedlings to 4-6in/10-15cm. To keep the crop going into the winter, cover the container with plastic, supported on wire hoops. Always keep container plants well watered.

Sowing Witloof

Sow seed in early summer in ½in/1.25cm drills, 6in/15cm apart. Thin seedlings to 6in/15cm when they can be handled easily. Hoe to keep the weeds down, and keep well watered, especially in periods of warm weather.

Forcing Witloof

In autumn or late autumn, lift the plants.

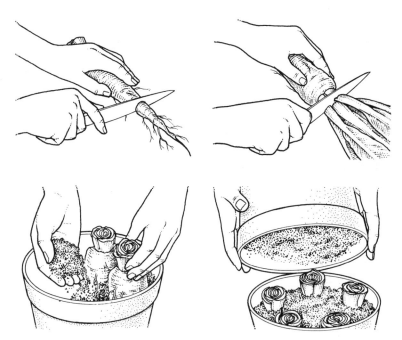

Cut off the tips of the roots and the top foliage to within about 1in/2.5cm of the crown. Store the roots in a cool place, placing them on their sides in a box of moist peat or sand. Remove a few of the roots at a time to force them. Fill a pot or box with quality loam potting compost and plant the roots close together with the crowns showing above the surface of the compost. Cover with another pot or box to exclude all light. Keep in a cellar or cupboard in a minimum temperature of 50°F/10°C.

After four to six weeks the chicons will be about 6in/15cm tall and ready for pulling. Snap them off carefully at the base, rather than cutting them. Put the cover over the box again and a second crop of smaller chicons will grow. Plants are thrown away after they have been forced.

Sowing Grumolo

In early summer, sow seed either in rows or broadcast, as for red and sugar loaf chicory. Thin to 3in/7.5cm. Leaves can be cut in late summer or early autumn as a cut-and-grow-again plant, but then they should be left to develop their rosettes of leaves for cutting the following spring. They are extremely hardy plants, and though they may look nothing in winter the small rosettes of leaves will appear for spring.

USING CHICORY

A common complaint about chicory is that it is bitter, but it is the very bitterness that provides welcome contrast to other salad leaves. Blanching removes excess bitterness. Chicons should be eaten as soon as possible after cutting. If you have to store them for a few hours, wrap them in foil or black polythene and put them in the salad compartment of the refrigerator. Remove the outer leaves and serve tossed in a rich oily dressing.

Whole chicons can be simmered in water for about ten minutes and served in melted butter, or braised in butter or vegetable oil for about 20 minutes.

The looseleaf chicory is used in mixed green salads, the red types adding colourful contrast.

Young tender cut-and-grow-again leaves may be stir-fried in oil for about two minutes. The larger leaves of mature plants are best sautéd in butter.

ENDIVE
(Cichorium endivia)

In Continental Europe, endive is an essential ingredient in any mixed green salad. Traditionally, the heads are grown to maturity and cut whole, but this can present a problem as they are large: there is a risk of wilting before the whole endive can be eaten. Instead, treat endive in the modern way as a cut-and-grow-again crop, cutting a few leaves from each plant as it grows, then leaving the head to mature. The heads may be smaller, but you will have had several cuttings of leaves to add variety to mixed salads. The broad-leaved, or Batavian, varieties are invaluable as a winter salad crop in place of lettuce. The curly-leaved varieties are more suitable for summer and autumn cropping.

Their large heads make endive impractical for growing in containers, though a possible exception is Fine Maraîchère, which has small heads of curly leaves. Most endive leaves are bitter and need blanching to make them more palatable; in this case, the variety Riccia Panacalieri is an exception.

Varieties

Curly-headed varieties include the very popular Green Curled and Moss Curled. Among the broad-leaved varieties there are Batavian Broad-Leaved, Batavian Green, Golda and Cornet de Bordeaux.

The plant's needs

Endive should be grown in rich, light but moist soil. In winter, dig in plenty of well-rotted manure or compost, which will break down by spring into moisture-retaining humus. Although sowing can start in spring, it is probably better to wait until early summer. Plants sown earlier tend to bolt, running to seed rather than producing leaves. Choose a sheltered part of the garden.

Sowing seed

Sow seed of curly-leaved varieties in late spring or early summer in drills ½in/1.25cm deep and 12in/30cm apart. Thin to 12in/30cm apart. Seed of the smaller Fine Maraîchère can be sown in rows 6in/15cm apart and thinned to 6in/15cm between plants. A further sowing of curly-leaved varieties can be made in summer. Sow seed of Batavian varieties for winter use in late summer.

Keep well watered at all times to prevent plants from running to seed. Cover those for winter crops with cloches. Plants come to maturity in three months, ready for blanching.

Blanching endive

Cover curly-leaved endive with a flower-pot or box to exclude light. In about three weeks it will be ready for cutting. Broad-leaved varieties can be blanched by tying the leaves together (only when dry) with soft string. This method will blanch only the inner leaves; for complete blanching, the plants must be covered with a pot or box.

The cut-and-grow-again technique

Sow seed as already described, or broadcast it. When leaves are about 3in/7.5cm, start taking a few leaves from each plant, cutting them just above the surface of the soil. This can be done several times and new growth will soon appear. After about six weeks stop cutting and thin the plants to 9in/22.5cm apart, leaving them to grow to full maturity.

Container growing

Sow seed of Fine Maraîchère in containers at least 12in/30cm wide, 6in/15cm deep and 2ft/60cm long. Either sow in two rows 6in/15cm apart and thin the plants to 6in/15cm apart, or broadcast them for cut-and-grow-again leaves, thinning out later to grow on to maturity. Keep container-grown plants well watered, especially in warm weather.

USING ENDIVE

To enjoy the full flavour and crisp texture of the leaves, eat endive raw. Wash and thoroughly dry it and then toss in a slightly sweetened dressing to counteract any bitterness. Serve it on its own or in a mixed green salad.

Heads of endive can be braised in a rich meat stock, with onion, for about 25 minutes.

MUSTARD
(Brassica negra/Sinapis alba)

and CRESS
(Lepidium sativum)

Mustard and cress are as near instant natural food as you can get.

Mustard will germinate and be ready to gather in ten days; cress is more tardy, needing about 14 days. They can be grown all year round, indoors, taking up little room. Outdoor sowings can also be made from spring to early autumn. These are true convenience plants, requiring no thinning – just sow and let them grow.

Varieties

There is hardly any choice in seed catalogues. Mustard is usually described as that and nothing more, but sometimes as white. Cress is described as curled or fine-curled. A new development to watch out for is the appearance of cress varieties with larger leaves and sturdier stems.

The plants' needs

Mustard and cress are grown in a tray on layers of paper towelling, flannel or other absorbent material, or in boxes of loam or peat compost. Indoors, a kitchen window-sill that does not catch direct sunlight is an ideal growing place.

Sowing seed

Nothing could be simpler. First dampen the absorbent material or compost, and then scatter the cress seed over the surface. Press down lightly and cover the surface of the container with paper or polythene. Four days later mustard seed can be sown in the same container, or in another one if you want to keep the tastes separate. When the seeds have germinated and the seedlings are about 1in/2.5cm high, re-move the covering. Make sure the compost or absorbent material is always damp. In about two weeks the crop should be ready for cutting when it is about 2in/5cm tall. Successional sowings will ensure a continuing supply. From spring to early autumn the containers can be placed outside, covering them in the same way until the seed has germinated.

USING MUSTARD AND CRESS

Raw mustard and cress are suprisingly nutritious, with reasonable amounts of protein, vitamin C and trace elements. They taste excellent in sandwiches, either alone, or with other fillings. The mustard provides the hot flavour in contrast to the milder cress. Use them in mixed green salads or as a garnish with hot dishes.

WATERCRESS
(Nasturtium officinale)

Watercress is a highly convenient cut-and-grow-again salad plant that will provide continuing supplies through the summer. You don't even have to buy seed to grow it yourself; a bunch of shop-bought watercress usually has some stems with roots attached and these can be planted. Alternatively take a few stems, trim the bottoms and place them in water. They will soon produce roots and are then ready for planting. Even running water is not necessary, for watercress will grow quite readily in the ground as long as it is always moist and out of direct sunlight.

Varieties

When seed is offered it will simply be described as watercress.

The plant's needs

A rich fertile loam soil, which retains moisture, will give the best results. In a place out of direct sunlight prepare a trench 12in/30cm wide and 12in/30cm deep. Dig plenty of well-rotted manure or compost into the bottom of the trench. Then put a 6in/15cm layer of manure or compost in the trench. Fill in the rest of the trench with soil.

Growing from plants

In late spring, plant rooted shoots 4in/10cm apart each way to form a block 28in/70cm by 12in/30cm, containing 32 plants.

The plants will soon spread to form a solid mat. Remove flower-heads as they appear. Keep well watered all the time, especially in warm weather, when twice daily watering will be needed. Keep picking the stems to encourage new growth. When the plants are no longer productive, replace them with fresh cuttings or successional sowings.

Growing from seed

In late spring, scatter the seed over the trench (see *The plant's needs*, above) and cover with a light sifting of soil. Thin seedlings to 4in/10cm apart and treat as for plants, keeping well watered.

Container growing

Containers should be 12in/30cm wide and at least 6in/15cm deep. Line the bottom and sides of the container with polythene to retain the moisture. Fill with quality loam potting compost. Plant the cuttings 4in/10cm apart each way, starting about 2in/5cm away from the edge of the container. Seed can also be grown in a container, as described above.

USING WATERCRESS

The attractions of raw watercress are its hot, tangy flavour – which should never be masked – and beautiful green colour; try mixing it with lettuce for an excellent green salad. Cooked, it makes a delicious soup. Simmer some onion in a rich stock until tender. Now add the watercress, but to retain its full flavour cook it no further. Liquidize, add cream and serve hot or cold.

LETTUCE
(Lactuca sativa)

What would a salad be without lettuce? "Much improved" may well have been the answer a few years ago, when limp and tasteless leaves were the order of the day. Today, however, the choice of types and the variety of taste and texture have never been wider.

Cabbage lettuce, divided into **butterheads** and **crispheads.** The butterheads are often the most disappointing, giving lettuce a bad name because of their flabby leaves and insipid flavour. Crispheads, which include the Iceberg types, are totally different. They produce large and extremely tight heads of crisp leaves, which are best served shredded.

Cos lettuce produce large and long heads almost meaty in flavour. Recent developments have concentrated on making the heads smaller with a sweeter more delicate flavour. Little Gem, with a small solid heart, is an excellent variety for close planting and for growing in containers.

Looseleaf lettuce boasts uniform-sized leaves, beloved of caterers since the leaves can be cut individually. This saves taking a whole head. For the gardener these varieties are ideal for the cut-and-grow-again technique, for close planting and for container growing. Individual leaves or whole heads can be cut just above soil level, allowing new growth to appear. The most fashionable cut-and-grow-again lettuce is an Italian import, Lollo Rossa, with crinkly red-and-green variegated leaves, guaran-

Lollo Rossa, a stylish variety.

teed to brighten up any salad bowl.

Lettuce can be grown outdoors all year round, but it will not survive in hard winters without protection under glass. By planning a programme of sowing it is possible to have leaf lettuce from late spring until autumn to provide all summer and autumn needs.

Varieties

Cabbage: butterheads The great and well-established favourite is All the Year Round, for sowings from spring until autumn. Musette, with a large heart, crops in early summer, and a later sowing will produce heads in autumn. It is resistant to mildew, mosaic virus and root aphid.

Hilde will also give early summer crops. For container crops and close planting, Tom Thumb is the best choice, producing heads the size of tennis-balls in summer and autumn. Soraya, resistant to virus and mildew, is one of the commercial crops now available to the gardener. For winter supplies grown under glass, varieties include Kwiek, Dandie and May Queen.

Cabbage: *crispheads* The old favourites are Webbs Wonderful, for summer, and Avoncrisp for supplies through to autumn. The commercially grown variety Saladin is now available for gardeners. It was bred to be resistant to tipburn (when the edges of the leaves turn brown, usually through rapid loss of water). Other commercial varieties now available include Lakeland – resistant to viral disease and root aphid; Great Lakes – resistant to bolting; and the

Below, Lobjoits Green, a Cos variety.

Above, Avoncrisp.

disease-resistant Malika, which is suitable for growing under glass for spring cropping. Marmer is also for winter use. And there is Iceberg, the most popular crisphead found on supermarket shelves.

Cos For large deep-green hearts grow Lobjoits Green, which can be grown through winter but is better protected. Winter Density can also be sown in autumn for spring supplies. Little Gem, with a small head, can be grown in blocks or containers for both summer and (given protection) winter crops.

Looseleaf Salad Bowl has large curled leaves – a little like those of endive. For contrast there is Red Salad Bowl, with brownish-red leaves.

27

The plant's needs

Lettuce needs a rich fertile, moisture-retentive soil. Dig in plenty of well-rotted manure or compost that will break down into moisture-retaining humus. The ideal pH level is about 6.5. For winter lettuce grown outdoors, choose a part of the garden most sheltered from the cold.

Cultivating leaf lettuce for a cut-and-grow again crop

This is the way to get a steady supply of leaves throughout summer and winter, rather than a summer glut of over-large hearts. Use leaf lettuce or cos varieties and grow them close together. Mark out an area of about one sq yd/90sq cm, and in spring broadcast the seed over it. Thin to only 2in/5cm apart. Keep well watered at all times.

After about six weeks leaves will be ready for cutting, about 1in/2.5cm above ground level. New growth will appear after a further six weeks. The most to expect is two cuttings from every sowing, so successional sowings must be made every week until late spring.

For a winter crop, sow seed of Lobjoits Green and Little Gem in late summer. Cover with a cloche for supplies through to early winter.

Container growing

A container should be 12in/30cm or more wide, 6-8in/15-20cm deep, and about 2ft/60cm long. Fill it with quality loam potting compost. In spring, sow seed for leaf

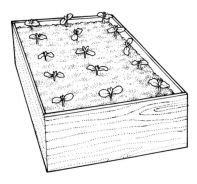

lettuce as already described. For small-hearted butterhead lettuce, choose Tom Thumb and for hearted cos lettuce, Little Gem. Mark out three rows 4in/10cm apart, starting 2in/5cm from the edge of the container. Sow seed thinly and cover with a

light sifting of soil. Thin seedlings to 4in/10cm apart – 18 plants in a container of that size. For larger heads, space plants 6in/15cm apart. Always keep container plants well watered; in warm weather twice daily watering may be necessary.

Growing the conventional way for large heads

For summer and autumn crops, sow seed outdoors in spring. Take out drills

½in/1.25cm deep, 12in/30cm apart for crisphead varieties, 10in/25cm apart for butterhead and cos varieties, and for Little Gem and Tom Thumb. Make a first thinning about 3in/7.5cm apart and finally thin to 12in/30cm (crisphead), 10in/25cm (butterhead and cos) and 6in/15cm for the small varieties, making uniform blocks of

plants for each type. Water the plants after thinning and keep well watered through the growing period. Make successional sowings every two or three weeks until summer.

For lettuce up to early winter, sow Avoncrisp in late summer in drills 12in/30cm apart and thin to 12in/30cm. Cover with cloches.

Lettuce for eating in winter and late winter must be grown under glass. Sow such varieties as Kwiek, Dandie and May Queen in seed trays in late summer or early autumn. Thin to 3in/7.5cm apart and

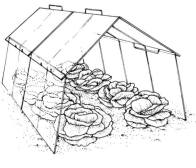

later transplant, 10in/25cm apart, in a greenhouse, frame, or open ground protected by cloches. To avoid attack by fungal diseases, keep the plants well ventilated.

For lettuce to eat in spring, grow varieties such as Malika and Winter Density. Only in mild areas are they likely to grow well outdoors without protection. In cold areas, they should be grown under cloches or in a frame. Sow seed in early autumn, thinning to 3in/7.5cm. In early spring, thin to 12in/30cm apart.

USING LETTUCE

Raw lettuce, especially the outer leaves, is a reasonable source of vitamin C, and there are traces of the usual minerals. It is not suitable for freezing.

For a simple salad, use lettuce on its own. For something more interesting, combine it with endive, chicory, watercress and celery tossed in a dressing of olive oil and wine vinegar. You could even add chopped tomatoes, cucumbers and seedless grapes.

Lettuce can be cooked · the

Victorians would do little else with it because of their fear of uncooked foods. Lettuce soup has a clean refreshing taste. Cook chopped onion in good chicken stock until tender. Add a shredded head of lettuce, some lemon juice and seasoning and simmer for one or two minutes. Liquidize.

The meatier lettuces, such as cos, can be stir-fried in oil, with finely chopped onion, for about two minutes.

SALAD PESTS AND DISEASES

Pests

Slugs and snails are the principal scourge of salad plants. They can be controlled with slug pellets or organic products that don't harm birds or pets.

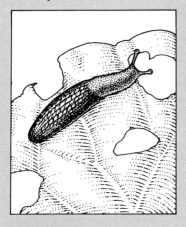

Root aphid attacks the roots of plants, covering them with white woolly deposits. Growth is generally stunted, the leaves may turn yellow

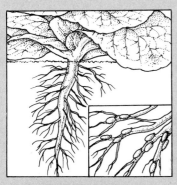

and the whole plant wilt dramatically. Water the plants around the soil with malathion. Organic growers may prefer to use a derris solution. Growing a resistant variety may lessen the problem.

Aphids can also be a nuisance above ground, covering the leaves with sticky honeydew and spreading mosaic virus. Spray with malathion, derris or soft soap. Cutworms attack

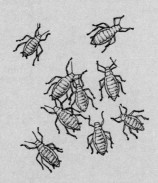

roots, causing leaf wilt. Sometimes they gnaw through the plants at ground level. Hoe round the plants, removing any of the offenders as they appear.

Diseases

Downy mildew is the most threatening disease. Damp is the major cause. Avoid trouble by never

watering directly on to the plants, always around them. If lettuces are grown under glass or cloches, make sure the ventilation is sufficient. Affected leaves will be covered with yellowish patches and areas of white mould on the undersides. Remove and burn them. If the leaves are only mildly affected, spray them with zineb. After an attack, wait several years before growing lettuce on the same patch. Try to lessen the problem by growing resistant varieties such as Little Gem, Great Lakes and Avoncrisp.

Grey mould causes plants to rot at the stems and collapse. It is easily recognized by the reddish-brown colouring of the stems. Whitish-grey fungal patches also appear on the leaves. As with downy mildew, avoid

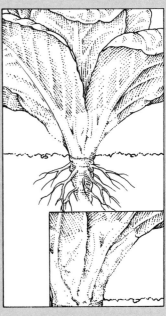

damp conditions. Remove infected leaves or the whole plant. Spray lightly affected plants with benomyl.

Mosaic virus, spread by aphids, causes yellow and pale-green mottling of leaves. There is no cure. Lift and burn infected plants.

SPROUTING SEEDS

From left to right, adzuki, soya, alfalfa, mung, sunflower and fenugreek seeds.

*T*he hour of the sprouting seed has come: it satisfies so many of the modern demands made of a vegetable that you could almost call it high-tech. It is nutritious, cooked or uncooked; it is versatile, a useful addition to many a vegetarian dish; nothing could be simpler to grow or give more rapid results. From sowing to harvesting is a matter of days, given the right temperature to induce germination. The only attention the seeds need while sprouting is thorough rinsing, usually twice a day, to prevent them from turning sour. And all this without having to move outdoors.

Almost all vegetable seeds can be sprouted, but some taste better than others. A few are harmful, in particular the poisonous seeds of potato and tomato, and their sprouts must not be eaten. Moreover, it is sensible to eat all sprouted seeds in moderation, since as well as being packed with vitamins and minerals they contain traces of toxic substances. These do no harm when the sprouts are eaten raw in small quantities and mixed with salad leaves, but platefuls of them tossed in oil and vinegar and eaten regularly will damage your health. Cooking – and this generally means a rapid stir-fry – reduces the toxicity, but the best idea is to use small amounts to add new and interesting flavours to dishes.

Seeds for sprouting can be bought at health food shops and nurseries. Make sure that they are seeds in-tended for sprouting and eating and not for sowing in the garden, for the latter are likely to have been treated with fungicides and insecticides. Health food shops and nurseries that include in their lists a section devoted to sprouting seeds are the safest sources of supplies.

The equipment for sprouting can be as simple as a jam jar and a little plastic tray. But there are plastic towers designed specifically for sprouting. They usually have several tiers so that different seeds can be sprouted on each level. The job of rinsing is also made easier: water is poured in at the top of the tower, channelled over the surface of each tier, the excess eventually collecting in the base. It is essential that the seeds never stand in water, or they will become mouldy and unusable. It is equally important that the seeds never dry out – the sure way to failure. A balance between the two is needed, so that the seeds are always in a moist atmosphere in the warmth (an airing cupboard may well provide the right temperature).

Under these conditions the seeds will germinate, producing white stems if grown in the dark and green stems if grown in the light, and the beginnings of seed leaves after a few days. This is the stage at which they are at their best for eating, usually no more than 1in/2.5cm long. After that they lose their flavour and become bitter and inedible.

Sprouting in a jar

Thoroughly wash the seeds, removing any that are obviously bad or discoloured. To hasten sprouting, soak the seed overnight. By the following morning they will have begun to swell. Rinse and drain them and put them in a jar to a depth of no more than ¾in/2cm. This will ensure that there is plenty of room for the seeds to grow to about four times their original volume. Don't put too many in the jar; if you have soaked too many, put them in another jar.

Cover the top of the jar with muslin or similar porous material and secure it with an elastic band. Place the jar on its side in a shallow container. Raise the bottom of the jar by putting a piece of wood under it so that any excess water can drain away from the seeds through the muslin. Put the jar in a warm place in a temperature of 55-70°F/13-21°C. If the seeds germinate in the

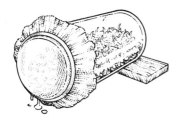

light, the sprouts will be green and soft, while those which are kept in the dark will be white and crisp. An ideal sprouting place is an airing cupboard, which provides both darkness and warmth. Seeds can be started off in the dark and moved into the light when they have begun to sprout, but not into direct sunlight, that will dry them out.

It is essential to rinse the seeds daily, usually twice - morning and evening. Empty the seeds into a fine kitchen sieve and rinse under a gentle flow of water

from the cold tap. (Rinsing under a strong jet of water is likely to part the developing stem from the seed.) Let them drain and then return them to the jar, covering the top again with the muslin.

Sprouting in a tray

Rinse the seed and soak overnight. Place several layers of dampened paper towelling in the bottom of a shallow tray. Scatter the seeds over the surface and cover with a further layer of dampened paper. Put the tray in a plastic bag and place it in a warm dark place. When the seeds have germinated, take the tray out of the plastic bag and remove the covering layer of paper. Leave in the dark for white shoots and move into the light for green ones. Rinse twice a day, morning and evening, making sure that excess water is poured away. With this method, the seeds will become embedded in the paper towelling. Both seed and stem may come away with a gentle tug, but it is more likely that the stems will have to be cut, so there will be some waste.

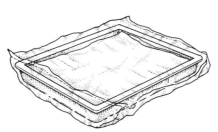

Sprouting in a purpose-built tower

After the layers of the tower have been spread with well-washed seeds, pour water into the tower twice a day. This will be channelled over the surface area of each layer and will eventually run through to collect in the base. The seeds need never be disturbed until they have sprouted and are ready for use. Each floor of the tower is detachable so that it can be removed, emptied, washed and filled with fresh seeds.

USING THE SPROUTS

Before using the sprouts rinse them thoroughly, especially if they are to be eaten raw. Add some to mixed-leaf salads or make them into a separate small dish after tossing them in vinaigrette, sour cream, or thinned-down mayonnaise dressings. A few can be added to soups and stews shortly before serving to vary the flavour and give a crunchy texture.

As a dish on their own, the best way of cooking them is to stir-fry as the Chinese do with mung bean sprouts. It is not necessary to have a wok to do this; a normal frying pan is just as good. Heat a little vegetable oil and add the bean sprouts, stirring all the time as they cook. Don't cook for more than two minutes so that they remain crisp and don't lose too much of their nutritional value. For added flavour, follow the Chinese method by stir-frying a little finely chopped onion, garlic or ginger in the oil before adding the bean sprouts. Sprouted seeds will keep for about a week in a refrigerator in a plastic bag or sealed container, but they should be rinsed every day. However, they are best eaten within two days. As they are so easy and quick to grow, they are not worth freezing. You will soon learn to judge how many seeds to start off for your everyday needs.

ADZUKI BEAN
(Phaseolus angularis)

The adzuki bean is popular in China and Japan. The beans can be cooked in a similar way to French or runner beans or dried and used in casseroles. When the beans are used for sprouting the shoots have a sweet nutty flavour and a crisp crunchy texture.

Use either the jar or tray method, placing the seeds in the dark to produce blanched shoots. Rinse at least twice a day, and three or four times if possible. Sprouting takes four to six days and the sprouts are ready to use when ½-1in/1.25-2.5cm long. Eat raw or lightly stir-fried.

ALFALFA
(Medicago sativa)

Alfalfa is rich in vitamins B and C and in minerals, which is why farmers grow it as cattle feed, but it makes a tasty salad ingredient for humans too. As a sprouting seed it has a sweet fresh garden pea flavour.

Use the jar method. When the seeds have germinated, place the jar in the light to turn the shoots green. Rinse twice a day. Sprouting takes three to four days and the shoots are ready to use when they are 1-2in/2.5-5cm long. Best eaten raw in salads and as a garnish in sandwiches.

BARLEY
(Hordeum vulgare)

Although barley is not usually thought of as an edible sprouting seed, when the sprouts are very small they have an interesting nutty flavour. They are also a source of vitamin B. In India and Japan

barley grown to maturity is a valuable food, but in Europe and the United States it is mainly used as malted barley for brewing or as pearl barley, an ingredient of substantial broths.

Use the tray or jar method, rinsing the seeds twice a day. They should sprout in three to four days. Eat the sprouted seeds when the roots are the same length as the seed; longer than that and they will taste unpleasant. Eat raw or briefly stir-fried.

BUCKWHEAT
(Fagopyrum sagittatum)

Buckwheat is used to make flour for cakes and pancakes in Russia, and in the United States for griddle cakes. In Russia it is also cooked in a similar way to rice.

To sprout buckwheat, use the jar method. After germination bring the jar into the light so that the shoots turn green. Rinse once a day. Sprouting takes two to four days. Eat the shoots when they are about ½in/1.25cm long. Use raw in salads, or add to soups and stews a moment before serving.

CHICK PEA
(Cicer arietinum)

Chick peas are widely grown in the Near East, North Africa and Mediterranean region. In India they are part of the staple diet, sometimes cooked with spices and tomatoes or made into a purée mixed with spices. While the cooked bean has a mealy texture the sprouts have a lighter texture and a more delicate flavour.

Use the jar method. The only disadvantage with chick peas is that they require frequent rinsing - four to five times a day. Sprouts will be ready in three or four days when they are about ½in/1.25cm long. Stir-fry the sprouts with onions and spices for about five minutes, or use them in soups, cooking for five to eight minutes.

FENUGREEK
(Trigonella foenum-graecum)

Fenugreek provides one of the distinctive spice flavours in curry dishes. The seeds are roasted before being ground to a powder. Roast them too long and the flavour becomes very bitter. Keep them too long after roasting and they will begin to smell unpleasantly of cheap Indian restaurants. When the seeds are first sprouted they tend to have a strong flavour, but when they are ready to eat this almost disappears, leaving a mild but spicy and unusual taste.

Use the jar method, rinsing twice a day. Bring the sprouts into the light to turn them green. If you like the curry flavour, eat them when they are about ½in/1.25cm long. If not, leave them until they are 2-3in/5-7.5cm long, when they will taste more mild. Use them raw, dressed in oil and vinegar, or stir-fried for about two minutes. Don't cook them any longer or they will be bitter.

LENTIL
(Lens esculenta)

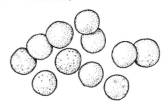

Lentil seeds come in two forms: the orange, split seeds, which cannot be used for sprouting, or the green-grey whole seeds, which can. Lentils are grown all over Africa, India and around the Mediterranean. In India they are the basis of dahl, a purée of the beans cooked with onion, garlic, ginger and tumeric. The sprouts have a high vitamin B content.

Sprout the green lentils in a jar in the dark, rinsing daily. They should be ready in about three or four days when they are about 1in/2.5cm long. Use them to make soup by simmering the sprouts in a rich meat stock with chopped onion for about ten minutes and then liquidizing. Or sauté them in oil with sliced onion, celery and chopped tomato and seasoning, as a vegetable dish.

MUNG BEAN
(Phaseolus aureus)

The mung bean is native to India, but is more familiar from its regular appearances on Chinese restaurant menus. In their sprouted form the beans are an excellent source of protein, minerals and vitamins. Beans can be bought already sprouted, but it is easy to sprout them yourself.

Use either the tray or jar method and sprout the seed in the dark to get crisp white shoots. Rinse two or three times a day. Sprouting should be complete in five days when the shoots are about 2in/5cm long. Stir-fry in oil with finely chopped onion and garlic for two or three minutes. Or serve raw, on their own with a vinaigrette dressing, or combined with shredded carrot, finely chopped cucumber and a few raisins, and dressed with vinaigrette or mayonnaise.

RADISH
(Raphanus sativus)

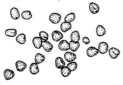

If you like the hot peppery taste of radish, try sprouting the seed instead of growing it to maturity for the roots.

Use the jar method and bring the sprouts into the light for a day to turn them green. Sprouts should be ready in three to four days when they are no more than 1in/2.5cm long. Use as a garnish in sandwiches, or on their own tossed in vinaigrette. They can also be added to mixed salads for contrasting flavour.

RYE
(Secale cereale)

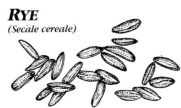

Rye started off life in Central Europe and was then introduced to the United States, where it was used to form the basis of the famous rye whiskey. Elsewhere the grain

is made into flour for bread, biscuits and cakes.

Use the jar method, sprouting the seeds in the dark. Rinse two or three times a day. They should be ready in three to four days and, like barley sprouts, are eaten when the roots are the the same size as the seeds. Eat raw dressed with vinaigrette. Or sauté them in oil or butter, with mushrooms and seasoning.

SOYA BEAN
(Glycine max)

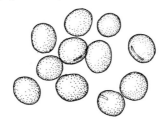

Soya beans are one of the richest possible sources of protein and vitamins. The Chinese have used these versatile beans for years: green soya beans are cooked in the pods and eaten hot; fermented beans are the basis of soy sauce; milk is extracted from them, and they are used to produce oil and flour. In the West we have used them as a meat substitute and as the basis of soya milk, but as a sprouting seed the superb qualities of the soya bean have yet to be fully recognized.

Use the tray or jar methods, in the dark for white shoots. Pick over the beans before adding water, rejecting broken seed. Remove any that have not started to germinate after the first day. Rinse frequently – three of four times a day – as they have a tendency to sour. After about five days, when shoots are around 2in/5cm long, they are ready for eating. Sweat them in oil with courgettes, peppers, tomatoes and seasoning for about 15 minutes.

SUNFLOWER
(Helianthus annuus)

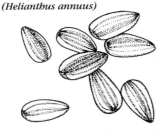

Like the soya bean, sunflower seeds have many uses. Oil, high in polyunsaturated fatty acids, is extracted from the seeds and

used for cooking and for making margarine. Cattle are fed on the stems, and oilcake, a by-product of oil extraction, is also used as animal feed. The seeds are fed to poultry and, when roasted, are also enjoyed by humans.

Use the jar method to sprout the seeds, keeping them in the dark. Rinse twice daily. After two to three days, when sprouts are ½in/1.25cm long, they are ready to eat. If left to grow bigger they will lose their sweet flavour, becoming coarse and strong. Serve raw with vinaigrette or stir-fry in oil for about three minutes.

TRITICALE
(Triticum/Secale)

Triticale is a hybrid cross between wheat and rye, with a sweet flavour not unlike corn.

Use the jar or tray methods, raising the sprouts in the dark. Rinse two or three times a day. Eat them when they are about 2in/5cm long, before the roots become tough and unpalatable. Eat them raw with vinaigrette or stir-fry in oil for about five minutes. They can also be added to soups.

WHEAT
(Triticum vulgare)

Wheat is probably the best of all sprouted grains for flavour. Its sweetness adds an interesting contrast to salads, soups and stews. It is also the most nutritious of all the cereals – high in carbohydrate content (therefore an invaluable source of energy), and in protein, minerals and vitamins.

Use the jar method, growing sprouts in the dark. Rinse two or three times daily. They should be ready in three to five days when the roots are no bigger than the seed; if left longer, they will be tough. Make them into a breakfast muesli, mixing wheat sprouts with chopped apple, raisins, sunflower seeds, yogurt or milk.

BRASSICAS

*T*he hardy brassicas have long been associated with a winter diet, pods and seeds taking their place in summer. Brussels sprouts are a typical winter vegetable, but how they have changed in recent years. No longer large and blowzy, today's small tight heads of leaves are something to look forward to. For a really marvellous taste, pick them at the 'button sprout' stage.

Even cabbage has emerged with a new reputation. Large heads of tough unappetizing leaves are a thing of the past. Now heads are small, ball-shaped or conical, and tender enough to be eaten raw. Some varieties that can make hearts are grown instead for individual loose leaves with the cut-and-grow-again technique.

Cauliflowers can be grown all the year round and the latest breakthrough is mini-cauliflowers. They take up far less room, make a helping for two persons (or one greedy one), and are easily frozen.

Sprouting broccoli is a winter vegetable rapidly being overtaken in popularity by calabrese. However, it is not hardy and in northern Europe can be raised only in spring and summer, even though it is available all the year round on supermarket shelves, jetted in from warmer climates.

BRUSSELS SPROUT
(Brassica oleracea var. *bullata gemmifera)*

*F*orget all about the old varieties of sprouts with their large unappetizing heads. Today's Brussels sprout is small but beautiful. Tight, tasty heads have been achieved through the development of F_1 hybrids but the gardener has an essential role – to pick them when they are at their best. This is the 'button sprout' stage, when they are no more than ¾in/1.9cm across, with leaves still tightly closed. Never leave them beyond this point – you will ruin an ideal crop.

By carefully selecting varieties it is possible to pick sprouts from early autumn through to early spring. Excess supplies should be frozen. If you want to grow sprouts specifically for freezing, choose a variety that matures in autumn, when the sprouts are uniform, perfect and untouched by frost. To ensure that all the sprouts are even in size the plants can be stopped when the sprouts are about ½in/1.25cm in diameter; this means removing the growing point and this should be done only to early-maturing plants.

All sprouts need plenty of room to grow and develop, so they are not suitable for close planting or container growing.

Varieties

The earliest-maturing sprouts, in early autumn and autumn, are Peer Gynt. They are medium-sized, solid and suitable for freezing. Mallard and Roger crop from autumn to early winter, with medium-sized sprouts. Both varieties are not given to toppling over. Widgeon will crop from late autumn to early winter. Citadel produces small sprouts from early winter, and is excellent for freezing. Rampart will crop from early winter to winter and Troika extends through to late winter. (Don't stop plants of Rampart and Troika; doing so will have little if any effect.) To take supplies through to early spring, sow seed of Fortress for medium, solid sprouts.

Make one concession to the old-established varieties by searching out the French variety Noisette, which has possibly the smallest sprouts, with a definite nutty flavour.

The plant's needs

Brussels sprouts need a rich fertile soil. It must also be solid to provide anchorage

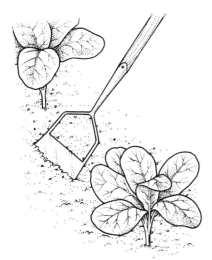

for these tall and heavy plants. In light sandy soil the plants are likely to rock in a breeze and eventually fall over. Choose a sheltered spot to limit the problem. Prepare the ground in autumn by digging in plenty of well-rotted manure or compost, being especially generous with it in sandy soils.

Like other brassicas, Brussels sprouts need an alkaline soil, with a pH level of 6.5 to 7.

Sowing seed

Early-maturing varieties (Peer Gynt, Mallard and Roger) can be sown in late winter in frames or under glass. Take out drills ½in/1.25cm deep and 6in/15cm apart. Sow the seed thinly, about 1in/2.5cm between each one. Cover with a fine sifting of soil. (If there is no protection available, wait until early spring is under way before sowing.) Thin seedlings to 3in/7.5cm and when they are about 6in/15cm tall transplant them, 20in/50cm apart each way in a block formation. A block 40in sq/100cm sq will contain nine plants. Firm and water the plants.

Sow seed of other varieties in a prepared seed-bed in spring, in drills ½in/1.25cm deep and 6in/15cm apart. Thin to 6in/15cm apart. In late spring or early summer transplant, spacing the plants 24in/60cm apart in a block formation. (These plants need more room to develop because they will be in the ground longer.) Firm and water the plants. Keep well watered throughout summer, especially in periods of warm weather.

In autumn, draw up the soil around the stems to support them. If tall-growing varieties such as Roger, Widgeon and Rampart seem rocky, stake them. Peer Gynt, Mal-

Brussels sprout, Widgeon variety.

lard and Fortress are medium-sized plants that may not need support. Remove any yellowing leaves.

Start harvesting the sprouts when they are still small and tightly closed. Either cut them off with a sharp knife or twist them away from the stem. Take a few sprouts from each plant, starting from the bottom where they are more developed. If the sprouts are to be frozen and the plants have earlier been stopped, the plants can be stripped. Discard any that have open leaves.

FREEZING AND COOKING BRUSSELS SPROUTS

Choose small evenly sized sprouts for freezing. Remove any blemished outer leaves. Blanch in boiling water for two to three minutes; the smaller the sprouts the less time they should be blanched. Drain, cool and dry thoroughly. Pack into plastic bags and freeze. As long as the sprouts have been thoroughly dried they will not stick together.

Before cooking Brussels sprouts remove any imperfect outer leaves.

Boil in salted water for six to eight minutes; by then they should be cooked, but still firm and crunchy. Never let them collapse to a watery pulp. Coat in melted butter and grind black pepper over them, or use freshly ground nutmeg.

If by mischance the sprouts should collapse, all is not lost. Purée them with cream and butter and season with pepper or nutmeg.

BROCCOLI

(Brassica oleracea var. botrytis cymosa)

White- and purple-sprouting broccoli used to be among the mainstays of winter and spring vegetables, but no longer. They have been pushed into the background by the appearance of calabrese (*Brassica oleracea* var. *italica*), and for that we have the Italians to thank.

Calabrese is not hardy, and the supplies that appear on supermarket shelves all year round are jetted in from Spain and other warm countries where it is possible to grow crops in all seasons. In colder areas a gardener has to be content with a summer and autumn crop, freezing any excess. The inferior white- and purple-sprouting broccoli are then grown for cropping from late winter to late spring.

In the past it has been recommended that the seed of calabrese be raised in a seed-bed and transplanted, but this often leads to arrested development of the plants, resulting in small heads. It is best to sow seed where it is to grow and thin the seedlings, or to sow in soil blocks so that the seedlings can be planted out without disturbance to the roots.

Calabrese will grow satisfactorily if planted closer than white- or purple-sprouting broccoli – indeed the current trend favours close planting, but not so close that it could ever be grown in a container.

Varieties

White- and purple-sprouting broccoli Both early purple-sprouting and early white-sprouting will crop in early spring. Late white-sprouting and late purple-sprouting will crop two to three weeks later. There is also a perennial variety, Nine Star Perennial, which needs plenty of room to develop.

Calabrese Most of the calabrese varieties are F₁ hybrids, bred for their reliability and consistency. Mercedes, with compact medium-sized heads, is one of the first varieties to mature; a sowing in spring should be ready in summer. (The blue-green heads turn dark green when cooked.) Citation is another early-maturer with large, domed, green heads. After the main heads have been cut, leave the plants to produce side-shoots of small tender heads. Green Comet will also crop early and produce small side heads after the large main heads have been cut. Emperor and Shogun are the latest F₁ varieties,

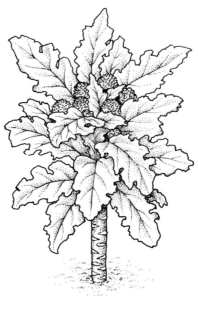

Emperor cropping early and Shogun, with blue-green heads, a later developer.

Finally there is Romanesco, different in appearance to the other varieties. It is almost a novelty plant with its tight, lime-green, cornet-shaped florets. It crops in late autumn, later than the others.

The plant's needs

The soil needs to be rich and fertile. Prepare it well in advance of sowing by digging in plenty of well-rotted manure and compost in autumn. This will break down into rich moisture-retentive humus, essential for successful crops of calabrese. Firm soil is also necessary, so sandy soil must have more manure and compost than other soils. Frequent watering will also be needed to keep the soil constantly moist. The ideal pH level is 6.5 to 7.

Sowing seed

In spring, sow seed of calabrese in drills ½in/1.25cm deep and 15in/37.5cm apart, where the plants are to grow. When the seedlings can be handled easily, thin to 6in/15cm. Seed can also be sown in soil blocks, planting the seedlings out in late spring or early summer when the plants are about 3in/7.5cm tall. Plants raised in this way can be moved without disturbing the roots, and it also makes planting out into block beds so much easier. Allow 10in/25cm each way.

Keep the plants well watered at all times. Twice daily watering may be necessary in spells of warm weather. Spread a mulch round the base of each plant to help moisture retention.

Cut the main head when the buds are still tight and have not started to open. Once they have, they are past their best. Leave the plants to produce side-shoots, which should be ready for picking about two weeks later. Treat the plants then as a cut-and-grow-again crop, taking only a few shoots to encourage more to grow. For a succession of plants, sow seed until summer to ensure crops through to late autumn. Sow seed of Romanesco in summer for the latest crop.

Sow seed of white- and purple-sprouting broccoli in a prepared seed-bed in spring. Drills should be ½in/1.25cm deep and 6in/15cm apart. Thin to 3in/7.5cm. In late spring or early summer, transplant the seedlings when they are about 4in/10cm tall to a sheltered part of the garden, spacing the plants 18in/45cm each way in a

block. Keep well watered at all times and apply a mulch around the base of the plants to retain moisture.

Before the onset of winter, earth up the stems and stake them so that they will not be rocked by the wind. Start cutting in late winter, taking the entire head first. This will encourage new side growths to appear. Cutting will be possible until spring or late spring when plants will start going to seed.

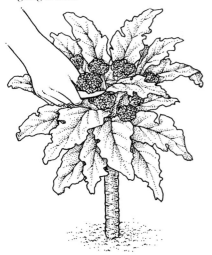

CABBAGE
(Brassica oleracea)

If you think cabbage has a bad name, it is time you tried growing some of the new varieties, which are as much a revelation as the new varieties of broccoli. There are many new F$_1$ hybrids among all types of cabbage – spring, summer, winter and savoy – that have been bred to produce tight heads with excellent flavour.

Some of the heads may be ball-shaped or conical, taking up far less room, so that close planting and even limited container growing is possible. The summer cabbage Minicole (with small, tight round heads) is one to try and the spring cabbage Pixie (with conical heads) is another. Close planting of Pixie will also produce spring greens instead of hearted cabbage by using the cut-and-grow-again technique. New varieties have also been bred to stand for a few weeks without deteriorating or splitting – the usual fate of older varieties if left too long in the ground.

Quality has improved so dramatically that there is no need to be afraid of using cabbage raw in green salads, or for making coleslaw. And for a totally different taste and texture, both raw and cooked, there is Chinese cabbage (see *Oriental vegetables*).

Varieties

Spring cabbage is sown in late summer for cropping the following spring. Spring Hero has solid medium-sized heads ready in late spring. Pixie can be raised for cut-and-grow-again leaves, and then left to heart-up in late spring. (This variety is suitable for container growing but only for leaves and not for hearted cabbage.) Offenham 1 – Myatts Offenham Compacta can be grown as greens or for hearts, producing medium-sized heads in late spring.

Summer cabbage is sown in spring, or in early spring under cloches, for cropping in summer or early autumn. Spitfire and Spivoy are early-maturing conical cabbages, with medium-sized heads, ready in early summer. Stonehead has small solid white heads that make excellent coleslaw. They will stand for three to four weeks. Minicole, which is suitable for close planting, matures around the same time and will stand for several weeks. Hispi, with conical heads maturing in early summer and summer, is tasty eaten raw in salads. Ruby Ball is a round red cabbage ready in

late summer. Autoro is another red cabbage, cropping later in autumn.

Winter cabbage is sown in late spring for winter use. The blue-green heads of Celtic have white hearts. They mature in early winter but stand well to late winter. Jupiter produces small round heads which can be used raw or cooked. They are ready in early winter, lasting through to winter. For late-maturing cabbage, there is January King – Hardy Late Stock 3, with medium-sized heads maturing in early winter but standing until late winter.

Savoy cabbage is sown at the same time as winter cabbage and ready for use at about the same time. New F$_1$ hybrids include Ice Queen with the familiar wrinkled and puckered dark-green heads, ready in early winter. Wirosa has solid dark-green heads, maturing in early winter but standing until late winter.

The plant's needs

Cabbage needs a rich, well-draining, solid soil prepared well in advance of sowing seed. Sowing on newly manured soil leads to all kinds of problems – poor soft growth and collapsing plants. Prepare the ground several months in advance by digging in well-rotted manure or compost that will break down into moisture-retaining humus in time for sowing. The soil will also have a chance to firm up again after the disturbance of digging. Choose a sheltered but sunny part of the garden. Lime is essential for healthy growth, so if the soil is acid, lime it in winter to achieve a pH level of 6.5 to 7.

Sowing seed of spring cabbage

In late summer, sow seed in a prepared seed-bed. Take out drills 1in/1.25cm deep and 6in/15cm apart. Sow seed thinly, aiming for about 1in/2.5cm between seeds. Thin seedlings to 3in/7.5cm when they can be easily handled. Transplant to where they are to grow in autumn when the plants have about four formed leaves. If the cabbages are being grown to produce heads, space them 12in/30cm apart each way. A block 4ft sq/1.2m sq will contain 20 plants. For greens, plants can be spaced at 4in/10cm intervals in rows 12in/30cm apart.

Heads should be ready for cutting in spring and late spring. Greens or individual leaves can be cut in spring. Take a few leaves from each plant to encourage new growth. If you want greens and hearts as well, don't cut any leaves from every third cabbage, but instead leave them to form a heart.

Sowing seed of summer and red cabbage

Seed can be sown in late winter or early spring in a frame or, if protected, under cloches. Otherwise wait until the early part of spring before sowing. Take out drills ½in/1.25cm deep and 6in/15cm apart. Space seed in the drills 1in/2.5cm apart. Thin to 3in/7.5cm. Transplant protected plants to growing positions in spring and the later-sown plants in late spring or early summer. Space plants

Cabbage, Ruby Ball variety.

14in/35cm apart each way, with the exception of the variety Minicole which need be only 10in/25cm apart. Keep plants well watered at all times.

Sowing seed of winter and savoy cabbage

In late spring, sow seed in a prepared seed-bed. Take out drills ½in/1.25cm deep and 6in/15cm apart. Leave 1in/2.5cm between each seed and thin to 3in/7.5cm when they can be handled easily. Transplant winter cabbage in early summer, and savoy cabbage in summer, both types at 18in/45cm each way.

Growing spring cabbage in containers

Non-hearting spring cabbage is the only type suitable for container growing. Choose a variety such as Pixie. Containers should be at least 12in/30cm wide, 10in/25cm deep and about 2ft/60cm long. Fill with quality loam potting compost. In late summer, sow seed in shallow drills 4in/10cm apart. Start the rows about 2in/5cm from the edge of the container so that there are three rows in a 12in/30cm-wide container. Sow the seed 1in/2.5cm apart in the drills. Thin seedlings to 4in/10cm apart, taking out the weakest.

In mild areas the containers need not be covered, but where there is a chance of frost cover with clear plastic secured to wire hoops. Container-grown plants must be kept well watered at all times. Start cutting in spring and late spring, taking a few leaves from each plant. This will encourage new growth.

KALE
(*Brassica oleracea* var. *acephala*)

You may be forgiven for thinking that today's plant breeders have concentrated on the appearance of kale rather than its taste, for the leaves have become ever more cut and curly. But the eating quality has also improved: no longer can it be dismissed as a stand-by between winter and spring when other vegetables are scarce, or simply as cattle food. Because supermarkets now scour the world to fill their shelves with a wide variety of vegetables during those once bleak months, kale is now hard to buy in shops. It is still worth growing to give a different and distinctively native flavour to all those foreign imports. The way to enjoy kale is to cut the leaves when they are small and young. Any left to grow large and coarse will be bitter and totally unappetizing. Kale can grow tall and needs space to develop; it is certainly not suitable for container growing on the patio.

Varieties

Curly-leaved types of kale include the very hardy Dwarf Green Curled, with tightly curled leaves. Tall Green Curled is similar, but taller. Westland Autumn is a small form, growing to about 18in/45cm, and Frosty is even shorter, about 12in/30cm. The latest F_1 hybrid is Fribor, very hardy with finely curled dark-green leaves.

The plant's needs

It is often said that kale is less demanding than other brassicas, but that is no reason to grow it on poor soil. The better the soil the better the crop. In autumn, dig in well-rotted manure or compost. By spring this will have broken down into moisture-retentive humus, essential for good growth. If the soil is acid, lime it to a pH level of 6.5 to 7. Choose a sheltered part of the garden. It may be hardy but, as with all winter vegetables, optimum growing conditions ensure a more rewarding crop.

Sowing seed

In late spring, sow seed in a well-prepared seed-bed. Take out drills ½in/1.25cm deep and 8in/20cm apart, and sow the seeds 1in/2.5cm apart. Thin to 3in/7.5cm, removing the weakest seedlings. In summer, transplant the seedlings to their permanent positions when they are about 6in/15cm tall, spacing them 15in/37.5cm apart.

COOKING AND FREEZING CABBAGE

White cabbage such as Stonehead, ready in late summer, can be used raw in coleslaw salad. Shred or chop the leaves finely. Add shredded carrot and diced apple. Toss all the ingredients in lemon juice, followed by a mixture of mayonnaise and sour cream until everything is coated.

Cabbage should be cooked as briefly as possible so that the end result is still crisp and not soggy. Equally important, the shorter the boiling the less the loss of vitamins and minerals. Boiling cabbage for 30 minutes loses more than half the available nutrients, so keep it short.

Shred the leaves and boil in salted water for four to five minutes. Even better, avoid water altogether and stir-fry in oil for two to three minutes for extra crispness.

Red cabbage can be shredded and braised with grated apples in white wine vinegar and butter. The vinegar keeps the cabbage red and stops it from turning purple.

To freeze cabbage, shred it and then blanch it for about one minute. Drain and allow to dry before packing into plastic bags. Frozen cabbage will take about one minute longer to cook than fresh cabbage.

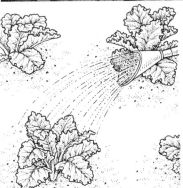

Curly Kale, Frosty variety.

Keep plants well watered during the summer months, especially in spells of warm weather. Taller varieties may need the soil firming around them to prevent their rocking in the wind.

Start cutting the leaves in winter, taking a few leaves from the centre of each plant. This will encourage side-shoots to appear, and these will be ready for cutting from late winter to spring. Always cut small young leaves; the large ones become bitter and inedible.

COOKING AND FREEZING KALE

Very young green leaves can be shredded and eaten raw with other salad leaves, covered in a vinaigrette dressing.

Before cooking kale cut away the tough ribs. Boil the leaves in a small amount of water, as for spinach, for between five and ten minutes, until it is tender but still crunchy. Drain, chop the leaves and mix with butter or cream to serve.

Kale can be frozen by blanching the leaves for about one minute. Drain and let the leaves dry before packing in plastic bags and freezing.

CAULIFLOWER
(Brassica oleracea var. botrytis)

No longer is this princely vegetable reserved for the spacious kitchen garden. The cauliflower has adapted well to the modern technology of close planting, using seed of a miniature variety. A mini-cauliflower head – about 3in/7.5cm in diameter – is enough for a single helping; an easily managed, elegant-to-serve vegetable compared with the large-headed type that has to be broken into florets for cooking.

The other development is the availability of cauliflowers all year round, not just in summer and autumn. This is achieved with varieties that, in very mild climates, will mature over winter; elsewhere they are produced in the special conditions of vast commercial greenhouses.

The ordinary gardener can in part simulate these conditions by sowing early-maturing varieties in heat during winter, but this is hardly the most efficient and cost-effective use of greenhouse space. A far simpler way to bridge the winter gap is to freeze the surpluses of summer and autumn crops, particularly of mini-cauliflowers.

Varieties

Summer cauliflowers For early crops seed of Alpha, Snowball and Dominant can be sown indoors or in a greenhouse in winter and planted out in early spring. These should be ready from early summer to summer. Dok Elgon matures in late summer from an outdoor planting in spring. The varieties Alpha, Snowball and Garant are the best choice for mini-cauliflowers that mature in the summer months. Predominant crops later in the autumn.

Autumn cauliflowers Outdoor sowings of Flora Blanca, Canberra and Barrier Reef from spring to late spring will be ready for cutting from autumn to late autumn.

Winter cauliflowers Viable only in mild areas where they will not suffer from frost damage. The most reliable are Walcheren Winter strains, producing cauliflowers in spring to late spring from sowings made the previous late spring or early summer.

The plant's needs

Cauliflowers do best in loam soils that are rich in humus. Choose a well-sheltered, sunny part of the garden to grow them in. The ground must be prepared thoroughly, well in advance, and that means starting the previous autumn. Dig over the soil, adding well-rotted compost or manure. During the winter any large clods of soil will have been broken down by frost. Raking over the surface will then achieve a fine tilth ready for sowing.

Cauliflowers prefer a lime soil; if it is acid, lime it in winter to achieve a pH level of 6.5 to 7.

Growing mini-cauliflowers from seed

Mini-cauliflowers take far less space in the garden, and though they are small (which is probably in their favour) there are far more of them. The secret is close planting in blocks, not widely spaced in long rows. Try for an early crop by sowing seed of the early-maturing varieties (Alpha, Snowball and Garant) indoors in winter, keeping a temperature of 55°F/13°C.

Either sow in a seed tray or, in preference, in small peat pots so that the seedlings can be transplanted with as little disturbance as possible. Seedlings in trays should be thinned to 2in/5cm between plants. In early spring, harden them off in a cold frame, or put the seed trays outdoors during the day, enclosing them in plastic sheeting but taking care that the plastic does not touch the plant.

A better alternative is to sow the seed in propagating trays with rigid plastic covers that have adjustable ventilation holes. When the seedlings are being hardened off, the covered trays can be placed outdoors and the ventilators opened a little more each day to acclimatize the plants to the cooler outdoor conditions. For a week or so (more if the weather is cold), remember to bring the trays indoors at night and to put them in a cool place.

Plant out in spring. Choose a block of ground about 4ft sq/1.2m sq, in which the young cauliflowers are planted 6in/15cm

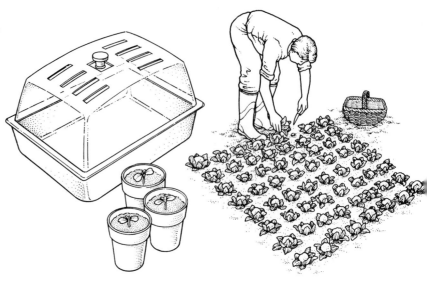

apart each way, as in a chess-board pattern. The whole block will contain 64 plants, compared with four plants in the same area if given the conventional spacing of 24in/60cm apart. These small cauliflowers should be ready for cutting in the early part of summer, depending on the temperatures while growing. Since the cauliflowers round the edges of the block get more light, they will be slightly larger than the others.

Using the same block method, seed can be sown directly into the ground from spring onwards. Take out drills ½in/1.25cm deep and 6in/15cm apart along the square. Thin the seedlings to 6in/15cm apart, choosing the sturdiest. Successional sowings can be made if the ground is available. Cauliflowers grown by the block method tend to mature at the same time, so if there are too many to eat immediately the rest should be frozen.

In planning a sowing programme you can reckon that spring sowings will take about 3½ months to reach maturity while the late spring and early summer sowings will take about 2½ months, because of the higher temperatures in which they are started off. Seed of the later-maturing Predominant, sown in early summer, will produce crops in early autumn and autumn.

Growing the conventional way for large heads

The methods of sowing seed for conventional growing of cauliflowers are the same as for mini-cauliflowers (see *Growing mini-cauliflowers from seed*). The difference begins when it comes to planting

out in the garden, with much greater spacing between the plants. The early-maturing varieties that have been grown indoors are planted out in spring 18in/45cm apart, with the same distance between the rows.

Seed can be sown outdoors in spring. Take out drills ½in/1.25cm deep and 6in/15cm apart. Sow seed thinly, covering with a fine sifting of soil. Thin seedlings to 3in/7.5cm and keep them well watered at all times. In early summer when they are 4-6in/10-15cm tall, transplant them to the prepared bed. Carefully lift them with as much soil as possible around the roots, and replant 24in/60cm apart. Canberra and Barrier Reef can be planted 20in/50cm apart. As the curd develops, bend large outer leaves over it so that it does not yellow in the sun. Water developing plants frequently so that the heads grow to their full size.

Autumn varieties should be sown in spring to late spring, and winter varieties in late spring to early summer. The growing methods are the same as for the summer varieties. Bend leaves over the developing curds of winter varieties to protect them from frost and snow.

Cauliflowers for freezing should have firm white heads. Mini-cauliflowers are frozen whole while large-headed ones should be broken into pieces of a similar size. Wash them thoroughly and blanch in hot salted water for about two to three minutes. If some lemon juice is added to the water, it will help to retain the creamy-white colour of the cauliflower. Drain and allow the cauliflower to get cold.

Dry thoroughly on kitchen paper · and place loose in plastic bags. As long as they have been dried properly they will not freeze together.

Raw cauliflower is not to everyone's taste but that is certainly the way to eat it if all the goodness is to be retained. Small florets can be tossed in vinaigrette or dressed with mayonnaise and added to salad

dishes. Cooked cauliflower loses over half its vitamin C. For that reason it should be cooked as briefly as possible: place it in boiling water, not cold water which has to be brought up to the boil. It should take no more than five minutes to bring it to a desirable tender but crunchy state. Cauliflower cooked from frozen will take about eight minutes.

BRASSICA PESTS AND DISEASES

Pests

Caterpillars If white-cabbage butterflies or cabbage moths hover over your brassica crops, watch out for trouble. Look on the undersides of leaves for eggs and remove them. If the caterpillars are allowed to

develop, they will eat holes in the leaves and deposit excrement, which is particularly unpleasant on white cauliflower curds. Pick off all caterpillars and spray the plants with liquid derris or pyrethrum.

Cabbage root fly lays its eggs in the soil. Developing larvae burrow into the stem and start to eat it. The result is stunted growth and possible death. Cabbages fail to heart, cauliflowers make poor-sized heads, and Brussels sprouts are rendered inedible because the larvae have burrowed into them. Protect plants

when transplanting by sprinkling bromophos around the base.

Flea beetle eats the leaves of seedlings, making small holes. Growth may be stunted or the seedlings die if badly infected. Dust with derris powder or pyrethrum.

Aphids can attack both seedlings and mature plants. They are often found on the undersides of leaves, but may attack almost any part of the plant. They suck the sap, stunting growth and eventually causing death. They are also a menace by spreading viral diseases as they move from plant to plant. Spray plants with liquid derris, pyrethrum or soft soap.

Diseases

Club-root is the worst brassica disease to be visited on the gardener. The roots of the plants swell and then rot, leaves wilt, stems are weakened and fall over. There is no treatment when the disease has

taken hold. Lift and burn the plants. Take preventive measures before planting seedlings: make sure the ground is adequately limed, rotate brassicas each year so that they grow in different parts of the garden, and dip the seedlings in calomel or benomyl solution before transplanting.

Downy mildew is a fungal disease. Yellow patches appear on the top surface of the leaves while the undersides are covered with white furry deposits · the fungus. Excessive damp encourages the disease. Spray with zineb.

Powdery mildew produces powdery white fungal growth on the upper surface of leaves. Remove the infected leaves and spray with benomyl.

Wire stem and damping off attack seedlings, turning the base of the stems black and making the seedlings topple over. Damped-off seedlings die; with wire stem they may survive, but never develop into plants. Prevention is the answer. Never sow seed in cold and wet soil and before sowing apply quintozene powder to the soil. Seed can also be dusted with thiram or captan.

Leaf spot may be a problem, causing brown spots on leaves. Remove affected leaves and burn them. Spray plants with zineb.

Swiss chard, not usually seen in the shops.

SPINACH AND OTHER LEAVES

As Popeye pointed out, spinach is nutritionally the tops, packed with minerals, protein and vitamins. Its one great vice, for the gardener, is its tendency to bolt. New varieties have sorted out that problem and have made it possible to grow spinach all year round, given some protection. The new cut-and-grow-again techniques can also be used to provide a succession of young tender leaves.

Spinach beet is not a bolter, but the leaves must be picked young. Here again the most tender leaves are produced by using the cut-and-grow-again technique. New Zealand spinach is another good substitute for spinach, with a milder flavour.

Other interesting leaves come from unfamiliar vegetables, seldom to be found in shops. Growing them yourself is often the only way to try them. Good King Henry is an ancient plant, with leaves that can be cooked like spinach. It looks attractive enough to be grown in a flower bed. Swiss chard has edible leaves and stems and ruby chard is another highly decorative plant with its red stems.

For gardeners with limited space, some of these leaf vegetables can be grown easily in containers.

SWISS CHARD
(Beta vulgaris)

Swiss chard, or seakale beet, is largely ignored by commercial growers so the only way to sample this hardy vegetable it to grow it for yourself. The tall thick white stems have crinkly triangular green leaves that can be cooked like spinach. The stems are steamed or chopped into pieces and boiled. It is also a decorative plant for the flower garden, as is ruby, or rhubarb, chard, with thinner rich red stems topped with dark-green leaves. The plants are large and need plenty of room to grow, so they are not suitable for container growing.

Varieties

It is often simply described as silver or seakale beet. Fordham Giant, as the name implies, has thicker stems. The red-stemmed type is known as rhubarb, or ruby, chard.

The plant's needs

Swiss chard is not fussy about the type of soil it grows in, but naturally crops will be that much better if the soil has been well cultivated and manured. Dig in plenty of well-rotted manure or compost in late autumn or early winter, leaving it to break down in preparation for spring sowing. A pH level of 6.5 to 7 is ideal.

Sowing seed

In spring, take out drills 1in/2.5cm deep and 15in/37.5cm apart. The seed is large and easy to handle, so it can be sown precisely at intervals of 4in/10cm. Thin out to 12in/30cm apart. The first stems will be ready in summer. As with rhubarb, they should be pulled and not cut. Take hold of the stem at soil level, twisting it away from the plant. Start with the outer stems of the plant, moving inwards. Don't wait until you have giant stems before pulling: they are for eating, not showing, and smaller stems will be much more tender and tastier.

For cropping in winter, make another

PESTS AND DISEASES: SWISS CHARD

Usually trouble-free, though slugs may be a nuisance. Lay slug pellets, or use an organic product that does not harm birds or pets.

sowing in summer or late summer. The plants will need some protection through the winter months. Cover with cloches in early winter or pile straw round the base of the plants. The stems will be ready for pulling in the following spring.

COOKING SWISS CHARD

Cook the stems within a few hours of pulling, the sooner the better, for they quickly go limp. For steaming choose smaller, thinner stems and cook for 20 to 30 minutes. The stems can also be simmered in water for a similar period. Serve with melted butter or a sauce. Larger stems should be cut into 1in/1.5cm pieces and boiled for about 15 minutes.

Very young leaves can be eaten raw in salads, but they are better cooked like spinach, boiled in a small amount of water for eight to ten minutes. Strain and chop the leaves finely, mixing with butter.

GOOD KING HENRY
(Chenopodium bonus-henricus)

There is certainly nothing new about Good King Henry. It has been around for centuries as a hardy perennial plant, grown because it looks attractive and has many culinary uses. The young stems can be blanched as they emerge, by earthing-up the soil in early spring. Leaves can be picked in spring and late spring and cooked like spinach. Small complete stems with flower buds and leaves can be sautéed in butter or oil. Nor does it look out of place in a flower bed. It needs little attention during the year and should be productive for several years before it needs replacing. It deserves to be more widely appreciated.

Varieties

Where it can be found in seed catalogues it will simply be known as Good King Henry.

The plant's needs

As it is an undemanding perennial, there will be a tendency to leave it to its own devices. However, if the soil is well prepared before sowing seed and the plants are regularly dressed with well-rotted manure or compost, the results will be much more rewarding. Choose a moist

part of the garden for it. In winter, dig in the manure or compost so that the soil will be rich in humus for sowing in spring.

Sowing seed

In late spring, take out drills ½in/1.25cm deep and 12in/30cm apart. Sow seed thinly and cover with a fine sifting of soil. Thin to 12in/30cm apart. Cut down the foliage when it turns yellow in the autumn. When growth first appears in spring the following year leave it to develop, perhaps taking a few leaves to cook like spinach.

The following year young shoots can be earthed-up in early spring ready for cutting in spring when they are about 6in/15cm high. Later, complete stems with leaves and flower buds can be cut, but stop this cutting in early summer to allow the plants to build up their strength for the next year's growth. However, some leaves can be picked until late summer as long as individual plants are not stripped.

Cut down yellowing foliage in autumn and dig in well-rotted manure or compost

Good King Henry, versatile and hardy.

Pests and diseases

Usually no problem.

COOKING GOOD KING HENRY

Cook the tender young shoots like asparagus, gently steaming them or simmering them covered with water. Sauté whole tender stems of small leaves or flowers in butter or use them raw in salad with an oil dressing. Like spinach, the leaves are a useful source of iron and can be cooked in the same way. Wash the leaves and simmer in water just covering the bottom of the pan. Cook until tender – about six minutes. Drain and press out excess water. Blend in melted butter for a creamy texture.

SPINACH
(Spinacea oleracea)

There was a time, and not long ago, when spinach had a bad reputation as an incorrigible bolter in dry summer weather, running to flower and seed instead of producing leaves. Today the problem is almost eliminated, thanks to the creation of new varieties that don't bolt so readily.

Excellent crops are produced by using the cut-and-grow-again technique and close-planting methods, with the advantage that they can easily be grown in containers. Spinach is high in protein and vitamins, low in calories, with generous helpings of minerals (sodium, potassium, calcium, magnesium and iron).

It does not do well in cold wet conditions, but can produce a satisfactory winter crop if protected by cloches.

Varieties

For summer and autumn cropping, the old-established favourites are King of Denmark and Long Standing Round, but both are likely to bolt in warm weather. Avoid these and go for Norvak, Sigmaleaf and the latest variety Medania. All are resistant to bolting and they have the added virtue that they can be sown in spring for summer cropping and in autumn for winter and spring cropping.

The plant's needs

A rich fertile soil is essential for healthy spinach, and it should hold water well as an added precaution against bolting. Dig in plenty of well-rotted manure or compost, in autumn for spring sowing and in spring for autumn sowing. Light sandy soil will need more manuring than other types to ensure good moisture retention. Spinach needs lime and the ideal pH level is 6.5 to 7.

The cut-and-grow-again technique

In spring, sow seed in drills 1in/1.25cm deep and 4in/10cm apart. Sow thinly so that there will be little thinning to be done later to get a final spacing of about 2in/5cm. When leaves have grown to some 3in/7.5cm, pick them leaving 1in/2.5cm of the stalk behind, from which new growth will appear. Take a few leaves from each plant rather than stripping a few plants bare. Further sowings can be made every three weeks until summer. If you want some larger plants thin them again to

6in/15cm, after taking two or three cuttings of the young leaves. Keep plants well watered, especially in warm dry weather.

Sow seed in late summer and early autumn for winter and spring cropping. Cover with cloches.

Container growing

Containers should be at least 12in/30cm wide, 6-9in/15-22.5cm deep, and about 2ft/60cm long. Fill with quality loam potting compost. Sow seed in drills as already described in the previous section or broadcast the seed, thinning plants to 2in/5cm each way. In late summer, clear the container and make another sowing for winter and spring. To protect the plants from late autumn onwards, cover the container with an improvised cloche of clear plastic supported on a wire frame.

Sowing seed for large heads of spinach

Prepare the ground as already described. In spring, sow seed in 1in/2.5cm drills, 12in/30cm apart. Thin seedlings to 6in/15cm when they can be handled easily. Further sowings can be made at three-weekly intervals until summer. Leaves should be ready for picking after about ten weeks. Sowings later in the season will be ready in about eight weeks. Take a few leaves from each plant rather than a lot from one; that way you will get further growth.

Make a sowing in late summer and again in early autumn for winter and spring supplies. Cover with cloches to protect the plants and raise the soil temperature.

PESTS AND DISEASES: SPINACH

Pests
Greenfly may attack. Spray with pyrethrum, derris or soft soap.

Diseases
Downy mildew produces yellow patches on leaves and grey mould on the undersides. Excessive damp and overcrowding are the usual causes. Pick off infected leaves and spray plants with zineb.

Spinach blight, caused by the cucumber mosaic virus, may attack the leaves, turning them yellow and making their edges roll inwards and

die. Pick off infected leaves and burn them. Prevent spread of the disease by controlling aphids that carry it from plant to plant.

COOKING SPINACH

Young cut-and-grow-again leaves are so small and tender that they can be used raw in salads. Serve on their own or with other salad leaves, tossed in vinaigrette. To cook, try stir-frying them in oil, but only briefly — about two minutes.

Larger leaves can be frozen. Blanch for two minutes, drain and gently pat leaves dry to get rid of most of the moisture. Pack into plastic bags and freeze.

To cook large leaves, steam them in a little water in the bottom of the pan for five to ten minutes. Drain and squeeze out as much water as possible. Chop and mix with butter and a little nutmeg to serve.

NEW ZEALAND SPINACH
(Tetragonia expansa)

New Zealand spinach has never been very popular, and it is not spinach at all. But it makes a good substitute, milder in flavour, and it will not run to seed, however hot the summer. It is not hardy and is grown only as a summer crop.

Varieties

Seed catalogues offer it only as New Zealand spinach.

The plant's needs

Soil should be prepared in the same way as for spinach. It needs to be just as rich and fertile, with a similar pH level – that is, 6.5 to 7.

Sowing seed

A start can be made in early spring by sowing seed indoors or under glass and at a temperature of about 55°F/13°C. Sow in a seed tray of loam seed compost and thin plants to 2in/5cm. Harden them off outdoors during the day, but bring them in at night.

Sow straight into the ground from late spring. The seeds are hard-skinned, so soak them overnight to improve germination. Sow seeds in groups of three ½in/1.25cm deep at 1ft/30cm intervals, with 2ft/60cm between rows. Thin by leaving only the strong seedlings, spaced 2ft/60cm apart. As they grow the plants will spread, taking up plenty of room. Pinch out growing tips for bushy growth.

From summer start cutting leaves, taking a few from each plant. New growth will keep coming and the plants will survive until the first frosts.

Pests and diseases

Usually no problem.

**COOKING
NEW ZEALAND SPINACH**

Young tender leaves can be stir-fried in a little oil for about two minutes. Cook larger leaves as described for spinach. Freeze the leaves in the same way.

SPINACH BEET
(Beta vulgaris)

Spinach beet, or perpetual spinach, does not suffer from the problems associated with spinach; it will not bolt and it is hardy through winter. If grown to maturity, the leaves will be larger and coarser than those of spinach but smaller tender leaves can be grown by using the cut-and-grow-again and close-planting techniques. It will also grow well in containers.

Varieties

Catalogues usually only offer it as perpetual spinach.

The plant's needs

Prepare soil in the same way as for spinach, and lime it if the soil is acid.

The cut-and-grow-again technique

In spring, sow seed thinly in drills 1in/2.5cm deep and 4in/10cm apart. If necessary, thin to 2in/5cm between plants. Start cutting leaves when they are about 3in/7.5cm tall, leaving 1in/2.5cm of stem from which new growth will come. Take a few leaves from among the plants; none must be stripped bare. Further sowings can be made at intervals but it should be possible to make several cuttings from each sowing. For winter and spring use, make a sowing in early autumn. Although spinach beet is hardy, this method of growing will be more successful if cloches are placed over the plants.

Container growing

Containers should be at least 12in/30cm wide, 6-9in/15-22.5cm deep, and about 2ft/60cm long. Sow the seed in quality potting compost as described above, or broadcast sow, thinning plants to 2in/5cm. Cut leaves as in the cut-and-grow-again technique. In early autumn, make another sowing for use in winter and spring. For protection, cover the container with a clear plastic sheet supported on wire hoops.

Sowing seed for large heads of spinach beet

In spring, sow seed in drills 1in/2.5cm deep and 12in/30cm apart. Thin to 9in/22.5cm. In summer, start cutting, taking only a few leaves from each plant, allowing them to develop. In late summer, make another sowing for winter use. Although spinach beet is hardy, the crop will be much better if protected under cloches. If that is not possible, pile straw round the base of each plant to give some protection.

Pests and diseases

Usually trouble-free.

COOKING SPINACH BEET

Stir-fry the small cut-and-grow-again leaves in oil for about two minutes. As these leaves are coarser than those of spinach, they may not be to everyone's taste raw in salad. Certainly mature leaves will have to be cooked in the same way as spinach.

STALKS AND SHOOTS

Rhubarb, Timperley Early variety.

*T*here has always been a tantalizingly long wait between starting an asparagus bed and cutting the first spears. The latest F₁ hybrids have now reduced this wait by a year. Admittedly nothing can be done to extend the harvesting period of six weeks (since in the nature of things the tender shoots then turn into the hard stalks of the fern), but a lot of asparagus eating can be crammed into that short time.

Celery growing has taken a new advance with the latest close-planting techniques producing tender and slender stems, without the chore of earthing-up. New varieties have also appeared, without the stringy stems of the old.

While there has been no great revolution in rhubarb, there is a growing appreciation among cooks of the virtues of the pink and forced stems, and a real-ization among a new generation of gardeners that forcing is a perfectly simple operation.

Gardeners are increasingly finding space for other vegetables in this group, among them the Continental favourite, the aniseed-flavoured Florence fennel. Growing it has been made easier and more popular with new F₁ varieties that are more likely to produce fat bulbs than to go prematurely to flower and seed.

The immature flower-heads of the globe artichoke are time-consuming to eat but they have their devotees. Cardoons, with their thistle-like stems, are similar in appearance, but it is their stems that are edible.

As a bonus some of these vegetables have highly decorative foliage that looks fine in a flower garden – Florence fennel, globe artichokes and cardoons among them.

46

FLORENCE FENNEL
(Foeniculum vulgare var. dulce)

Florence fennel, as its name suggests, is a native of Italy and thrives in a warm climate. Even so, more northerly gardeners may well find it worth a try. The plant has a tendency to bolt and produce seed but no bulb, but new varieties are now available that do much to curb this tendency.

Florence fennel has a sweet aniseed flavour and a crunchy texture that add a new dimension to the conventional range of vegetables. Use it raw in salads or cooked and served hot. If left to cool and covered with a rich oily dressing, it is the perfect vegetable for a cold summer meal.

Varieties

Varieties include Perfection, producing medium to large bulbs, Sirio and Zefa Fino. The last named is said to be the most bolt-resistant.

The plant's needs

Florence fennel must have a sunny sheltered position in rich, well-draining but

Florence fennel, Zeta Fino variety

moisture-retentive soil. A light and sandy soil will ensure that it is well draining, and by digging in manure, which breaks down into humus, the soil will be made more fertile and able to hold more moisture. A moist soil is essential in the summer months when the developing bulbs need plenty of water or they will not swell. Heavier soils will also give reasonable results, but avoid growing florence fennel in heavy clay.

Prepare the ground in late autumn or early winter by digging in plenty of well-rotted manure or compost.

Sowing seed

Sow seed in late spring when all chance of frost is over. Take out drills ½in/1.25cm deep and 12in/30cm apart. Sow the seed thinly and cover with a light sifting of soil. Thin out seedlings to 8in/20cm. A succession of sowings can be made until summer, but the later developing plants will need protection under cloches.

Keep the plants well watered, especially during periods of hot weather, when twice daily watering may be necessary. Applying a mulch around the base of the plants will help to retain moisture. When the bulbs are golf ball size, soil can be drawn up around them. This is not essential but blanching the bulb will make it

more tender.

Start cutting the bulbs in late summer when they are tennis-ball size. Do not leave them so long that they grow into tough woodiness.

Pests and diseases

Seldom give trouble.

FREEZING AND COOKING FLORENCE FENNEL

Whole bulbs should not be frozen. It is possible to freeze the individual overlapping leaves, but they look unappetizing compared with the attractiveness of the whole cooked bulb. It is best not to bother with freezing.

To cook whole, cut off the ferny top leaves and trim the base of the bulb. Simmer in near-boiling water for 15 to 20 minutes until the bulb is tender but still crunchy. Serve hot with melted butter, or cold with an oil dressing.

A bulb can also be eaten raw in a salad. Simply separate the overlapping leaves and cut them into small pieces.

ASPARAGUS
(Asparagus officinalis)

The good news for today's asparagus grower is that the new F$_1$ hybrid varieties mean you can now cut at least a few spears a year after planting the one-year-old crowns instead of having to wait the usual two years. These varieties also reduce waiting from three years to two if you grow from seed. Over the years they may also go on to produce twice as many spears.

Although supermarket shelves may suggest that asparagus spears grow all the year round, this is only because spring comes at different times in the United States, South America, the Far East, Spain and other countries from which asparagus is expensively imported. Tinned asparagus is also always available, but that is hardly worth a mention. The best and most delicious way to eat asparagus is straight out of one's own garden. That opportunity lasts for only a brief six weeks or so in late spring and early summer when the spears are young and ready to eat. Nevertheless, it is well worth waiting for.

Asparagus imported from the United States is usually fat-speared, but thinner from other sources, and mostly a uniform pale green. This is because the spears are allowed to grow in the light, about 8in/20cm above soil level. White spears are produced by being grown in the dark, usually by ridging the soil over the crowns. The spears are then cut just as the tips emerge from the soil. Commercial growers increasingly produce green asparagus, but blanched white asparagus is both more tender and more aesthetically pleasing.

Varieties

Connovers Colossal is the universal favourite, producing fat spears with succulent, tender, purple-tinted tips. It does well on sandy soil and crops early. Martha Washington is a long-established American variety that also has tender purple-tinted tips. Lucullus, an F$_1$ hybrid, produces male plants only, giving heavier crops than varieties with male and female plants.

New varieties are regularly introduced, available as seed or crowns. Look out for the all-male varieties that are becoming increasingly popular because of their high yield - sometimes almost double that of older varieties.

The plant's needs

Asparagus should be grown in a warm, sheltered, sunny part of the garden. This is especially important for early varieties that can be damaged by frost. The secret of a productive asparagus bed is a well-draining rich soil, so preparation is all-important. In autumn, dig in plenty of well-rotted compost or manure to make the bed ready for planting in spring.

Asparagus will grow in any type of soil as long as it is well draining. Digging in manure helps sandy soil to retain water, and clay soils to drain freely. A pH level of about 5.8 is ideal.

Planting crowns

Since asparagus needs plenty of room to develop, container growing is not suitable. In spring, dig trenches in the plot manured in the autumn – 12in/30cm wide, 8-10in/20-25cm deep and 3ft/90cm apart. This allows the roots room to spread. Place the one-year-old crowns 18in/45cm apart in the trench with the roots well spread out, and cover with 3in/7.5cm of soil.

During the first summer, gradually draw in the soil from the sides of the trench so that it is filled in level by the autumn. Hoe to keep down the weeds. Water well in dry weather.

In autumn when the foliage begins to turn yellow, cut down the stems to just

above soil level. Apply a mulch around the cut stems to suppress weeds and enrich the soil. The following early spring apply a general fertilizer at 3oz per sq yd/90g per sq m. Follow the same routine into the third year, the first time that spears should be cut. (If you have planted new F$_1$ hybrid varieties, a few spears can be cut in the second year.)

For white (blanched) asparagus, ridge up the soil over the crowns in spring to a depth of about 6in/15cm.

If you want green spears, leave the soil level. When the tips show about 4in/10cm above the soil, using a special asparagus knife or sharp kitchen knife, cut the spears about 4in/10cm below the surface of the soil. In the first year of cutting, cut only one or two from each plant. The following year you can cut as much as you like but only for about six weeks, stopping by the middle of early summer. The remaining spears must be left to develop into fern, which will build up the plant's strength to produce the following year's crop. Keep the bed watered if the summer is dry.

PESTS AND DISEASES: ASPARAGUS

Pests

Asparagus beetle This yellow-and-black insect lays its black eggs on the newly emerging spears in spring. The grubs, and later the beetles, feed on the foliage, if allowed to develop. Spray with derris.

Slugs and snails can be controlled by laying pellets that contain methiocarb or metaldehyde, but these can be harmful to pets. Ask your supplier about organic alternatives.

Diseases

Violet root rot is a fungus that leaves a purple deposit on asparagus roots. If the bed becomes diseased, plants must be lifted and burned. That area of the garden must not be used to grow asparagus again.

In the eighth year of the current bed's life, start a new one, in a different spot, to ensure continuing supplies.

Sowing seed

Before sowing in spring, soak seed over-night to encourage germination. Take out drills ½in/1.25cm deep and 12in/30cm apart. Sow thinly. Cover with a fine sifting of soil. Thin to 6in/15cm and plant out into the trenches the following spring.

An earlier sowing in late winter can be made indoors at 55-65°F/13-16°C either in trays or, preferably, peat pots. Thin the seedlings raised in trays and transplant to individual pots when they can be handled easily. Harden off in early summer and plant out in autumn. It may be possible to cut a few spears the following year, but it is better to wait.

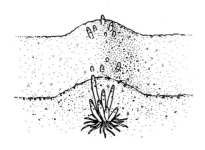

FREEZING AND EATING ASPARAGUS

The harvesting period is so short that yields from the average bed seldom produce a surfeit to be frozen. But if you do have any spare spears, they are easy to freeze. Wash them, cut off the woody ends, and blanch in hot salted water for two to

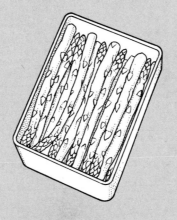

string. Lay a mug on its side in a pan of boiling water as a support to keep the tips out of the water. Simmer for

three minutes. Allow to cool and pack them in a plastic container in layers separated by wax paper. For easy storage, the spears are best placed tips to ends in alternate layers.

Asparagus contains a fair amount of protein and vitamins B and C, but as with many vegetables the vitamin content is halved with cooking.

Steaming is the best and simplest way of cooking asparagus. The only problem is to get the tougher part of the spears tender enough while not overcooking the delicate tips. There is a special, and expensive, steamer designed to do this – a tall narrow saucepan with a basket to hold the thicker part of the spears upright in boiling water while the tips are out of the water and gently steamed.

More cheaply, the same effect can be achieved with an ordinary saucepan. Make bundles of the spears, using elastic bands or soft

about 10 to 15 minutes depending on the thickness of the spears. Frozen spears will take a little longer. Serve with melted butter or hollandaise sauce.

A simpler method – heresy to the purist – is to immerse the whole of the spears in water. Use a large deep frying pan. Arrange the spears, not tied together, so that they are all facing the same way. Place the pan with the thick ends of the spears above the heat. Adjust the heat until the water there is all but boiling. The tips, being further away from the heat, will be gently simmering. With a little practice both stems and tips can be cooked to perfection without too much trouble.

GLOBE ARTICHOKE
(Cynara scolymus)

Globe artichokes are a form of perennial thistle, about 4ft/1.2m tall. With their decorative silvery-grey leaves and violet-blue flower-heads they don't look out of place in a flower garden. The edible part of the plant is the immature flower-head that must be cut when it is still tight and before the fleshy scales start to open.

The labour of eating a globe artichoke is probably greater than growing it. After cooking, the scales are pulled away one at a time and the soft inner flesh sucked out. Eventually the hairy central choke is revealed. This is removed and thrown away. Underneath is the so-called heart or fond, the most delectable part of the vegetable. Whether you have the patience to extract what there is from the scales before reaching the reward of the heart is up to you.

It is best to replace the plants after three years but there is a by-product at this stage before they are finally dug up. After removing the globes the foliage is cut down and fresh shoots, or chards, grow. These can be eaten raw or cooked.

Varieties

The usual varieties offered as seed are Green Globe and Purple Globe. The latter has purple-tinted heads, and is hardier. Plants may be obtained from garden centres. Vert de Laon is claimed to have the best flavour.

The plant's needs

Artichokes require a sheltered sunny spot in rich well-draining soil. In winter, they will require some protection from frost, with a covering of straw. In the autumn, before planting, dig into the soil plenty of well-rotted manure or compost. Then in spring spread a general fertilizer at the rate of 3oz per sq yd (90g per sq m).

The ideal soil is light and sandy or rich loam. Results will be poor on heavy clay soils. A pH level of 6.5 is required. If the soil is acid, it should be limed in winter.

Raising from plants

Plants are the quickest way of getting a crop of artichokes. These will usually be suckers removed from established plants, so in future years you should have supplies from your own plants. Plant groups of three or four 2ft/60cm apart. Keep well watered. In the first year, cut off any

Globe artichokes.

flower-heads before they have a chance to develop. When the foliage begins to die down in the autumn, cut it off to ground level. Cover the crowns with straw or leaves to protect them from frost, though in mild areas they can be left uncovered.

The following late spring apply a mulch round the stems. Water well throughout

the summer. Flower-heads will be ready from summer onwards - the main terminal head first, followed by the smaller lateral heads. Cut them, with about 2in/5cm of the stem, before the scales begin to open. When the foliage begins to die in autumn, cut it down and protect the crowns from frost.

After three years of cutting start raising new plants. In spring, select suckers about

9in/22.5cm tall. Cut downwards into the soil by the side of the shoot, making sure that each sucker has enough roots to support it. Plant out to final growing positions, in groups of three or four.

Sowing seed

Raising plants from seed means waiting 2½ years before the first globes can be cut. In spring, take out drills 1in/2.5cm deep and 12in/30cm apart. Thin to 9in/22.5cm and plant out to final positions the following spring. Flower-heads will not be produced the first year.

The wait can be cut a little by sowing seed in late winter in heat, 55-60°F/13-16°C. Sow thinly in trays or in peat pots. Thin out the seedlings growing in trays and transplant to individual pots when they are easily handled. Plant out in a prepared bed in spring when all chance of frost is over, leaving 9in/22.5cm between plants. Cut out any flower buds as they develop. Plant out to final positions the following spring.

Growing in containers

As the plants are decorative, one could be grown in a large pot on a patio, with the bonus of up to 12 globes to eat. Plant a sucker in a 12in/30cm pot of quality loam compost. Treat the plant in the same way as already described, but remember that frequent watering will be necessary, especially in warm weather.

Producing chards

Plants about to be replaced can first be used to produce chards. When the last globes have been removed in early autumn, cut down the foliage to within 9in/22.5cm of the soil. New shoots will soon appear. When they are around 2ft/60cm tall, tie them together and ridge up the earth so that the foliage shows above the soil. After about six weeks the stems will be blanched and ready to cut.

Purple Globe, a hardy variety

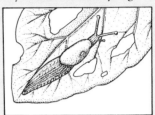
FREEZING AND COOKING GLOBE ARTICHOKES

Before freezing, remove the tough outer scales. Trim the pointed tips of the remaining scales. Remove the inedible hairy choke. Blanch for about six minutes, adding lemon juice to the water to prevent the cut scales from turning black. Cool, drain, and place each globe in a small plastic bag or container.

The usual way to cook globe artichokes is by boiling, but the small ones can be deep fried or baked whole. Before boiling the large globes cut off the stem and remove any coarse outer scales. Cut off the points of the remaining scales and rub the cut areas with lemon juice to prevent them from turning brown. Cook in salted boiling water for 30-40 minutes until the leaves are tender. To eat them, pull the scales away one by one, dip in melted butter or hollandaise sauce, and suck out the tender flesh. Remove and reject the hairy choke and eat the heart.

Stuffed artichokes are prepared in the same way, but the chokes are removed before the stuffing is added. They are then baked.

The chards can be eaten raw or boiled, like celery.

CELERY

(Apium graveolens)

The days are gone when family fights broke out at the table for the small, tender, succulent sticks of celery among the large, tough, stringy outer stems. At least they should be, for new self-blanching varieties and new techniques of close planting have made it easy to grow the kind of small, tender-hearted celery to be seen on supermarket shelves.

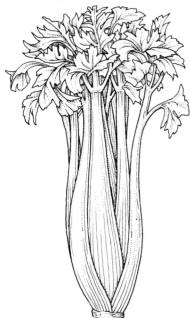

Very close planting – 6in/15cm apart – will produce slender celery hearts, and slightly wider spacing – 10in/25cm – will still give excellent results. The use of self-blanching varieties removes the need for earthing-up to make the stalks tender. The only drawback with self-blanching celery is that it is available only between summer and autumn: the first frosts kill it off. The ordinary trench celery, which is frost-resistant, is available from autumn to late winter. Its drawback is that it needs earthing-up to make it tender - a chore for the gardener. Both self-blanching and trench celery can be frozen to be used for braising or for making soups.

Varieties

Self-blanching Lathom Self-blanching, which is resistant to bolting. Celebrity matures earlier and has larger stems. American Green Greensnap has long, green virtually stringless sticks. Golden Self-blanching is a yellow variety with a short compact head. Ivory Tower is a new stringless variety.

Trench celery All have a stronger flavour than the self-blanching types. Giant White has large heads. Giant Red and Giant Pink, with red and pink flushed sticks, are hardier.

The plant's needs

Best results are achieved in a peaty moist soil. However, if the soil is not water-retentive it can be improved by digging in well-rotted manure or compost. For self-blanching celery, prepare the soil in spring. These varieties are almost stringless and to stay that way they must have plenty of water while growing.

The ideal pH level for all celery is about 6 to 6.5.

Growing small-hearted self-blanching celery

In early spring, sow seed in trays of loam seed compost at a temperature of 50-55°F/10-13°C. Don't cover the seed as it requires light to germinate. Enclose the tray in a plastic bag. Prick out the seedlings into a tray of loam potting compost, spacing them 2in/5cm apart. Harden off the plants in late spring by placing them outside during the day and bringing them indoors each evening. Plant out in early summer in a block, spacing plants 6in/15cm apart. A block 4ft sq/1.2m sq contains 64 plants, producing slender, tender hearts.

This close spacing ensures that the plants blanch themselves. Only those on the outside of the block and partly exposed to the sun will not be fully blanched, but fixing a strip of black polythene round the plants on the edges of the block will solve this problem.

Keep the plants well watered during the growing period, especially during warm weather. Daily or twice daily watering may then be needed to prevent the celery from becoming stringy. Feed weekly with liquid fertilizer.

Harvest from late summer onwards, cutting as required until the first frosts are imminent. Any celery still in the ground should then be lifted for freezing.

If you want larger heads of celery, space them 10in/25cm apart, but no more. Treat them in the same way as the small-hearted plants, placing black plastic all round the outside plants in the block.

Growing in trenches

This method takes more time and effort in preparing the ground before planting and in earthing-up the soil to blanch the growing sticks. However, it does supply celery until late winter, until the ground freezes.

Preparing the trench

In spring, dig a trench 15in/37.5cm wide and 12in/30cm deep. Fork plenty of well-

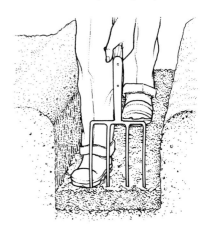

rotted manure or compost into the bottom of the trench. Then fill the trench with soil to within 6in/15cm of the top.

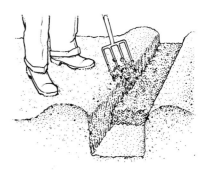

Sowing seed

Sow seed as for self-blanching celery. Plant out in the trench in early summer, spacing the plants 9in/22.5cm apart in a single row along the centre of the trench. Water and keep well watered throughout the growing period. If the roots dry out the stems become stringy and inedible. Feed weekly with liquid fertilizer. Remove any suckers (side-shoots) that grow.

Start earthing-up in late summer when

plants are about 12in/30cm tall. Tie black polythene round the bunched stems so that soil does not get between the indivi-

dual stalks. Earthing-up is done by drawing the soil around the plants from both sides of the trench until it is half way up the stems. Make sure that the soil is moist before earthing-up otherwise it will not stay in place. About three weeks later earth-up the soil again to form a sloping ridge so it reaches the top of the plastic, but does not spill over into the leaves.

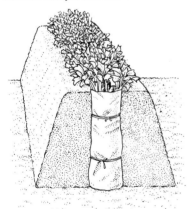

In autumn, about two months after earthing-up began, the celery will be ready for lifting. Start at one end of the trench and dig up plants as they are needed. Carefully earth-up the exposed end of each trench as the plants are removed. Celery will survive short frosts but not a long stay in ground that remains frozen hard: it is then likely to rot. Some protection can be given by covering the plants with a tunnel cloche.

PESTS AND DISEASES: CELERY

Pests

Celery flies lay eggs on the leaves from late spring. The maggots that develop burrow into the leaves, causing brown blisters. Infected leaves can be picked off and burned. Spray the rest with malathion. Minor infestations will not harm the celery itself as long as the leaves are removed. If badly infected the whole plant will die.

Slugs and snails can be controlled with slug pellets or an organic alternative: ask your supplier for details.

Diseases

Celery leaf spot This fungus is the most serious celery disease. The leaves and stems develop brown patches. But since most seed is treated with a thiram solution before it is sold, this disease should not be a problem. If leaves do become infected, spray with Bordeaux mixture.

FREEZING AND COOKING CELERY

A stem of celery is mostly water, contains little in the way of vitamins or minerals, and next to no protein. But with its sharp nutty flavour it is one of the tastiest of raw vegetables. If you grow the small tender-hearted celery most, if not all, of the stems can be eaten raw. Cut off the leaves and base of the stems, wash them, and they are ready to eat.

Celery can be frozen for use in cooked dishes, although when thawed it becomes limp and so is not suitable for eating raw. To prepare for freezing, cut the stems into 1in/2.5cm pieces, blanch for three minutes, cool, drain and store in plastic bags.

Cooked celery makes an excellent sharp thick soup if liquidized. Small hearts of celery are best braised complete in stock, butter or vegetable oil. The stems of large heads can be destringed with a vegetable peeler, cut in short lengths and simmered in stock until tender. Boiling in water alone tends to leave celery flavourless.

SEAKALE
(Crambe maritima)

You don't need to find a space in your garden to grow seakale as it can be grown equally well indoors in a cellar or cupboard. In fact, if you want a crop that lasts all through the winter, this is the only way to grow it. If you decide to grow seakale outdoors you will find that, like the globe artichoke and the cardoon, it is an attractive ornamental plant that does not look out of place in a flower bed.

Seakale has never been in the mainstream of popular vegetables; it is rarely, if ever, seen on the shelves of supermarkets. But it has a good reputation among gardeners who have grown it themselves. The blanched stems have a sweet nutty flavour when cooked and the raw leaves are an interesting addition to salads.

Varieties

As it is not a popular vegetable, there has been little development of new varieties. Lily White is the usual one on offer.

The plant's needs

Since seakale is a perennial, the ground must be well prepared before planting. In autumn, dig in plenty of well-rotted manure or compost. It does best in a well-draining sandy soil with a high lime content (pH 6.5).

Planting root cuttings or thongs

This is the quickest way of obtaining a crop of seakale; growing from seed adds a year's wait. Thongs should be available from garden centres or seed merchants. One end of each thong will have been cut on the slant while the other end is straight, and it is the slanting end that is planted bottom down. The best time to plant them is early spring. If planted in rows, the thongs should be 12in/30cm apart with 18in/45cm between rows. Set them about 1in/2.5cm below the surface of the soil. Keep the plant well watered throughout the summer and give them a liquid feed every two weeks. Remove any flowering shoots as they appear so that the plant concentrates on building up good growth. Cut down the foliage when it begins to die in autumn.

Sowing seed

Sowing seed is much cheaper than buying thongs, but adds a year to the wait from the

Seakale, at home in a flower bed.

first crop. Take out drills 1in/2.5cm deep and 12in/30cm apart. Sow seed thinly in early spring or spring. Thin to 6in/15cm. Leave the plants until the following spring when they are planted out to their permanent positions.

Forcing outdoors

In winter, cover the plants with pots or boxes and put a layer of leaves or compost over them to raise the temperature. Or soil can be ridged up over the plants to a depth of 10in/25cm. Whichever method you use, it is essential to exclude light. In spring, the stems are ready for cutting.

Forcing indoors

Select mature plants for forcing indoors as they will have to be discarded afterwards. However, first they will have provided cuttings from which to raise new plants.

In autumn, dig up the roots of the selected plants. First take the cuttings by removing the side-shoots, or thongs, from the main root. They should be about 6in/15cm long. Make a slanting cut at the end of the shoot furthest from the main root and a straight cut at the other end. You will then know which way up they have to go when you come to plant them the following early spring. Pack them in bundles, place in a box and cover them with sand or potting compost. Keep in a cool place. Before planting out the cuttings take off all but the most prominent

bud, which will have developed over the winter.

Start the forcing by planting the roots in pots of quality loam potting compost with the crowns showing just above the surface. Cover with a box or another pot ensuring that all light is excluded. Keep at a temperature of about 50°F/10°C, in a cellar or cupboard. The stems should be ready for cutting in about five weeks. Discard the plants after forcing. To maintain a succession of forced stems during the winter, store roots in a box, cover them with sand or compost, keep in a cool place and for forcing bring them out as required.

Pests and diseases

Seldom a problem, but if anything strikes, it will be one of the usual brassica pests and diseases (see page 41).

(see page 41)

FREEZING AND COOKING SEAKALE

Freezing is not recommended.

To prepare for cooking cut off the base and small leaf at the top of each stem. Simmer or steam for 20 to 30 minutes until tender. Serve in melted butter.

Leaves of unforced seakale can be used raw in salads. Shred them finely and dress with vinaigrette. They can also be boiled whole for eight to ten minutes. Cut up finely and mix with butter, serving like spinach.

CARDOON
(Cynara cardunculus)

Cardoons, like globe artichokes, are a type of thistle but, in their case, it is the blanched stems rather than the globes that are eaten. The plants are very

Cardoon, an attractive vegetable plant.

decorative, with deeply incised blue-grey leaves and purple thistle flowers, but they need plenty of room as they spread to 3ft/90cm and grow to 8ft/2.4m tall.

Like the globe artichoke the cardoon is a perennial, but it is best treated as an annual, discarding the plant after cutting the stems. For that reason and because it needs earthing-up it is not a suitable plant for growing in a container. But its decorative appearance means that one or two could well qualify for a dual role in the flower garden.

Varieties

As cardoons are one of the less common vegetables, they will not be found in all seed catalogues. The usual varieties are Ivory White, with spineless leaves, Gigante di Romagna, and Tours, with spiny leaves. If you grow a spiny-leaved variety, wear stout gloves when tying the plants before earthing-up.

The plant's needs

Cardoons need a rich, well-draining soil in a sheltered but sunny part of the garden. The best results will be achieved in loam soils. Sand and clay soils can be improved by digging in well-rotted manure.

Sowing and growing

In spring, sow seed, one to a pot, and place in a frame or unheated greenhouse. In readiness for planting out, dig a trench in the garden 12in/30cm wide and 18in/45cm deep. Dig in plenty of well-rotted manure until the trench is 12in/30cm deep. Growing in a trench ensures that the plants will have ample moisture during the summer months.

In late spring, harden off the seedlings and plant them out in the trench at the beginning of early summer, 18in/45cm apart. Water the seedlings and keep the plants well watered in summer. Give weekly doses of half-strength liquid fertilizer.

In early autumn, start the blanching process. Make sure the leaves are thoroughly dry or they may rot when tied together. Remove any dying leaves and tie the stems together with soft string at the

Cardoon's thistle-like flowers.

top and bottom of the plant. Cover the whole length of stems with a piece of black plastic and secure it with string, with the leaves just protruding at the top. Draw

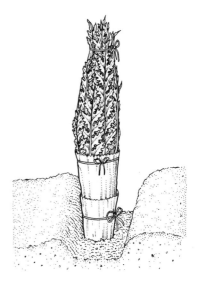

soil around the plant to the top of the plastic. In four to six weeks, blanching will be complete. From then until the frost arrives, plants may be dug up as required.

Pests and diseases

Seldom give trouble.

FREEZING AND COOKING CARDOONS

It is unlikely that you will grow more cardoons than you eat but if you do want to freeze them, this can be done quite easily. Discard all the coarse outer leaves and use only the inner tender young stems. Peel away any obviously stringy parts. Blanch for three minutes in water with lemon juice to prevent the stems from discolouring. Drain and allow to dry. Pack into bags and freeze.

For cooking, prepare the stems in the same way as for freezing, leaving them in water with lemon juice if they are not to be cooked immediately. Boil in salted water for 15 to 20 minutes. Drain and toss in butter. They can also be served with cheese sauce or left to cool and tossed in vinaigrette.

RHUBARB
(Rheum rhaponticum)

You will need a fair-sized garden to grow rhubarb as, with its tall stems and enormous umbrella leaves, it could never be called space-efficient. If you do have the space, it is worth considering growing forced rhubarb. The first bright-pink sticks, with their sharp but delicate flavour, should appear in time for, or just after, Christmas and can be enjoyed for several weeks before the coarser unforced rhubarb takes over from spring to summer.

The trouble is that to grow forced rhubarb you must have a bed of mature rhubarb to provide the roots for forcing, and such a bed takes several years to establish. Furthermore, once a root has been forced there is no further use for it. But given a large enough garden the return from a rhubarb bed makes it a good investment, especially as, once established, a bed needs little attention.

The quickest way to establish a rhubarb bed is from plants – this allows a few sticks to be picked in the following year. Raising from seed, though simple, adds a futher year before the first crop can be pulled. Once established, a bed, if not over-picked, should be productive for about five years. Raise new plants in time to take over from the old bed.

Varieties

Champagne Early or Timperley are the varieties to choose for forcing. One of the most popular main-crop varieties is Victoria, with thick sticks. Glaskins Perpetual can be pulled late in the season.

The plant's needs

As the bed will last for several years, the ground must be well prepared before

planting. Choose a sheltered part of the garden. In winter, dig holes 2ft/60cm deep and spaced to allow 3ft/90cm between the crowns. Dig plenty of well-rotted manure or compost into the soil at the bottom of the hole. Add a further layer, 6in/15cm deep, of manure or compost and then fill the hole with soil. Rhubarb will grow in any type of soil, but rich heavier loam or clay soils give the best results. The pH level should be 5 to 6.

Raising from plants

In early spring, remove soil from the prepared holes so that there is plenty of room to spread out the roots. The depth of planting should be enough to ensure that the buds are just below the surface of the soil when the holes are filled in. Keep the plants well watered in warm weather; applying a mulch around the crown of the plants will help to retain moisture. Remove any flowering shoots as they appear.

The following spring to summer pulling can begin, but only one or two sticks from each crown.

In following years, feed with a general fertilizer throughout the summer months. More sticks can be pulled but always leave a few on each crown. Stripping a plant completely will mean a poor crop the following year. In late winter each year, fork in some well-rotted compost or manure taking care not to damage the crowns.

Sowing seed

In spring, take out drills 1in/2.5cm deep and sow the seed thinly. Thin to 6in/15cm. In autumn, lift the plants and move them to their permanent positions, having prepared the ground as already described. Don't pull any sticks the following year. The year afterwards pull only a few.

Forcing outdoors

Crowns that have been pulled regularly for at least three years are those to choose for forcing. In the middle of winter, place a bucket or box over the selected crown, and cover with straw or compost to raise the temperature inside, encouraging the crown to grow. Sticks should be ready for pulling in early spring. The same plants should not be forced every year as this weakens them.

Forcing indoors

If there is room, rhubarb can be forced indoors. Choose plants that are due to be re-

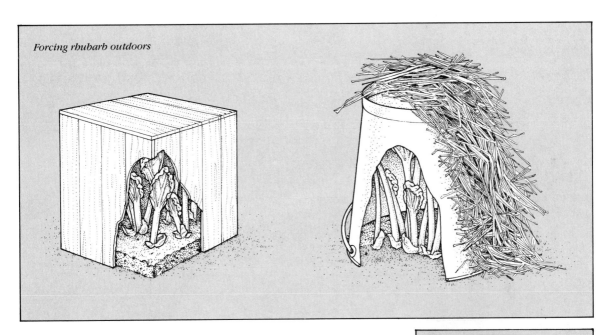

Forcing rhubarb outdoors

placed: once they have been forced in-doors they will have to be discarded. When the leaves have died down in autumn and late autumn, dig up a plant and leave the roots exposed outdoors for about two weeks. Plant the crown in a box, just covering with soil. Water well and

cover with another box or black poly-thene supported on a wire frame: the plants must be in the dark. Keep in a tem-perature of 50-55°F/10-13°C. Sticks will be ready for pulling in about six weeks. Throw the plant away when all the sticks have been pulled.

FREEZING AND EATING RHUBARB

There is unlikely to be any surplus of forced rhubarb to freeze, but there may well be more of the main crop. Trim the sticks and remove any strings. Cut into 1in/2.5cm pieces. Blanch in boiling water for about a minute. Drain and allow to dry before packing into bags for freezing.

Forced rhubarb needs no more than gentle simmering. Trim the sticks, removing the leaves and the base. Cut into 1in/2.5cm pieces. Add sugar to it in the pan and just cover with water. Simmer gently for two to three minutes; if cooked too long it disintegrates.

Main-crop rhubarb can be gently stewed with sugar, adding ground cinnamon to enhance the flavour. It will take about five minutes to cook.

Main-crop rhubarb makes an excellent crumble. Put 1in/2.5cm pieces of uncooked rhubarb in a fireproof dish. Add sugar and a little water plus, perhaps, a touch of white rum or Cointreau. Instead of a pastry topping make a mixture of coarse rolled oats, brown sugar and melted butter or margarine, with powdered cinnamon if liked. Cover the rhubarb with this topping and bake for about 40 minutes.

PESTS AND DISEASES: RHUBARB

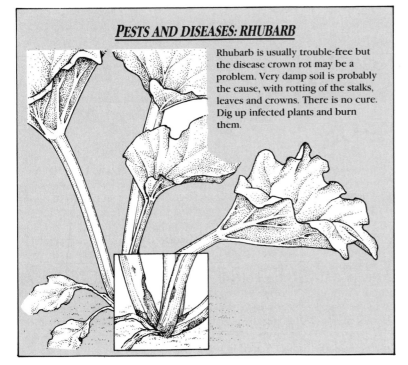

Rhubarb is usually trouble-free but the disease crown rot may be a problem. Very damp soil is probably the cause, with rotting of the stalks, leaves and crowns. There is no cure. Dig up infected plants and burn them.

PODS AND SEEDS

*F*or the countless fans of fresh, home-grown peas (pick them small and you may never want to eat a frozen pea again) the ultimate achievement of modern seed technology is the mangetout. It not only relieves you of podding; it gives you more for your trouble and is the perfect stir-fry vegetable.

Scarcely less significant to lovers of the runner bean is the development in recent years of the new, almost stringless varieties. Infuriating, inedible strings are a thing of the past as long as you pick these new varieties young. The giant runner bean belongs in the local show, not in your kitchen. The same is true of the delicious French bean.

Broad beans have had a bad name in the past for growing only one or two to the pod and having thick dry, sometimes bitter-tasting skins. New varieties can be depended upon to contain a respectable number of beans; pick them young, small and tender, and they vie with peas for full, sweet, juicy flavour.

Sweet corn, too, thanks to recent developments, is sweeter than ever, and new varieties contain ever larger numbers of kernels.

These are all vegetables that lose both flavour and texture in freezing; to get the best out of pods and seeds, today's kitchen gardener uses the new varieties and treats them for what they are: summer vegetables, pure and simple, to be enjoyed for the moment – and anticipated in winter.

SWEET CORN
(Zea mays)

In Continental Europe sweet corn is grown for animal fodder. Elsewhere it is considered to be one of the most succulent of vegetables, particularly since breeding has now made the cobs fatter with more closely packed and sweeter kernels. A variety with about 12 rows of kernels is now considered inferior to those with between 16 and 20 rows. The new F_1 hybrids also have sweeter kernels, and some of them even retain that sweetness a day or two after picking.

Sweet corn is a warm-weather plant and seed cannot be sown directly in the ground until late spring, but a head start can be made by an early sowing indoors or in a heated greenhouse. They are too large to be grown in containers, but the modern technique of close planting in blocks is satisfactory and ensures that the plants are pollinated efficiently by the wind.

Varieties

Early-maturing varieties, taking about four months from sowing to harvesting, include the long-established favourite Kelvedon Sweetheart, with 12 rows of kernels; Sunrise (up to 14 rows); and for sweetness Early Extra Sweet (14 rows). Reward matures a little later, with cobs bearing 18 to 20 rows of kernels. Earlibelle, with 14 rows of kernels, has long chunky cobs. Aztec and Sundance are both considered reliable for rich sweet flavour. Sweet 77 is an extra sweet variety with 16 rows of kernels, which retain their sweetness for a day or two after picking. Incredible (18 rows) is a late-maturing variety that also keeps its sweet flavour after picking.

The plant's needs

Sweet corn requires a sunny sheltered part of the garden because it is a tender plant. For the best results the ground should be fertile, well-draining but moisture-retentive. Dig in plenty of well-rotted manure or compost the previous autumn so that it has time to break down into moisture-holding humus. All types of soil are suitable and a pH level of 6.5 is ideal.

Sowing seed

Seed cannot be sown outdoors until late spring but it can be sown indoors in spring, given a temperature of 55°F/13°C.

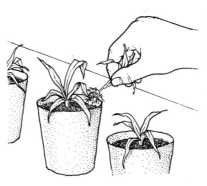

Don't sow seed in trays because sweet corn does not transplant well. Instead, use peat pots filled with loam seed compost, two seeds to a pot. After germination remove the weaker of the two seedlings. Harden off the seedlings by putting them outdoors during the day – in a propagator for some protection but with the vents open – and bringing them indoors each evening.

They should be ready for planting out in the latter part of late spring or in early summer. Space plants 15in/37.5cm apart each way so that a block 4ft sq/1.2m sq will contain 16 plants.

Sow seed directly into the ground in late spring, two seeds together every 15in/37.5cm each way. Thin by removing the weaker of the two seedlings. This close planting will help to ensure successful pollination. Keep plants well watered, especially in periods of warm weather. Spreading a mulch around the base of the plant will help to retain moisture.

Cobs should be ready for harvesting from the end of late summer. By this time the silks at the end of the cob will have withered and turned brown. Press one or two kernels from among the plants. If a clear liquid emerges the cob is not quite ready. A milky liquid indicates perfection, and no liquid at all means it has gone beyond its best. Give the cobs a sharp twist to remove them from the stem.

Pests and diseases

Seldom troubled.

COOKING AND FREEZING SWEET CORN

Remove the outer sheath and cut away the silks from the top of the cob before cooking. Boil in unsalted water for no more than six to eight minutes until the kernels are tender. Drain and serve coated with melted butter and cope with eating them. The cooked kernels can be stripped off the cob with a fork for serving – if you don't want the fun (and the mess) – of gnawing them straight off the cob. Kernels stripped from the cob can also be served cold with raw diced red and green peppers, coated with a vinaigrette dressing or mayonnaise.

Cobs are frozen whole after they have been prepared as for cooking. Blanch for about four minutes, drain and allow to cool. Wrap each cob in foil and pack into plastic bags. Allow frozen cobs to thaw out thoroughly before cooking.

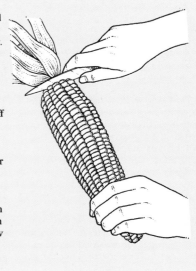

PEAS

(Pisum sativum)

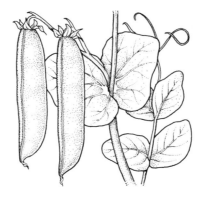

Many of today's pea varieties have been bred with the frozen food market in mind – each pod must be tightly (and profitably) packed with peas and the plants must mature at the same time for mechanical harvesting. That may be a virtue for the commercial grower but it is a curse for an ordinary gardener. Faced with a surfeit of peas all ready for eating the choices are to freeze them or waste them, whereas what the ordinary gardener wants is a steady supply of garden fresh peas to be picked at their peak. The way to get round this problem is to choose the new varieties for their bursting pods and make small successional sowings so that they mature at different times, or sow a number of varieties with a range of maturing dates.

At least the gardener can be grateful that various diseases, such as downy mildew, have been bred out of new varieties. But breeding does not control pests and nobody has yet managed to eliminate the major pest, the pea moth.

As well as the garden pod peas, which need tedious shelling, there are labour-saving mangetout or sugar peas, which are cooked and eaten whole. This delicacy used to be the preserve of Continental Europe, France in particular, but no longer. Since mangetout have become increasingly popular in the shops, more and more gardeners are taking to growing their own. They must be picked while the pods are tender and have not become stringy; at this stage the peas inside are visible only as tiny bumps. Both pods and peas have a sweet delicate flavour.

Snap pea varieties can also be treated like mangetout as long as they are young. If allowed to mature, strings like those of beans will have to be removed from the pods before cooking.

Petit pois varieties have the smallest, sweetest peas. Peas are sown closely together so they are ideal for container growing. The harvest will not be large, but if there is no other space available at least a few boilings of really fresh peas will be well worthwhile.

Varieties

Round-seeded varieties of peas are hardy and can be sown in winter for early crops the following year. Wrinkled-seeded varieties are sown in spring for early and main crops later in the year.

For sowing in early winter the favourite varieties are Feltham First and Meteor, both growing to about 18in/45cm. These provide the first crops in late spring.

Feltham First can also be sown in early spring to crop in early summer followed by Kelvedon Wonder and Little Marvel (both 18in/45cm). Hurst Beagle (18in/45cm) is another early, maturing in about three months after sowing. This variety freezes well. Hurst Green Shaft has tightly packed pods, with up to ten peas in each one. It crops heavily and the peas have an excellent flavour. It grows to 2½ft/75cm, with the pods concentrated at the top of the plants.

Tristar and Multistar are the varieties to sow in spring if you want to freeze peas. They crop heavily with uniform peas, all maturing at the same time.

Onward (24in/60cm) is probably the most widely grown pea for the main crop, followed by Senator (3ft/90cm).

Mangetout varieties for sowing in spring and late spring include Oregon Sugar Pea (3ft/90cm) and Dwarf Sweet Green (18in/45cm). Snap pea varieties, for sowing in spring to late spring, include Sugar Snap (6ft/1.8m) and the dwarf Sugar Ann (2ft/60cm). The main petit pois variety offered is Waverex (18in/45cm).

The plant's needs

Peas need a rich, well-draining soil. Dig in plenty of well-rotted manure or compost in autumn so that there is time for it to break down to moisture-retaining humus. If fresh manure is applied to the soil immediately before sowing, it will encourage lush foliage growth instead of pod development. Peas prefer a limy soil, so acid soils should be limed to achieve a pH level of 6 to 7.

Sowing seed

Sow the seed of round-seeded varieties, such as Feltham First and Meteor, in early winter. Make a trench about 6in/15cm wide and 2in/5cm deep. If several rows are being planted, the distance between the rows should be the same as the height to which those varieties of peas are expected to grow. Space the seed 2in/5cm apart each way, making three staggered rows in the trench. Press the peas into the soil and cover them immediately.

At this stage birds are a great problem and the peas must be protected from them. Cover the rows with small mesh pea guards or plastic mesh, supported on wire a little way above the soil. In mild areas these first sowings will not need protection from the cold, but elsewhere they will be successful only if cloches are placed over the trench. Seedlings and plants under cloches need to be well ventilated at all times.

When the plants are about 3in/7.5cm tall, they will begin to need support. Make a row of short twigs along both sides of the trench for the plants to climb up. Soon they will need taller support. Wire netting or rows of string can be attached to upright stakes at the expected height of the plants. Keep the ground well watered and apply a mulch round the base of the plants to retain moisture.

In early spring, sow seed of Feltham First, Kelvedon Wonder, Little Marvel, Hurst Green Shaft and Hurst Beagle. In spring and the early part of late spring sow Tristar, Multistar, Onward and Senator. If the weather is cold and wet, wait until it improves and the soil has warmed up before sowing seed. For successional

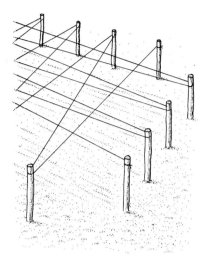

crops, seed can be sown every three weeks until early summer.

Start picking the pods when they are plump and well filled, but before they have become too large and past their best. Pick regularly and freeze them if there are too many for everyday use.

Sow seed of mangetout, snap peas and petit pois in spring or late spring, making one or two succesional sowings.

Mangetout peas will be ready for picking when pods are 2-3in/5-7.5cm long and the peas can be just seen or felt inside. Snap peas should be picked at around the same size if they are to be eaten like mangetout. Left to mature the pods will require stringing, but at that stage they are best treated like pod peas and shelled. Petit pois are best eaten when the pods feel plump, but remember that they will not grow to anything like the size of other varieties.

Growing in containers

It is best to concentrate on a main-crop sowing, of varieties such as Senator or Onward; there will be more peas than the meagre handful from an early sowing. Also always go for the taller varieties that yield more than the dwarfs. The mangetout variety Oregon Sugar Pod and the snap pea Sugar Snap are also suitable for container growing. Containers should be at least 12in/30cm wide, 10in/25cm deep and no less than 3ft/90cm long – the longer the better if practicable. Fill the container with quality loam potting compost.

In spring, take out three ½in/1.25 drills, 4in/10cm apart, and starting 2in/5cm from the edge of the container. Space seeds 2in/5cm apart. Press into the compost and cover. Protect the peas from birds by covering the top of the container with plastic netting. When plants are about 3in/7.5cm tall, support with twigs, and as they grow provide netting attached to canes for the plants to twine upwards. Always keep container plants well watered; twice daily may be necessary in spells of hot weather.

Pick sugar snap and mangetout peas when the pods have barely started to swell. Main-crop peas will be ready when the pods feel plump.

PESTS AND DISEASES: PEA

Pests

Pea moth is the biggest menace. It lays its eggs on the leaves, and when the larvae hatch they burrow into the pods and feed on the peas. Shelling a pod and finding the

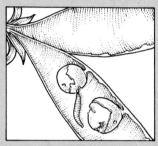

unwelcome visitors there already is probably the first inkling you will have of their presence. At this stage there is nothing that you can do; the crop is lost. However, you can take preventive action when the plants have just started to flower – spray with fenitrothion or dust with carbaryl.

Pea thrips lay eggs on leaves and flowers. The hardly visible nymphs that emerge feed on both leaves and pods, leaving silver-coloured patches. If the plants are badly infected growth will be retarded, affecting flowering and drastically reducing the number of pods. Spray with dimethoate or a more acceptable mixture of derris and pyrethrum.

Birds can be a problem, both immediately after sowing and when pods are developing. Cover newly sown seed with fine mesh nylon netting and, if necessary, net mature plants.

Aphids are a threat in warm humid summers. Spray with derris or pyrethrum.

Diseases

Downy mildew was once a major disease, but it has been bred out of many of the new varieties. If it does strike, the leaves will be covered with white powdery patches. Spray with zineb or Bordeaux mixture.

COOKING AND FREEZING PEAS

Peas are one of the best vegetable sources of protein and contain reasonable amounts of B vitamins and vitamin C. They are at their best freshly picked and then cooked and served simply. After shelling, boil the peas in a small amount of salted water along with sprigs of mint, for eight to ten minutes. The smaller the pea the less cooking it will need. Large peas take longer and rarely seem to get tender all the way through. Drain and coat the peas with melted butter.

Petit pois will take only some five minutes to cook.

Cook young snap peas and mangetout in boiling salted water for about five minutes, so that they are still crunchy. More mature snap peas must be stringed before cooking. They will take at least ten minutes' boiling if they are being cooked whole. Mangetout can also be stir-fried in butter or oil for about five minutes.

To freeze peas, shell them and blanch for about one minute. Drain, cool, pack into plastic bags and freeze. Mangetout peas should be blanched for about two minutes. Drain, cool and pack into plastic bags or rigid containers. Frozen peas take about two minutes longer to cook than fresh peas.

BROAD BEANS
(Vicia faba)

Home-grown broad beans bear little relation to the beans found in market stalls or supermarkets. By growing them yourself you can make sure that you pick them when they are small and juicy instead of large and coarse, and you can also choose to grow the new, longer varieties with more beans to the pod.

What the plant breeders still have to achieve is a bean with a less tough outer skin. Admittedly broad beans are easy to skin after they have been partially cooked, but it makes a tedious job.

Broad beans take up a good deal of space, so they are not suitable for container growing. But if your space is limited, there are a few dwarf varieties that can be grown more closely, 9-12in/22.5-30cm each way. They are ideal for growing in blocks instead of the usual double rows. In fact, it is not necessary to sow in double rows; single rows with closer planting have been shown to be just as productive.

Varieties

In mild areas it is possible to make a sowing in early winter, to crop in early summer, but this is advisable only in frost-free areas. The usual variety sown then is Aquadulce Claudia, producing white beans. Early-maturing varieties from sowings in late winter and early spring include Express, with 8in/20cm pods containing up to six greenish-white beans. Jubilee Hysor, later-maturing, has long pods holding up to nine beans. Hylon pods have up to eight white beans and Revlon a similar number of green beans.

Among the dwarf varieties the most popular is probably The Sutton, which grows to about 12in/30cm. Expect about four white beans from each pod. In between the dwarf and tall varieties there is Feligreen, producing 8in/20cm pods of green beans. All these beans freeze well

Broad beans, The Sutton variety.

and some people think that the flavour improves with freezing.

The plant's needs

Broad beans will grow in all types of firm, fertile, well-draining soil. Heavier soils seem to suit spring-grown crops, while early winter sowings will do better in lighter soils. They are not so wet and cold, and give the plants a better chance of survival. These early winter sowings should also be confined to a sunny, sheltered part of the garden, digging in well-rotted manure or compost about three months before sowing. For spring sowings, the manuring should be done the previous autumn. Apply lime to acid soil to achieve a pH level of about 6.5.

Sowing seed

In mild areas sow seed of Aquadulce Clau-

Broad beans, Aquadulce Claudia variety.

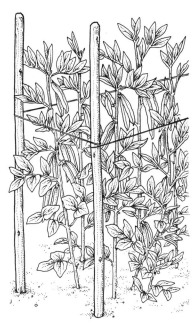

dia in early winter. Take out drills 2in/5cm deep, 15-18in/37.5-45cm apart. Sow the beans 8in/20cm apart. The dwarf variety, The Sutton, can also be sown at this time of the year. Make drills 2in/5cm deep, 9in/22.5cm apart and sow the beans at 9in/22.5cm intervals. A block 3ft sq/90cm sq sown at these distances will contain 25 plants. Plant a few extra beans to replace any that may not germinate in the block. As the plants grow, pile up soil around their base to protect them against bad weather.

In colder areas an early start can be made by sowing under glass. In late winter, sow the beans in seed boxes (2in/5cm apart each way) or peat pots (one bean to a pot) using loam seed compost. Place in a frame or unheated greenhouse. Harden off the plants gradually in spring by placing them out of doors during the day or lifting the lid of the frame. Bring the pots and boxes indoors at night or close the frame. They should be ready for planting out in a block (as already described) a week or two later.

Tall-growing varieties will eventually need support. Place two canes at the end of each row and tie string, running the length of the row, around them, at about 12in/30cm above the soil level. As the beans grow taller tie more lines of string higher up the canes.

When plants are in full flower and the pods have started to form, pinch out the growing tips both to encourage pod development and to discourage blackfly. Greater control of this pest can be achieved by removing the top 4-6in/10-15cm of tender growth, which the blackfly find most appealing.

The first beans should be ready for picking in early summer. At this stage they should be young and tender, about 8in/20cm long. Pick them regularly so that the plant is encouraged to put out more growth.

Sow the main crop of broad beans from early spring onwards, using sowing distances already recommended, depending on whether they are dwarf or tall varieties. Successions of sowings can be made every three weeks until late spring for crops through to early autumn. When plants are no longer productive, make use of the nitrogen they have generated in the nodules attached to the roots. Either cut off the foliage at ground level and dig the roots into the soil or remove the whole plant and put it on the compost heap to rot down.

COOKING AND FREEZING BROAD BEANS

Among beans only haricots have a higher protein content than broad beans, and the skins of broad beans also provide a rich source of dietary fibre.

To cook broad beans, shell them and cook them in boiling salted water for about six minutes until they are tender. If the outer skins seem tough they can be removed. Toss the beans in butter. If the beans are large and past their best, boil them for about 15 minutes and pureé them in a liquidizer. Add butter, cream, lemon juice and seasoning. Serve them cold in a salad with cooked peas and French beans dressed with mayonnaise or vinaigrette.

To freeze, blanch the shelled beans for two to three minutes. Drain, cool and pack in plastic bags. Beans cooked from frozen take about eight minutes.

RUNNER BEANS
(Phaseolus coccineus)

Runner beans have always been a popular addition to any kitchen garden. They look attractive and taste delicious. Their only disadvantage has been their tough strings that need to be removed before cooking. But now plant breeders have solved this problem by producing several varieties of stringless bean – some totally stringless, others only when young.

Other good news is that experiments have shown that close planting produces a heavier crop. But when considering how many to plant, remember that runner beans should always be picked when they are young and at their best. Even a few plants can provide more than enough fresh beans for a single family. Any surplus can be frozen. Like peas, they will not taste as good after freezing but they will still taste better than beans allowed to mature to their full length that are tough and tasteless.

Rows of runner beans are decorative and tall enough to grow as screens in the garden. They can be grown on patios in containers, either rectangular or circular. A wigwam structure of canes in a circular container will eventually make a dense ornamental cone of flowers, leaves and beans.

Varieties

Stringless varieties include Polestar, with red flowers, and beans up to 10in/25cm long. Red Knight, red flowers and beans 10in/25cm long, has been bred for disease resistance. Pickwick is a dwarf variety growing to 12in/30cm, which should not need any support. Flowers are red and the beans are 8in/20cm long. Desirée is white-flowered with 10in/25cm beans. If you must grow beans for showing, try some of the latest varieties such as Enorma, with beans up to 14in/37cm long. Picked long before that stage, they should also be stringless and worth eating. Bokki is an early variety with beans growing to 12in/30cm long. If picked when about 8in/20cm long, they too are usually stringless.

The plant's needs

Runner beans must have fertile well-draining soil if crops are not to be disappointing. Choose a sunny sheltered part of the garden and prepare the ground in autumn before sowing the following year.

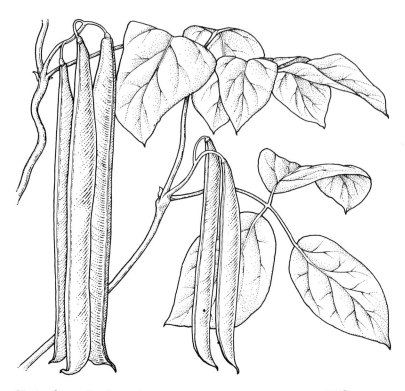

Dig in plenty of well-rotted manure or compost. The ideal pH level is about 6.5.

Supporting the crop

Most runner beans are tall-growing so, apart from the dwarf varieties, they will need support soon after they start growing. It is important to be prepared well in advance with plenty of canes, wire and string ready for the day.

For most systems of support, reckon that each bean will need one cane, longer than the usual height of the variety being grown. Further long canes will be needed to reinforce the structure so that it does

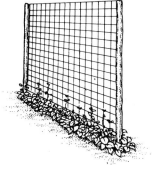

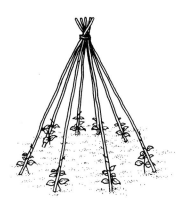

not fall over. Runner beans are generally sown in double rows. One cane is pushed into the soil beside each plant at an angle so that opposite canes meet over the middle of the two rows to form an inverted V. Pairs of canes are tied together a little distance from the top. Long canes are then laid horizontally in the small V shape at the top of the pairs of canes and firmly secured.

Single rows of beans can be planted against a wall. Fix a horizontal batten to the wall just above soil level and another 10ft/3m above it up the wall. Screw hooks into the battens at 6in/15cm intervals and stretch wire or string between them.

To save room, plants can also be arranged in a circle. Canes then need to be put in place to make a wigwam shape. Take as many canes as there are plants and tie them together about 12in/30cm from the tops of them. Space out the canes one to each plant and push them firmly in the ground alongside each plant. For extra support for the beans and to secure the wigwam, circle the bottom of the wigwam with wire and run strings from this wire to the top of the canes.

Sowing seed

It is usual to wait until late spring before sowing seed outdoors, but an earlier start can be made by sowing seed indoors in spring. Use peat pots filled with loam seed compost, sowing one bean in each pot. Seedlings can then be transplanted to their growing positions with the minimum of disturbance. Keep at a temperature of 55°F/13°C.

In late spring, start to harden off the seedlings, placing the pots in a cold frame or propagating tray with the ventilation holes left open during the day. Remember to bring the seedlings in each evening. They should be ready for planting out in the prepared bed in the latter part of late spring or early summer. Plant them 6in/15cm apart in a double row with 12-15in/30-37.5cm between each row.

From late spring to early summer sow seed in the ground where it is to grow. Take out two drills 2in/5cm deep and 12-15in/30-37.5cm apart. Sow the seed 6in/15cm apart in the drills. When the seedlings have two leaves, tie them loosely to the canes that are to support them. Keep the ground well watered at all times, especially when flowers first appear. Apply a mulch round the base of each plant to help to retain moisture.

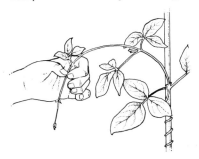

If you don't want 6ft/1.8m or more monster plants, pinching out the growing tip of each plant will reduce its potential height.

Wait until the plants are about 12in/30cm tall and then pinch out the main tip. This will encourage side-shoots to appear. These too can be pinched out to make the plants even bushier. In any case, pinch out the growing tip when the plants reach the top of the canes.

Beans should be ready for picking from summer to early autumn, or even autumn if a late sowing has been made in summer. Pick the beans when they are 6-8in/15-20cm long. At this stage they will be tender, and strings will not have developed on Enorma and Bokki varieties. Keep picking them regularly, every other day, to ensure continuing supplies of young tender beans. It should be possible to pick for several weeks.

Growing in containers

Containers should be a minimum of 12in/30cm wide for a single row of beans, and 18in/45cm wide for a double row, 10in/25cm deep and a minimum of 2ft/60cm long. Circular containers must be a minimum of 12in/30cm in diameter to make the crop at all worthwhile; half barrels are ideal.

Fill the container with quality loam potting compost a week or so before sowing to allow the compost a little time to settle. Add more if necessary to bring it up to within 1in/2.5cm of the top of the container. In early summer, sow seed for a single row 6in/15cm apart. For double rows, make two drills 12in/30cm apart, starting 3in/7.5cm from the edge of the container and sow the beans 6in/15cm apart. In round containers sow seed in a circle starting about 2in/5cm from the edge. Stake them as already described.

Earlier sowings can be made in containers indoors in late spring. Harden them off gradually and place them outdoors permanently in early summer. When two leaves appear, stake the plants as described. Pinch out the growing tip, and later the side-shoots to encourage bushiness. Pick regularly for crops of young tender beans.

COOKING AND FREEZING RUNNER BEANS

To cook runner beans, top and tail them and slice diagonally into ½in/1.25cm lengths. Remove any strings. Cook in boiling salted water for about five minutes (if the beans are young); when cooked they should be tender but retain a crunchy texture. Drain and cover with melted butter before serving. Cold cooked beans can be combined with cold cooked broad beans and peas to make a salad. Coat with vinaigrette or runny mayonnaise.

To freeze beans, top and tail and remove any strings. Slice into ½in/1.25cm pieces and blanch for two minutes. Drain, cool, pack into plastic bags and freeze.

FRENCH BEANS
(Phaseolus vulgaris)

French beans are rapidly catching up in popularity with runner beans, not least because they can be jetted in to our supermarkets almost all the year round. They also look more attractive than runner beans, since they can be cooked and served whole instead of having to be cut into small pieces. In fact, breeding has concentrated on producing these smaller pods, about 4in/10cm long. These are excellent for cooking whole and more of the nutrients and flavour will be retained that way. They will not need stringing unless you let them grow too old.

Plant breeders have also been experimenting with shape and colour, producing round as well as flat pods, and attractive yellow beans that keep their colour when cooked (although the purple pod varieties unfortunately turn to green).

Although there are climbing varieties of French beans, which have to be staked like runner beans, most are dwarf and need little support. French beans can be grown using close-planting techniques, which produce heavier crops than conventional wider spacing. They are also ideal for growing in containers.

Varieties

Dwarf varieties The smallest pods, about 4in/10cm long, and round and stringless, are produced by Pros Gitana. They mature in three months and are excellent for freezing whole. Tendergreen has round stringless beans, about 6in/15cm long, which are also good for freezing. Loch Ness, with round stringless pods, take about three months to reach maturity. Another new variety is Aramis, with slender 6in/15cm pods, which matures at about 70 days. Older-established, flat-podded varieties include Masterpiece (8in/20cm pods) and The Prince. Purple Queen has stringless round purple pods that turn green when cooked. Kinghorn Wax has 6in/15cm flat yellow pods that keep their colour when cooked. Another popular yellow bean is Mont d'Or.

Most of these dwarf varieties will grow no more than 18in/45cm tall.

Climbing varieties These require staking in the same way as runner beans. Hunter has flat beans up to 10in/25cm long. For round beans there is Largo. Of the long-established varieties Blue Lake, with rounded pods containing white seeds, is the most popular.

The plant's needs

The ideal soil is medium to light, rich and moisture-retentive. Loam, peaty and sandy soils are suitable, but growing French beans on clay soil is not worthwhile. Choose a sunny, sheltered part of the garden. Dig in plenty of well-rotted manure in the autumn to give it time to break down into humus.

Sowing seed

French beans are not hardy and must not be sown outdoors until late spring after the soil has had a chance to warm up. For early crops, a start can be made by sowing seed indoors in late winter or early spring. Sow the beans singly in peat pots filled with loam seed compost and keep in a

temperature of 55°F/13°C. Gradually harden off the plants, placing them outdoors during the day and bringing them in at night. It is best to give them some protection outdoors during the day by placing them in a propagating tray with the ventilators open. Plant out to final positions in early summer, spacing the plants 6in/15cm apart each way.

An early outdoor sowing can be made in spring if the soil has had a chance to warm up by then. Place cloches over the sowing area three weeks before you intend to sow. After the seed is sown leave the cloches in place until early summer, but keep the plants well ventilated.

Unprotected sowings can start in late spring. For the highest yields, grow the plants close together in a block formation. Take out drills 2in/5cm deep, and 6in/15cm apart along the square. Sow the beans at 3in/15cm intervals in the drills. Thin seedlings, removing the weakest, so that there are 6in/15cm each way between plants. A block 4ft sq/1.2m sq should contain 64 plants, and picking the beans should not involve too much stretching. If

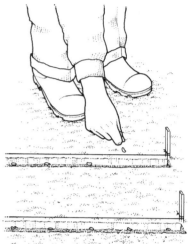

room is restricted, sow in rows 18in/45cm apart with 4in/10cm between each seed. Successional sowings every three weeks until the beginning of summer should provide beans until autumn, given protection under cloches. Even dwarf plants may need support from twigs or string.

Keep plants well watered at all times: if the soil dries out the pods will not develop fully. Applying a mulch round the base of the plants will help to retain moisture.

Start picking the beans when they are young and tender, say about 4in/10cm long. Pick them regularly so that none is allowed to grow large, coarse and ultimately stringy. If there are too many for everyday use, freeze the surplus beans while they are still at their best. Regular picking will also encourage fresh pod growth. When pulling the beans from the plants, beware of wrenching up the whole plant. Hold the stem securely before pulling away the beans, or cut them off.

Growing climbing plants

In late spring, take out two drills 2in/5cm deep and 12-15in/30-37.5cm apart. Sow the beans 6in/15cm apart. When the plants have two leaves, stake them by pushing a cane into the soil by each plant at an angle so that the canes meet over the middle of the two rows to form an inverted V shape. Pairs of canes are tied together a little distance from the top. Secure canes along the top of the structure, resting them in the small V shape at the top of the canes, to give added strength.

When leading stems reach the top of the canes, pinch them out. This will encourage side-shoots to develop and make the plants bushy.

Pick the beans when they are no more than 6in/15cm long for the tenderest crops.

Growing in containers

Containers should be a minimum of 6in/15cm wide for a single row and 12in/30cm for a double row, 10in/25cm deep and at least 2ft/60cm long. Fill the container with quality loam potting compost and allow the compost to settle. Add more compost before sowing to bring it to within 1in/1.25cm of the container top.

For a single row, make a drill 2in/5cm deep and, starting 3in/7.5cm from the end of the container, sow the beans 6in/15cm apart. A 2ft/60cm container will hold seven plants. For a double row, make the drills 6in/15cm apart, starting the first drill 3in/7.5cm from the edge of the container. Support the stems with twigs or short canes. Containers for climbing French beans should be 18in/45cm wide to grow a double row and 12in/30cm wide for a single row. For a double row, make the drills 6in/15cm apart, starting 3in/7.5cm from the edge of the container. Support with canes when the plants have two leaves (as described under *Growing climbing plants*).

COOKING AND FREEZING FRENCH BEANS

Top and tail the beans and cook whole in boiling salted water for about seven minutes. If the pods have grown longer than 4in/10cm, slice them into 1in/2.5cm pieces as for runner beans and boil for about five minutes. For an interesting colour contrast, cook and serve green and yellow beans together. French beans can also be served cold with a vinaigrette or mayonnaise dressing.

To freeze French beans whole, top and tail them and blanch for three minutes. Drain, cool and pack into plastic bags. Sliced beans should be blanched for two minutes.

French beans, Royalty variety, which produces purple beans

HARICOT BEANS
(Phaseolus vulgaris)

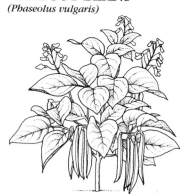

There is nothing complicated about growing haricot beans as they are only the ripened and dried seed of certain varieties of French beans. In the different stages of their growth the beans can be put to different uses. In their young state they are picked and cooked just like other French beans. At the half-way stage they are called flageolet beans and it is the green beans inside the pods that are eaten. Finally, in their fully ripened and dried state the now white beans are called haricots. They are probably best known as the irreplaceable ingredient of *cassoulet*, a traditional but infinitely varied French dish that includes various meats, fowl and sausage.

Haricot beans need space to develop and ripen and are therefore not suitable for container growing.

Varieties

Some varieties of French bean are better for drying than others, and the one usually recommended is Chevrier Vert.

The plant's needs

A medium to light moisture-retentive soil is ideal; haricot beans do badly on clay. For the beans to ripen, a sheltered but very sunny part of the garden is essential. In the autumn before sowing, dig in plenty of well-rotted manure or compost so that it breaks down into rich humus by spring.

Sowing seed

Haricot beans need more space to develop than French beans. In late spring, take out drills 2in/5cm deep and 12in/30cm apart. Sow the beans at 12in/30cm intervals along the drills. A block 4ft sq/1.2m sq will contain 20 plants,

giving a reasonable crop of ripened beans. Keep the plants well watered, especially in warm weather. A mulch around the base of the plants helps to retain moisture.

By early autumn the pods will have turned yellow and the swollen beans should be visible as bumps. They are now ready for harvesting. Never pull up the plants when they are wet with rain; always wait until they have dried off. Then pull them up and hang them in a shed to dry out thoroughly. When the outer skins are shrivelled and bone dry, shell the beans and store them in ventilated cardboard boxes so that the beans continue to dry. Storing them in enclosed jars tends to make them sweat.

COOKING HARICOT BEANS

To make the traditional *cassoulet*, leave beans to soak in water overnight. Then simmer them in gently boiling water with sliced onion and bouquet garni for about 30 minutes.

Partly roast the meat and fowl being used – probably pork and mutton, and duck. (This is where the expense and time come in.) Drain the beans, removing the onion and bouqet garni.

Put a layer of beans in the bottom of the casserole dish, followed by layers of the different meats, plus preserved goose and boiling sausage, with a final layer of beans. Fill the casserole with a good rich stock and finally cover with a layer of breadcrumbs. Bake in the oven very slowly for two to three hours. Top up with more liquid if the beans are drying out. Fewer meats can be used, of course, but boiling or Toulouse sausages are considered essential.

OKRA
(Hibiscus esculentus)

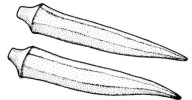

Okra is becoming an increasingly familiar sight in European supermarkets. In India, tropical Africa, the Deep South of the United States and the

West Indies it is as common as the various types of bean are in Europe. Okra grows best in a warm, humid climate, but in cooler areas it can still have a place in the kitchen garden. The plants will have to be started off under glass and then brought outside only in warm weather.

Okra makes an attractive plant, with its bright-green leaves and unusual seed pods looking like small furled umbrellas. An okra would look well in a container on a patio, although the yield of pods would not be large; or in warm areas it could be grown in a sheltered flower bed.

The pods can be used in soups and curries or as a vegetable. The famous New Orleans Creole dish, Gumbo, is a stew of okra, green peppers, celery and onions.

Varieties

One of the old-established varieties is Clemson's Spineless. New varieties include Long Green, Green Velvet and Annie Oakley. All may grow up to 4ft/1.2m tall.

The plant's needs

The ideal soil is light sandy and well draining. But it must not dry out rapidly in hot dry weather, because lack of water affects pod growth and development. Therefore prepare the soil in advance the previous autumn by digging in plenty of well-rotted manure or compost. By spring this will have broken down into rich humus, which retains moisture well. Grow okra outdoors only in warm areas and then in a sunny sheltered part of the garden. Plants in pots should be grown in quality loam potting compost.

Sowing seed

Sow seed indoors in late winter or early spring, two seeds to a peat pot of loam seed compost. Keep at a temperature of 55°F/13°C. Thin by removing the weaker of the two seedlings when they can be handled easily. Seed can also be sown thinly in seed trays in loam seed compost and thinned. When seedlings are about 4in/10cm tall, transplant to 6in/15cm pots. If the plants are to be kept most of the time in the greenhouse, transplant finally to 8in/20cm pots. Pot grown plants may spend some of the summer outdoors on a patio.

In warm areas where plants are to be grown outside they must be properly hardened off in readiness for planting out in early summer. Hardening off should start two to three weeks before then, but only if the weather is suitable. Place the pots outside in a propagator with the ventilators open, and bring them indoors at night. Don't take risks as a result of rushing this step: for example, if there have been night frosts don't put plants outside the following day. When hardening off is complete and the weather suitable, plant out at spacings of 12in/30cm each way.

Sowing directly into the ground in warm areas can begin in late spring, but warm up the soil first by covering the ground with cloches three weeks before sowing. Take out drills 1in/2.5cm deep, 12in/30cm apart, and sow two seeds at 12in/30cm intervals. Replace the cloches until the seed has germinated. Remove the weaker of each pair of seedlings. Keep the plants well watered – they must never be allowed to dry out. This is most important with container-grown plants that may need twice daily watering in hot weather.

From early sowings in heat the first pods should be ready to pick in late summer. Pick them when they are no more than 2in/5cm long, otherwise they will be tough and stringy. If the tip of a bean breaks when it is bent, that is the time to pick; if it just bends without snapping you are too late. Keep picking the pods regularly to encourage new growth, which continues until the first frosts. Later sowings will not be ready for harvesting until early autumn or autumn.

Pests and diseases

Seldom cause trouble.

COOKING AND FREEZING OKRA

Trim the okra pods, removing the stems and tips. Boil in just enough salted water to cover the okra for about 10 to 15 minutes. Slice onions and tomatoes and fry briefly in oil with a little cayenne pepper. Drain the okra and add to the tomatoes and onions. Alternatively, the okra can be parboiled for about eight minutes and then fried with the other ingredients. The Indian way with okra is to fry in oil with cumin, tumeric and cayenne pepper for about 10 to 15 minutes until tender.

To freeze, trim the pods and blanch for about four minutes in boiling water. Drain, cool, and pack in plastic bags.

BEAN PESTS AND DISEASES

Pests

Blackfly is the most likely pest to affect bean crops. The flies colonize the tender tips of the plants, suck the sap and stunt growth. They are easily seen and the time to watch out for them is from late spring to summer. On broad beans infestations can largely be avoided by removing 4-6in/10-15cm of the growing tips when the pods have started to form. Plants should also be sprayed with derris and pyrethrum. If the flies attack French and runner beans, spraying is the only answer.

Bean-seed flies lay eggs in the soil and they emerge as maggots, which attack seeds (they fail to germinate) and seedlings (they wilt and die). There is no cure. Take preventive measures when sowing by dusting the drills with bromophos.

Diseases

Chocolate spot is a fungal disease that attacks both broad and runner beans. In its less serious stage the leaves, pods and stems are covered with small brown spots. If the disease takes hold, leaves turn black and wilt and eventually the plant will die. Extremely wet conditions are the main cause. At the first signs spray with benomyl or organic Bordeaux mixture. Pull up and burn infected plants.

Anthracnose may affect runner beans making unsightly brown markings on leaves, stems and – worst of all – the beans themselves. They look most unappetizing. Badly infected plants should be removed and burned. If the beans have not been attacked, spray plants with benomyl.

Halo blight is a French and runner bean disease that produces brown spots surrounded by yellow rings on the leaves and beans. Lift and burn any infected plants. There is little that can be done to stop its spread, but spraying with Bordeaux mixture may help.

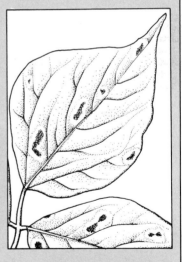

Various diseases attack the roots of beans, causing leaves to yellow and growth to be stunted, with the eventual death of the plant. If you see early signs of such root diseases, water the soil with zineb or captan but if they have taken hold, pull up and burn the plants. Never put diseased plants on a compost heap.

Chinese artichokes, something of a rarity.

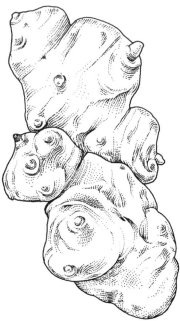

JERUSALEM ARTICHOKE
(Helianthus tuberosus)

TUBERS

*T*he best-known of the tubers is undoubtedly the potato, a vegetable that rightly deserves its traditional place in the kitchen garden. Today potatoes are recognized as being highly nutritious and a rich source of dietary fibre. They are also extremely easy to grow.

There are dozens of varieties of potato, but few are available except from specialist seed merchants. Each year sees new varieties superseding the old, and many of them are an improvement. You can now choose varieties specifically suited to different methods of cooking. Some are better for chipping and sautéing, others for boiling, baking and roasting. One or two are outstanding for cold potato salad.

Less well-known tubers are the Jerusalem and Chinese artichokes. These are quite different in taste and texture to potatoes but are nevertheless delicious. They are difficult to find in the shops, so it is well worth having a go at growing them yourself.

*M*any gardeners view Jerusalem artichokes as something of an unknown quantity but they can make an excellent alternative to potatoes. They have a sweet flavour and a texture that is less floury than that of potatoes.

The objection to them is that the old varieties produce very knobbly tubers that are irritating and time-consuming to peel. Newer varieties are a godsend because they have reasonably smooth surfaces and a shape rather like dumpy parsnips. The problem is tracking them down. It is, indeed, hard enough to find any tubers listed in seed catalogues and often the only way to get hold of them is to buy them when you see them on sale as a vegetable. They are usually in the shops around late autumn and early winter. They should be kept in a cool dry place until ready for planting in late winter and early spring.

Jerusalem artichokes are members of the sunflower family and they grow to similar heights – about 10ft/3m. They make a good windbreak or screen but there is unlikely to be a great show of yellow flowers unless there are extended periods of hot sunny weather in summer. Because of their eventual height and the depth of soil needed for the tubers, they are not suitable for container growing.

Varieties

It is worthwhile searching out a named variety from a seed merchant. The varieties usually offered are Silver Skinned, with a mild flavour, and Fuseau, the best from the cook's point of view because most of the knobbles have been eliminated. However, you may have no choice but to buy some anonymous tubers from the greengrocer.

The plant's needs

Jerusalem artichokes need a rich free-draining soil; if grown in poor soil the result will be puny, poor-flavoured tubers. The ideal soil is light and sandy, but most types will produce successful results. In the autumn, dig in well-rotted manure or compost to give it time to break down before planting in late winter or early spring. Choose a sheltered spot so that they don't get too much battering by the wind, or make sure that they are well staked if they are in an exposed position. Acid soil should be limed to achieve a pH level of about 6.

Planting tubers

In late winter or early spring, make a trench 6in/15cm deep and plant the tubers 12in/30cm apart. If there is more than one row, there should be 3ft/90cm between them. Plant tubers whole if they are the size of a small egg. Divide larger ones, ensuring that they have several growing eyes.

When the plants are about 9in/22.5cm tall, earth up the soil to form a low ridge and stake the plants. Either drive a stake into the ground by each plant or place stakes at each end of the row. Fix wires between the stakes at 2ft/60cm intervals and secure the stems to the wires with soft twine. To restrict the growth of the plants, pinch out the growing tips in summer. This should keep their height down to about 6ft/1.8m.

From autumn onwards the tubers can be lifted. By that time the foliage will have started to turn yellow and die. Cut stems down to within 8in/20cm of the ground. Lift the tubers as they are required through the winter. If you are pleased with your results and are keen to grow this vegetable again, remember to save some for planting next year's crop.

Pests and diseases

Seldom cause trouble.

COOKING JERUSALEM ARTICHOKES

The artichokes have to be peeled, either before or after cooking. If you want them hot it will have to be before. Add some lemon juice to the water in which they are to be boiled to prevent the tubers from turning brown. Cooking them unpeeled will help to contain browning, but still add lemon juice. Boil in salted water for about 20 minutes. Tubers can be sliced and sautéd in butter or oil, with added lemon juice, for about five minutes, or roasted in oil, like parsnips, for about half an hour.

They make a delicious creamy soup. Cook sliced onion, chopped celery and peeled Jerusalem artichokes in a rich chicken stock for about 20 minutes. Liquidize and add a generous dollop of cream.

Not suitable for freezing.

CHINESE ARTICHOKE
(Stachys affinis)

If it is difficult to find Jerusalem artichokes, then it is doubly hard to find Chinese artichokes. At one time sources were restricted to experimental horticultural establishments, but Jerusalem artichokes are slowly creeping into a few seed catalogues, and what a discovery they are if you have not tasted them before. They have a striking nutty flavour coupled with a crisp texture. If you cannot find them in a seed catalogue, you will probably come across them in specialist Chinese food shops in late autumn or early winter. Try some first and if you like the taste save some for planting.

Unlike the towering Jerusalem artichoke they grow to some 18in/45cm only, so they don't need staking. However, they need a good depth of soil and room to develop, so they are not suitable for container growing.

Varieties

In seed catalogues they are simply described as Chinese artichokes.

The plant's needs

For heavy cropping and large tubers, the soil must be rich, fertile and light. Improve the texture of heavy soil, such as clay, by digging in peat. To make the soil more fertile, dig in well-rotted manure or compost in the autumn in readiness for planting the tubers in early spring.

Planting tubers

In early spring, dig a trench 4in/10cm deep, with 12-18in/30-45cm between trenches if there is more than one. Plant the tubers 10in/25cm apart. Keep the plants well watered at all times, or the tubers are likely to shrivel. A liquid feed every two weeks from summer onwards will improve the size of the tubers. From autumn the foliage yellows and dies down. When it is dead, cut it off about 4in/10cm from the ground. Lift the tubers as they are needed and cook them straight away; they deteriorate within a few hours. If there is a chance of frost, they should be protected under cloches. Keep back some tubers for planting in early spring.

Pests and diseases

Seldom give trouble.

COOKING CHINESE ARTICHOKES

Chinese artichokes have even more awkward shapes than Jerusalem artichokes, but they are somewhat less difficult to prepare. To remove the skins, trim the ends of the tubers and drop them into boiling water to blanch them for about a minute. Remove them and the skins should rub off easily. Simmer the tubers for about 15 minutes in water (or stock) to which salt and lemon juice have been added. Drain and toss in butter. The tubers can also be made into soup in the same way as Jerusalem artichokes.

They are not suitable for freezing.

POTATO
(Solanum tuberosum)

Black plastic sheeting has now taken most of the hard grind out of home potato growing. It is an innovation that could not be simpler. When the potatoes have been planted, the soil above is covered with the plastic. As the potatoes grow the sprouts show as bumps under the sheeting, and holes are made in it to let the potatoes through. No earthing-up, no weeding; nothing much more to do until the crop has to be harvested.

Now that it has been made so easy there is every reason for growing your own potatoes. It means that you can grow more varieties than the limited number on sale, and choose them for both their taste and for their use.

Furthermore home-grown 'new' potatoes just dug out of the ground and cooked straight away have a flavour never found in shop-bought potatoes. Added to this, the main-crop potatoes out of the garden will not have to undergo the battering they get from mechanical harvesting and washing that often leaves them badly bruised and blackened inside.

Even if the garden is too small for a potato bed some container growing is possible, using wood or plastic barrels, or special barrels with sliding panels for easy harvesting. Early varieties make the best choice for containers. Yields will not be very large, but even a few helpings of early Jersey Royals from a container in an unheated greenhouse would make your efforts worthwhile.

Varieties

Potato varieties are grouped into first-early, second-early and main-crop varieties.

First earlies These are planted in early spring and will be ready for harvesting in early summer and summer. Concorde has yellow waxy flesh, excellent for sauté and chipped potatoes. Maris Bard has creamy-white flesh, suitable for boiling, chipping, roasting and salads, as is Vanessa, a new red-skinned variety with creamy flesh. Lola has yellow waxy flesh, suitable for sauté and chipped potatoes.

Second earlies are planted in spring and are ready for lifting in summer and late summer. Foremost straddles early and second-early varieties; it has firm white flesh turning floury on cooking, useful for mashed or baked potatoes. Marfona has

cream to light-yellow flesh, excellent for boiling and baking. Wiltja, with pale-yellow flesh, makes tasty sauté and chipped potatoes.

Main-crop varieties are planted towards the end of spring, and will be ready from summer onwards. All should be removed from the ground by autumn and stored. Désirée is red-skinned with pale-yellow flesh, excellent for all uses. Maris Piper, with creamy-white flesh, is rated top for baking, chipping and sautéing, closely followed by boiling and mashing. Kondor, developed from Wiltja, has creamy-yellow flesh and red skin, a good boiler. Romano, developed from Désirée, is another red-skinned variety, suitable for all methods of cooking. Kirsty, with creamy flesh, is best baked or roasted. Cara has taken over in popularity from the old King Edward, the long famous potato from which Cara has been derived. Few King Edwards are now grown and those so labelled are far more likely to be Cara, a good all-rounder that cannot be faulted for any cooking use.

Finally, one of the oldest varieties, Pink Fir Apple, is grabbing the limelight and is even in fashion in some supermarkets. It is the best variety of all for potato salad.

The plant's needs

Potatoes will grow in all types of soil, preferably in an open position. The richer the

soil the better the crop, so manure the ground well. In autumn, dig in plenty of well-rotted manure or compost. In time for spring planting it will have broken down into rich moisture-retentive humus. A pH level of about 5.6 is ideal – more acid than for many vegetables.

Sprouting the tubers

Tubers are usually despatched by nurseries in winter. They cannot be planted immediately because they would probably be damaged by frost. However, early despatch allows time for the tubers to be sprouted: encouraging them to sprout in protected conditions for about six weeks before planting out gives them a head start. Arrange the tubers in egg trays, with the ends that have the most growing eyes uppermost. Alternatively, use shallow boxes with a layer of dry peat at the bottom in which the tubers will sit upright (most growing eyes uppermost). Keep the tubers in a light frost-free room, but not in the warmth since that would encourage weak growth. Expect sturdy 1in/2.5cm shoots.

Growing tubers under black plastic

Plant first-early tubers in early spring, second earlies in spring and main-crop tubers towards the end of spring.

Make V-shaped drills 5in/12.5cm deep and 24in/60cm apart for first-early varieties, and 30in/75cm for the others. Plant first-early tubers 12in/30cm apart in the drill and the rest 15in/37.5cm apart, the sprouted ends facing upwards. Carefully fill in the drills so that the shoots are not damaged. Cover the ground with a sheet of black plastic, which should extend 12in/30cm either side of the planted area.

To secure the plastic, use a spade to make continuous slits into the soil along both sides and ends of the sheet of plastic. Push the plastic into the slits by hand or with the spade and weigh down the edges with soil. If more than one row of potatoes is planted, leave a space between the strips of plastic for access.

By late spring the shoots of the potatoes will be visible as bumps under the plastic. Carefully make holes in the plastic to allow the shoots to grow through.

Early and second-early potatoes will be ready for lifting when the plants are in flower. At this stage the potatoes will be no bigger than jumbo-sized eggs. Dig up only as many as you want for immediate use. First cut off the tops of the roots to be dug up, then fold back the plastic and with a fork ease the potatoes out of the ground.

Leave main-crop potatoes in the ground until the top growth has turned yellow and died down. Cut the top growth down and wait for what promises to be a fine spell. Remove all the plastic covering. Lift the potatoes with a fork, taking the greatest care not to damage them. Any that are damaged should be put aside for immediate use. The rest should be stored in trays covered in black plastic to exclude the light (which turns them green) and kept in a frost-free but cool place. Never store potatoes in a sack: there is no quicker way for one damaged potato to taint the rest. Inspect the trays regularly and throw away any that are going rotten.

Growing in containers

One space-saving method is to grow potatoes in layers on top of one another in a wooden barrel or plastic tub. For a worthwhile crop, the container must be at least 2ft/60cm deep and 2ft/60cm in diameter. At the bottom of the container put a 4in/10cm layer of a mixture of quality loam potting compost and well-rotted manure or compost. For a container of this size, arrange four sprouted tubers on the surface of the compost, equal distances apart, and about 4in/10cm in from the edge of the container. Cover them with a 4in/10cm layer of compost.

When the shoots of the first layer of potatoes are about 6in/15cm tall, add another 4in/15cm layer of compost and place four more tubers at equal distances between the shoots showing above the compost. Put another 4in/15cm of compost on this second layer of potatoes. Carry on in this way until four layers of tubers have been planted.

Keep the compost well watered at all times. A container with sliding panels makes harvesting much easier.

For an early crop of Jersey Royal potatoes, plant sprouted tubers in a container in winter or late winter and keep them in an unheated but frost-free greenhouse. They should be ready by late spring.

Growing the conventional way

In well-prepared ground, plant the sprouted tubers as described under *Growing tubers under black plastic*. After filling in the drills draw up the soil a little to make a gently sloping ridge along the row. When the top growth is about 8in/20cm tall, ridge up the soil around the plants by drawing it inwards from either side of the row. This will help to keep weeds in check and prevent potatoes that are growing near the surface of the soil from turning green, which makes them unfit to eat. Keep well watered. Harvest as described (see *Growing tubers under black plastic*).

COOKING AND FREEZING POTATOES

There are numerous ways of cooking potatoes but two of the most popular ways are as chips and as roast potatoes. With a little care it is is easy to get crisp results. Cut the potatoes into slender chips and leave them to soak in cold water for about an hour to remove some of the starch. Drain and dry thoroughly on absorbent paper or a cloth. The oil in the chip pan must be hot but not smoking; if you have a cookery thermometer, let the fat reach 350°F/177°C before lowering the chips in their wire basket into the oil. They should start to sizzle immediately. Cook for about five minutes. Remove them from the oil and drain them. Heat the oil again, rather hotter this time (385°F/196°C) and watch them rapidly turn golden brown. Drain them and put them on absorbent paper in a serving dish. (Chips can be made by single frying, but double frying makes them crisper.)

For crisp roast potatoes, parboil them for about five minutes. Drain and vigorously shake the potatoes in the pan to roughen up their surface; this will make them brown and crisp better. Place in a roasting tin in pre-heated fat or oil and cook for about an hour in a hot oven. The tastiest roast potatoes are those cooked in duck fat, but a little of the crispness may be lost.

It is hardly worth the effort of freezing potatoes, except possibly for small new ones. Blanch in boiling water for about three minutes and allow to cool before packing them in rigid containers.

PESTS AND DISEASES

Pests

Potato eel-worm is the worst pest that attacks potatoes. Top growth becomes weak and stunted, often dying down completely and the crop will be poor or non-existent. There is no treatment. Lift and burn all plants. Grow potatoes in a different part of the garden every year. If the ground is badly infested with eggs, it may not be possible to grow potatoes for several years.

Wireworms bore into the tubers, tunnelling all the way through and leaving none of the potato edible. Again there is no cure once they have struck. If they have attacked, rake bromophos into the soil the following year before planting the tubers (in a different part of the garden).

Slugs can be a real problem for potatoes grown under plastic. Before covering the plants, prepare the soil with a slug killer - ask your supplier about organic alternatives.

Aphids will eat the foliage in warm weather, killing plants completely in extreme cases. Spray with derris and pyrethrum to keep them down.

Diseases

Potato blight is a fungal disease that turns the foliage yellow, with dark-brown patches on leaves and stems.

Then the tubers rot. Excessive wet is the cause. At the first sign of yellowing, spray the foliage with maneb, zineb or the more organically acceptable Bordeaux mixture.

Scab looks unpleasant, but affects only the skin of the potato. It is encouraged by over-limed soil. Help to prevent its presence by not liming before growing potatoes, but instead digging in compost or manure to produce humus.

New varieties of beetroot – an even richer purple colour.

ROOT CROPS

Nowadays, when you can buy so many vegetables all the year round, plant breeders have to work hard to make familiar root vegetables a competitive alternative. Carrots are a good example of their success. They used to be large and rather woody, but the new varieties are juicy finger-sized roots of a strong orange colour. Both flavour and appearance have improved and even main-crop carrots are now smaller and more tender.

The flesh of new varieties of beetroot has become a richer, deeper red-purple colour, and the plants have now been made resistant to bolting.

Today's vegetable gardener might also want to try the recently introduced Japanese and Chinese radishes, with their long, white tapering roots. They can be eaten raw; but if you try stir-frying them, as they do in the East, you will discover an entirely new vegetable taste.

There are other new tastes that are worth trying too – salsify and its sweet-flavoured companion, scorzonera; Hamburg parsley; celeriac, a knobbly root with a celery flavour; and kohlrabi, a cabbage/turnip cross which has long been enjoyed in Continental Europe. With this range of flavours and improved quality, roots are well able to maintain their position in the modern kitchen garden.

BEETROOT
(Beta vulgaris)

Today's better-bred beetroots are a godsend to both gardener and cook. For the gardener the major advance has been the breeding of varieties that are resistant to bolting, when the plants perversely flower and seed instead of developing the swollen roots. Other new varieties have reduced the chore of thinning. The older varieties had up to three seeds stored in a 'packet' that was part of the flower-head, so when they germinated all but one of the seedlings had to be removed. Now there are new labour-saving varieties that produce just one seed instead of a probable surfeit of seedlings.

For the cook it is the colour that has changed – to an even deeper red-purple. Early sowings will produce small tender and succulent globes, but always choose a bolt-resistant variety. Later sowings give larger globes, some of which can be stored for winter use.

Beetroot is suitable for close planting, either in blocks or rows, and can be grown in containers.

Varieties

For early sowing The old favourite is the bolt-resistant Bolthardy, with dark-red flesh. Monopoly, a single-seeded variety, and Regala are also bolt-resistant.

For summer sowing Among these are Detroit Little Ball, which has small globes that can be pickled, and Detroit New Globe. For a change of colour, there is Burpees Golden, which tastes like a red beetroot but has yellow flesh that does not bleed. For a change of shape, there are cylindrical beets, Cylindra; or tapering-rooted Cheltenham Green Top, Forono; and the single-seeded Cheltenham Mono.

The plant's needs

The ideal soil for beetroot is light and sandy, but it will grow in any type. Choose a sunny sheltered spot and dig in compost or well-rotted manure during the previous autumn before sowing seed in spring. Lime acid soils for a pH level of about 6.5.

Sowing seed

Sow seed of bolt-resistant varieties in early spring. If the soil has not warmed up, sow under cloches. Take out drills 1in/2.5cm deep and 8in/20cm apart and sow the seed of the multi-seeded varieties in pairs 4in/10cm apart. Thin, removing the weaker seedling of each pair. Seed can also be sown in a block, spacing 4in/10cm each way, so an area 2ft sq/60cm sq would contain 49 plants. Single-seeded varieties should be sown at 2in/5cm intervals in rows 8in/20cm apart and thinned to 4in/10cm apart, or in blocks 2in/5cm each way, thinning to 4in/10cm each way.

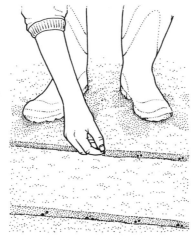

For main-crop and long-rooted varieties, sow seed in late spring or early summer, spacing rows 12in/30cm apart, with 4in/10cm between seeds. If planting in a block, space seed 6in/15cm each way. For successional cropping, sow seed every two or three weeks. The last sowing should be in summer.

Plants will need frequent watering in periods of warm weather or the globes are likely to be woody.

Lift the globes as they are needed from summer to late summer. They should never be allowed to grow larger than the

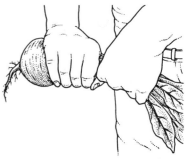

size of tennis-balls. The main crop is lifted in early autumn or autumn. Pull them out of the ground by hand to avoid damaging the flesh with a spade or fork and twist off the leaves. Long-rooted varieties may need easing out with a fork. Store the roots in boxes of sand or peat and keep in a frost-free place.

Growing beetroot in containers

Containers should be at least 12in/30cm wide, 8in/20cm long and 2ft/60cm long. Fill with quality loam potting compost. Sow seed of bolt-resistant varieties in early spring 4in/10cm apart each way, starting 2in/5cm from the ends and sides of the container. A container 2ft/60cm long will then hold 18 plants.

In late spring or early summer, sow the main-crop variety Detroit Little Ball, using the same spacings.

PESTS AND DISEASES: BEETROOT

Seldom a problem. Aphids may attack but are usually kept under control with derris or pyrethrum sprays.

COOKING AND FREEZING BEETROOT

One of the problems with serving beetroot is that the juice tends to stain other food. The alternative is to grow yellow-fleshed beetroot, which does not bleed.

Prepare the roots by trimming off the leaves, taking care with the red beets not to cut into the flesh, causing bleeding. Boil in salted water for about 45 minutes, until tender. The skin should then peel away easily. Try serving beetroot diced and added to chopped celery and apple. Toss in a dressing of yogurt, lemon juice and seasoning. The classic beetroot dish is the rich soup called bortsch. Shredded raw beetroot, onion, cabbage, lemon juice and tomato purée are cooked in a rich beef stock for about 30 minutes. Add sour cream just before serving.

Beetroot are hardly worth the trouble of freezing.

CARROT
(Daucus carota)

The most popular modern carrots are small, slim and sweet. They have a strong colour – indeed, plant breeders have concentrated on producing carrots that are bright orange throughout without any green rings, and that continue to look good after cooking. These are the carrots that have taken over supermarket shelves.

Home gardeners will also rely largely on these early varieties, fresh from the garden from early summer and from the freezer for the rest of the year. But there are many other choices, especially of shape, among the main crops. Ignore the long-rooted conical-shaped monsters fit only for the show bench. Instead, choose the main-crop varieties with short conical or blunt-ended roots, or even round roots. These are the larger carrots most useful for stews.

Carrots in general can be planted close together and thinned according to the size required. They can also be grown in containers – choose Amsterdam Forcing and Nantes Tiptop.

Varieties

Earlies Amsterdam Forcing will provide the earliest crops in early summer from a protected sowing in late winter or early spring. From spring onwards sow unprotected for cropping between summer and early autumn. Other varieties include Mokum, with slender cylindrical roots; Early Nantes and Nantes Tiptop, with cylindrical blunt-ended roots; and the round-rooted varieties Parmex, Parisian Rondo and Early French Frame. F_1 hybrid varieties with a uniform orange colour running the length of the root include Nandor and Clairon with cylindrical roots.

Main crop Chantenay Red Cored produces stumpy carrots in autumn from sowings in spring to late spring. James Scarlet Intermediate is one of the old-established reliable varieties with tapering roots. Berlicum Berjo produces cylindrical blunt-ended carrots and Autumn King's are cylindrical stump-ended. The variety Beacon with long, tapering stump-ended roots has a strong orange colour. F_1 hybrids in this group include Camus, with stump ends and uniform orange colour, and Cardinal, with cylindrical roots and strong colour. If you must grow the giants of the carrot world, go for St Valery and the F_1 Fedora.

Sowing seed

For early-protected sowings of Amsterdam Forcing, warm up the soil for about two weeks before sowing in early winter by placing cloches over the area to be sown. Take out drills ½in/1.25cm deep and 6in/15cm apart. Sow the seed thinly and cover with the cloches. When the seedlings are about 1in/2.5cm tall, thin to 2in/5cm apart. At this stage carrot root fly can be a menace – it is attracted by the smell of the thinnings. These, therefore, must never be left lying about, and should be buried deep in the compost heap, or, far better, burned. To lessen the risk of attack, thin in the evening, when the flies are less active, and water well the remaining seedlings. Cloches can be removed completely in spring or late spring.

The first unprotected sowings of the early varieties can be made in early spring, with the spacings already described. If there is room, make another sowing two or three weeks later.

The first sowing of main-crop varieties is made in spring. Sow in drills 6in/15cm apart, thinning to 2in/5cm, and later to 4in/10cm if larger carrots are wanted. Successional sowings can be made from late spring to summer. The final sowing will provide tasty young carrots in late autumn. In the final weeks they may need to be protected under cloches.

Early varieties are ready for harvesting from early summer onwards and main-crop from autumn onwards. They taste better if they are pulled just before they are needed. Pull them up by hand. Reluctant roots can be eased with a fork.

In mild areas carrots can be left in the ground in winter as long as they are well protected under straw or leaves. Where frost is likely the roots should be lifted for storage indoors in a frost-free but cool place. Twist off the top foliage by hand or cut it off with a knife. Store in layers in large boxes or plastic bins filled with sand or peat. Store only sound carrots, and make sure they don't touch each other.

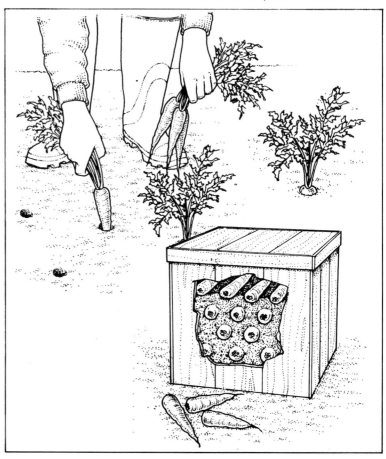

Growing in containers

Containers should be at least 12in/30cm wide, 10in/25cm deep, and 2ft/60cm long. Fill with quality loam compost. From spring onwards sow seed of the early varieties Amsterdam Forcing and Nantes Tip-top. Take out drills ½in/1.25cm deep and 4in/10cm apart, starting 2in/5cm from the side of the container, giving three rows of carrots. Sow seed thinly. When seedlings are about 1in/2.5cm tall thin to 2in/5cm. Main-crop varieties should also be sown and thinned to the same spacings. They will never grow to be show specimens, but smaller carrots make sweeter and more tender eating. Keep containers well watered at all times. In warm weather twice daily watering may be needed.

PESTS AND DISEASES: CARROT

Pests

Carrot fly is the major pest, most likely to attack at thinning time. The signs are wilting and then dying foliage. The grubs burrow into the roots and render them inedible. As a precaution before sowing, rake bromophos into the soil and after thinning sprinkle more bromophos along the row. Early sowings are unlikely to be attacked, and container-grown plants should also escape if the containers are raised above ground level.

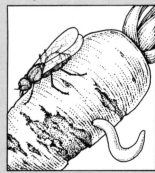

Diseases

Sclerotinia rot is a major problem, attacking stored carrots. An unpleasant white fungus develops on the stored roots, harbouring groups of black spores. There is no cure and any affected carrots should be removed and burned. Never store damaged roots.

COOKING AND FREEZING CARROTS

Carrots are rich in carotene, which the body converts into vitamin A; it is hardly diminished by cooking. Cook young finger-sized carrots whole. Top and tail them but don't peel; scrubbing is all that is required. Just cover them with salted boiling water and cook for about ten minutes. Larger carrots will take a little longer, but they should still be firm and crisp. Drain and toss in melted butter. Older carrots may need peeling and slicing before cooking. Try them stir-fried. Cut into fine slices and cook in oil, along with ginger, for about ten minutes, stirring all the time.

Carrots make excellent soup. Simmer sliced carrots and onion with the juice and grated rind of oranges in a good chicken stock for about 20 minutes. Liquidize and serve hot or cold.

Use raw grated carrot in coleslaw or on its own with a vinaigrette dressing.

To freeze young carrots, blanch them in boiling water for about three minutes. Drain and dry and pack into plastic bags.

CELERIAC
(Apium graveolens)

The leafy tops of celeriac look like celery, but underground there is a large knobbly turnip-shaped root, not a bit like celery to look at but with a celery flavour. It has a taste many gardeners are experiencing for the first time, and it is becoming deservedly popular. For the gardener, celeriac has the advantage over celery in that it does not have to be earthed-up. However, it does need a long growing season for the root to develop to a decent size, and it also needs plenty of room, which makes it unsuitable for container growing. Both tops and bottoms of the plant can be eaten, the roots either cooked or raw.

Varieties

The varieties are limited. Marble Ball is one of the oldest-established varieties, producing large roots that can be stored in peat or sand over winter. Globus also has large roots with a distinctive strong flavour. Both Jos and Snow White (a new variety) mature earlier. Iran and Tellus have medium-sized roots that retain their white colour after cooking.

The plant's needs

Choose a warm, sunny and sheltered part of the garden. In autumn, dig in well-rotted manure or compost so that the ground is ready for sowing in the following spring. Lime acid soil for a pH level of about 6.

Sowing seed

Start seed off indoors or in a greenhouse in spring. Sow seed thinly in pots or trays of loam seed compost. Firm the compost, sprinkle the seed thinly over the surface and cover with a fine sifting of compost. Keep at 50-55°F/10-13°C. When seedlings are about 1in/2.5cm tall, prick them out into trays of loam potting compost, spacing them 2in/5cm apart.

In late spring, start hardening off the plants by placing the trays outdoors during the day. Either put them in a propagator with the vents left open or cover each tray with plastic supported with wire to prevent it from touching the plants. Remember to bring the trays in each evening. After about two weeks they should be ready for planting out, in early summer.

Plant out in block formation, spacing plants 12in/30cm each way. A block 3ft

Celeriac, Marble Ball variety.

sq/90cm sq will contain 16 plants. The slightly bulbous base should be planted at ground level and not buried beneath the soil. Keep the plants well watered at all times and apply a mulch around their base to retain moisture. As the root develops some side-shoots may appear. Cut them off to force the plant to concentrate on producing one large bulb.

The roots can be lifted from autumn onwards. In frost-free areas plants covered with straw can be left in the ground until used. Otherwise lift all the roots in autumn and store in peat or sand in a frost-free place.

PESTS AND DISEASES: CELERIAC

Pests

Carrot fly can be a problem, causing wilting and dying foliage (see under carrots). Before planting out, rake bromophos into the soil.

Celery flies should not be as troublesome as they are with celery itself. They lay eggs that hatch into maggots, burrowing deep into the leaves and causing brown blisters. Pick off and burn infected leaves and spray with malathion.

COOKING AND FREEZING CELERIAC

Grate raw celeriac and add it to mixed green salads or serve it on its own, dressed with vinaigrette or mayonnaise.

Before cooking celeriac trim off the top leaves, which can be used for adding flavour to soups. Scrub the bulb and then peel to remove the knobbly surface. Slice or dice into cubes and cook in salted boiling water for about 10 to 15 minutes until tender. Add some lemon juice to the water to help retain the whiteness of the flesh. Toss in melted butter before serving or purée it with cream.

Celeriac also makes a tasty soup. Simmer with onions and fines herbes in a good chicken stock. Liquidize with cream or milk, garnishing the surface with chopped celeriac leaves.

To freeze celeriac, trim off the leaves and peel. Cut into cubes and blanch in boiling water for three minutes. Drain, cool and dry before packing into polythene bags.

HAMBURG PARSLEY
(Petroselinum crispum)

The parsley-flavoured leaves of Hamburg parsley top a long parsnip-like root with a taste between parsnip and celery. This is another vegetable favoured on the Continent, now gaining fans elsewhere. From sowing seed to maturity takes about six months, with major root growth in autumn.

Varieties

This is not an easy vegetable to track down. It may be described only as Hamburg parsley, but a few named varieties include Berliner and Hamburg Turnip-rooted.

The plant's needs

Choose a sunny sheltered part of the garden. Prepare the soil in autumn by digging in well-rotted manure or compost. Lime acid soil to achieve a pH level of about 6.5.

Sowing seed

In spring, take out drills 10in/25cm apart and ½in/1.25cm deep. Thin seedlings to 8in/20cm apart. Keep well watered. Apply a mulch round the base of the plants to retain moisture. Roots will be ready for lifting in autumn or late autumn. Dig them up as required over winter or lift them and store in boxes of peat or sand.

Pests and diseases

Seldom give trouble.

COOKING AND FREEZING HAMBURG PARSLEY

Remove the leaves and scrub, but don't peel, the surface of the roots. Slice them lengthways in half and roast in meat juices. The roots can also be sliced and cooked in boiling salted water for about ten minutes. Serve tossed in butter or they can be puréed with milk or cream. They can also be eaten raw, grated in salads. Use the tops to flavour soups.

Freezing is not recommended.

KOHLRABI
(Brassica oleracea)

Kohlrabi, a cross between cabbage and turnip, has been enjoyed on the Continent for years. Now, at last, its popularity is spreading to other countries. Better varieties have surfaced on its travels. Once the globes would turn tough and woody if they were allowed to grow too large, say above the size of a tennis-ball. New F₁ hybrids have put an end to that.

Kohlrabi can be grown in containers, but closer spacing means that the globes have to be harvested when they are smaller, around the size of a golf ball. Since they grow conveniently on the surface of the soil it is easy to judge their size.

Varieties

Old-established varieties include White Vienna, with pale-green globes, and Purple Vienna, which has purple skin but white flesh. The new F_1 hybrids that will not turn woody are Rowel and Lanro.

The plant's needs

Kohlrabi requires rich fertile but light soil and a sunny position. Dig in well-rotted manure or compost in autumn before sowing seed the following spring. Lime acid soil to achieve a pH level of about 6.5.

Sowing seed

In spring, take out drills 12in/30cm apart and ½in/1.25cm deep. Sow seed thinly. Thin seedlings to 6in/15cm apart. Successional sowings can be made every three weeks until summer. Start pulling the globes from summer onwards, when they are no bigger than a tennis-ball. The final sowings should be of the purple-skinned variety, and they will be ready for eating in early winter. Don't store the globes of these late sowings because they shrivel: leave them in the ground and pull as required.

Growing in containers

Containers should be at least 12in/30cm wide, 10in/25cm deep and 24in/60cm long. Fill with quality loam potting compost. In spring, take out drills ½in/1.25cm and 4in/10cm apart, starting 2in/5cm from the edge of the container, making three rows. Sow seed thinly and cover with a sifting of compost. Thin seedlings to 4in/10cm apart. Keep well watered es-

Kohlrabi, Purple Vienna variety.

pecially in warm spells, when twice daily watering may be needed. Unlike other root vegetables, kohlrabi will tolerate hot and dry conditions if necessary. Start lifting in summer when the globes are no bigger than a golf ball.

Pests and diseases

Aphids can be troublesome. Spray with derris or pyrethrum.

Brassica pests and diseases may strike (see page 41).

COOKING AND FREEZING KOHLRABI

Prepare the globes for cooking by cutting off the top leaves. Scrub but don't peel the surface to retain the full rich flavour of the flesh. Cut into slices or strips and cook in salted boiling water for about ten minutes, until tender. Serve tossed in butter, or puréed with cream.

Kohlrabi may also be eaten raw in salads. Grate and toss in vinaigrette or dress with mayonnaise.

Globes can be frozen whole, but choose small ones. Blanch in boiling water for three minutes; drain, cool, dry, and pack into plastic bags. Larger globes can be diced before blanching.

PARSNIP
(Peucedanum sativum)

Parsnips are one of the world's ancient vegetables; indeed they were the staple diet until potatoes arrived on the scene. They are still a truly labour-saving vegetable, requiring little or no attention once they have been thinned. On the other hand, the ground in which they grow is tied up for much of a year, from sowing in spring to harvesting from autumn onwards.

In the past canker, a fungal disease, has been a major drawback to growing parsnips; it causes the crown and shoulder of the roots to rot just when they are ready to harvest. The newest varieties now cope with this and close-planting techniques help to control the disease.

The long-rooted varieties are best avoided as they need a depth of fertile soil not found in many gardens. Choose a variety such as Avon Resister, which has small bulbous-shaped roots that can be grown close together. Such close planting, coupled with a later sowing date, ensures a crop of small, sweet, tasty parsnips, favoured in the kitchen if scorned on the show bench.

Varieties

The smallest roots come from Avon Resister, which has a good resistance to canker. For medium-sized roots, Cobham Improved Marrow produces white smooth-skinned roots, also with a high canker resistance. Gladiator is the latest F_1 hybrid variety, with wedge-shaped roots and canker resistance.

The giants of the parsnip world are Tender and True, Improved Hollow Crowned and White Gem, all of which need deeply cultivated soil. If you want to grow these varieties, deep pockets of soil will have to be prepared in advance of sowing or else the roots are likely to fork.

The plant's needs

Parsnips must have a rich fertile soil and a sunny position. Don't dig in manure or compost before sowing, but use a part of the garden that has been manured for a previous crop: the roots will fork if they are grown in newly manured soil. Lime acid soils to achieve a pH level of about 6.5, as soils that are too acid encourage canker.

To grow long-rooted parsnips, further preparation is needed. Make holes 18in/45cm deep and at least 3in/7.5cm in

diameter and fill them with a mixture of finely sifted soil and peat. Mark each hole with a stick to aid sowing.

Sowing seed

Indoors an early start can be made by sowing seed in peat pots in late winter. Sow three seeds to a pot, filled with loam seed compost and keep at 55°F/13°C. Thin, leaving the strongest seedling in each pot. In spring plant out, allowing 3in/7.5cm between plants and 8in/20cm between rows for Avonresister; and for all other varieties 6in/15cm apart and 12in/30cm between rows.

If the weather is mild, an early sowing can be made outdoors in late winter, but it is wiser to wait until early spring or spring when the soil has begun to warm up. Take out drills ½in/1.25in deep, 8in/20cm apart for Avonresister and 12in/30cm apart for other varieties. Sow three seeds of Avon-

resister at intervals of 3in/7.5cm and other varieties at 6in/15cm. Thin to the strongest seedling of each group. Apply a mulch round the base of the plants to help retain moisture and keep the weeds down. There is no need to hoe, which can easily damage the crowns.

Roots should be ready for lifting from autumn onwards, when the top foliage has started to die down. If an early sowing of Gladiator has been made, that should be ready in early autumn. Lift the parsnips as they are required, and in mild areas this may continue through the winter. In colder parts the parsnips survive in the ground but if it becomes frozen, the roots become difficult to lift. Therefore, it is better to lift the remainder of the roots in late autumn or early winter and store them in boxes of sand or dry peat. Don't attempt to store damaged parsnips and make sure that stored ones are not touching each other.

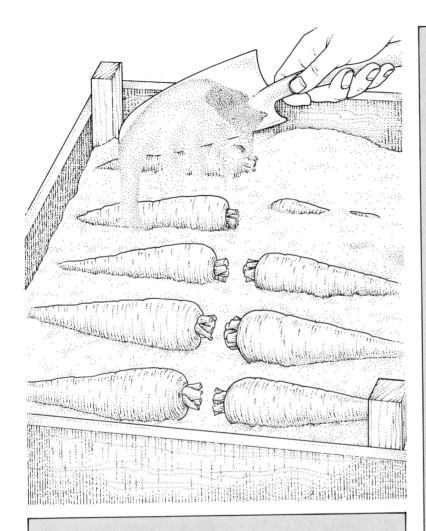

A roasted parsnip is far superior to a boiled one. Remove the top and tail and scrub the root but don't peel it. That way the skin will become crisp and the flesh will be sweet and floury. Cut the root lengthwise into halves or quarters, depending on its size, and bake in oil for about 45 minutes.

If you want to boil parsnips, cut them into rings or short sticks. Serve as a purée with butter or cream, adding a little lemon juice to counteract the sweetness.

To freeze parsnips, cut into slices and blanch for two minutes. Drain, cool and dry before packing into plastic bags.

PESTS AND DISEASES: PARSNIP

Pests
Celery flies lay eggs on the leaves in late spring. The resulting maggots burrow into the foliage, causing brown blisters. Pick off affected leaves and spray the plants with malathion.

Diseases
Canker is the main threat. A fungus attacks the crown and shoulders of the roots turning them black and then rotting them. There are several causes – lack of lime; growing on freshly manured ground; damage to the crowns of the root; and prolonged drought. Once diseased the crop is lost, so preventive measures must be taken. Sow only canker-resistant varieties. Lime soil adequately. Don't sow on newly manured ground. Keep the plants well watered in periods of warm, dry weather.

RADISH
(Raphanus sativus)

If the familiar small red globes of sum-mer radishes are a little too hot for your taste, there are now milder and more subtle alternatives available. The long white and weighty but succulent roots of Chinese and Japanese summer and winter radishes have now arrived on the scene. They can be eaten both raw and cooked, and gardeners are taking to them enthusiastically.

The traditional radishes still have their place, of course, not least because they mature so quickly – as little as four weeks from sowing to harvesting. They are the ultimate, space-efficient catch crop. They can be fitted in between rows of slow-germinating and maturing vegetables, such as parsnips, using space not re-quired by the main crop until later stages of growth.

All radishes can be grown in con-tainers, providing successions of crops through the summer, followed, perhaps, by the often-neglected winter varieties. However, long-rooted varieties grown in containers will have to be pulled before they grow too long.

Varieties

Summer For those with a traditional taste in radishes, French Breakfast provides the red cylindrical roots and Cherry Belle the red, small round ones. Scarlet Globe has all-red skin, with crisp, white mild flesh. For early sowing under cloches there are Saxerre Robino and Ribella. For the adventurous, the latest introducton is the Japanese radish or mooli. F₁ hybrid var-ieties include April Cross and Minowase Summer; both have white tapering roots up 12in/30cm long. They don't grow as rapidly as traditional varieties, but they can be left in the ground for six weeks after maturing without deteriorating. Long White Icicle also has a white root, not as long as the Japanese radish, but if it is allowed to grow to more than 6in/15cm, the flavour will be hot and peppery. Mun-chen Bier is the odd one out, because it is not grown for its roots but for its seed pods. The plants are allowed to flower and the seed pods follow. They have a sharp spicy flavour and can be used raw in salads or stir-fried.

Winter The winter varieties are sown in summer and should be ready from autumn onwards. Black Spanish Round has large globes with black skin and pure

Radish, Cherry Belle variety.

white flesh, while China Rose has long cylindrical rose-red skin with white flesh. Japanese varieties include Mino Early with white, mild-tasting roots up to 12in/30cm long. Leave some winter radish in the ground all through the winter and try the pods produced after the plant has run to seed in spring.

The plant's needs

Even if you are growing summer radishes only as a catch crop, make sure that the ground has been well prepared. The best soils are fertile, light and sandy, but mois-ture-retentive. If the soil dries out for any length of time, the radishes will be hot and peppery. To avoid this, sowings in high summer should be made in a slightly shaded part of the garden that will not dry out too quickly. Dig the soil over before sowing, breaking it down to a fine tilth.

Winter radishes will grow in heavier soils (but not thick clay), though it pays to improve such soils by digging in plenty of peat. Sow in ground that has been manured for a previous crop, never in freshly manured ground. Lime acid soils to a pH level of about 6.5.

Sowing seed

Summer varieties In late winter, make sowings of Saxerre, Robino and Ribella under cloches. Take out drills ½in/1.25cm deep and 6in/15cm apart. Sow seed 1in/2.5cm apart and if the seedlings look overcrowded, they can be thinned to 2in/5cm apart.

The main summer crops are sown out-doors unprotected, from spring onwards, using the same distances. Japanese sum-mer radishes should be sown at 3in/7.5cm intervals in a row, and thinned if neces-sary. Make successional sowings every three weeks for supplies throughout the summer. Keep well watered, especially in warm weather.

Harvest the cylindrical varieties when the roots are no more than 1in/2.5cm long and the globes when they are about ½in/1.25cm in diameter. At that stage they will be mild and crisp, and not the all-too-familiar peppery hot and spongy roots that ruin many a salad. Japanese radishes are best used when about 6in/15cm long.

Winter varieties Sow seed of winter radishes in summer or late summer. Drills should be ½in/1.25cm and 9in/22.5cm apart. Sow the seed at 3in/7.5cm intervals and thin to 6in/15cm.

Unless the winters are severe, winter radishes can be left in the ground and

Radish, Minowase variety.

pulled as needed. The only problem can be lifting them when the ground is frozen. To avoid that, cover the ground with straw. If winters are likely to be severe, lift all the roots in late autumn or early winter and store in boxes of peat or sand.

Growing in containers

Containers should be at least 12in/30cm wide, 10in/25cm deep and 24in/60cm long. Fill with quality loam potting compost two days before sowing to allow it to settle. Add further compost if necessary to bring the level within 1in/2.5cm of the top of the container.

Sow summer radish from spring onwards. Take out drills ½in/1.25cm deep and 4in/10cm apart, starting 2in/5cm from the edge of the container so that there are three rows. Sow seed at 1in/2.5cm intervals in the rows and thin to 2in/5cm if necessary. Sow Japanese varieties at 3in/7.5cm intervals, thinning if they look overcrowded. Water well at all times; in warm weather twice daily watering may be necessary.

Sow winter varieties in summer or late summer. Take out drills ½in/1.25cm deep and 6in/15cm apart, starting 3in/7.5cm from the edge of the container, so there are two rows. Sow seed at 3in/7.5cm intervals and thin to 6in/15cm. Pull roots in late autumn or early winter; they are at their best when no more than 6in/15cm long.

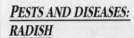

PESTS AND DISEASES: RADISH

Diseases are seldom a problem. However, if seedling leaves are nibbled, the flea beetle is to blame: it finds radishes almost irresistible. Dust the rows with derris or pyrethrum to discourage them.

COOKING AND FREEZING RADISHES

Radishes are usually eaten raw, topped, tailed and sliced. They can then be added to mixed salads, tossed in vinaigrette. Sliced radishes may also be dressed on their own. Try a yogurt dressing, mixed with lemon juice, seasoning and a selection of chopped fresh herbs – parsley, chives and chervil, for example. For a change, try grating or shredding radishes into mixed salads and sandwiches, or make a dip with soy sauce.

The large Japanese radishes may be eaten raw, sliced or shredded, but they really come into their own when cooked. Thinly slice radish and cucumber and stir-fry with a little oil and garlic for about three minutes. You can also try stir-frying radish with shrimps as the Chinese do. Use the seed pods of Munchen Bier raw in mixed salads or stir-fry them in oil for about five minutes.

Freezing of radishes is not recommended.

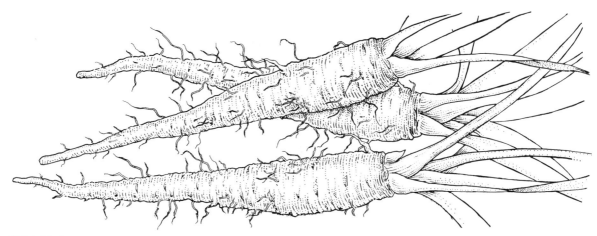

SALSIFY
(Tragopogon porrifolius)

The parsnip-shaped salsify, a native of Southern Europe, is a vegetable that has been largely neglected until recently. It has an interesting, subtle flavour and is sometimes described as the vegetable oyster or oyster plant. If you haven't grown it before, you may well find it worth a try.

Because of the depth of its tapering roots (about 12in/30cm) and the planting distances needed, it is not suitable for container growing.

Varieties

There is a limited choice of varieties, most of which have been around for decades. Those usually offered are Giant, Sandwich Island or Mammoth Sandwich Island.

The plant's needs

The best roots are those grown in fertile light soil that has been deeply dug. Choose a part of the garden that has been manured for a previous crop; never sow salsify in newly manured ground. Nor should they be grown in clay soil, but other heavy soils can be lightened by digging in plenty of peat. Lime acid soil for a pH level of about 6.5. Remove stones because they encourage the roots to fork.

Sowing seed

In spring, take out drills ½in/1.25cm deep and 10in/25cm apart and sow the seeds in groups of three at 6in/15cm intervals. Remove the weakest of the seedlings when they can be handled easily. Keep the plants well watered at all times. Apply a mulch round the base of the plants to help conserve moisture. Do not hoe as this may permanently damage the plants' crowns.

The roots will be ready for lifting in autumn. This needs care as cuts on the roots will cause them to bleed. Only in very mild areas can the roots be left in the ground in winter and lifted as needed. Elsewhere, lift them and store in boxes of peat or sand in a frost-free place.

Pests and diseases

Usually no problem.

COOKING AND FREEZING SALSIFY

Salsify can be grated and used raw in salads. Scrub the surface, peel thinly and then grate and mix with lemon juice so that it does not discolour. Dress with vinaigrette or mayonnaise. You can also use it with other raw grated vegetables, such as cabbage and carrot, to make coleslaw.

If you are going to cook salsify, first scrub and peel the roots, cutting off the tops and bottom. Boil in water with a little lemon juice to help retain the colour for about 20 minutes. Toss in butter or serve covered with an olive oil and lemon dressing.

Freezing is not recommended.

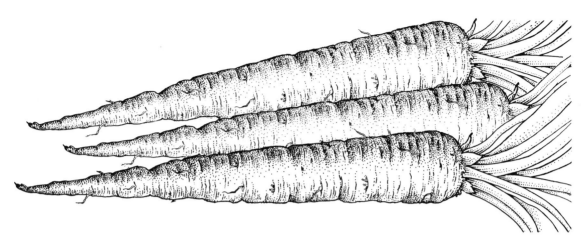

SCORZONERA
(Scorzonera hispanica)

Scorzonera is the companion to salsify and in recent years has been just as neglected. The thin roots have black skins, but their flesh is creamy-white like salsify, and their sweet flavour is considered by many to be superior. Seed suppliers are waking up to the current demand for this unusual vegetable, so the seed should be easy to track down.

The length of root and the planting distances make it unsuitable for growing in containers.

Varieties

The seed may be sold simply as scorzonera, but there are now a few named varieties. The old-established one is Russian Giant, but newer varieties include Lange Jan and Habil.

The plant's needs

Scorzonera needs a rich, well-draining but moisture-retentive soil. Deep digging is needed to prepare the ground as the roots grow to 12in/30cm long or more. Choose a part of the garden manured for a previous crop. Freshly manured ground encourages the roots to fork. So do stones in the soil and as many as possible should be removed when digging. If necessary, dig in plenty of peat to make the soil more moisture-retentive. Acid soil should be limed to reach a pH level of 6.5.

Sowing seed

Don't sow seed too early in the year because the plants have a tendency to bolt, developing flowers and seed instead of a

reasonably sized edible root. In the late part of spring, take out drills ½in/1.25cm deep and 10in/25cm apart. Sow the seed in groups of two or three at intervals of 6in/15cm. As the seedlings develop, remove the weakest one of each group. Don't hoe to keep down weeds as this may

damage the crowns. Instead apply a mulch around the base of each plant to suppress weeds and retain moisture.

The roots should be ready for lifting in autumn or late autumn. They can be left in the ground all through the winter, but if the ground freezes the roots will be hard to lift, because of their length. Take care when lifting that you don't slice the root: ease the soil round it before lifting. Alternatively, the roots can be lifted in late autumn and stored in a box of peat or sand in a frost-free place, but they will have lost the full flavour of just-pulled roots.

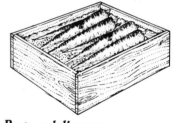

Pests and diseases

Seldom a problem.

COOKING AND FREEZING SCORZONERA

To use it raw in salads, prepare it in the same way as salsify (see opposite).

When cooking, use herbs to bring out the full flavour. Scrub and peel the skin and slice the root into 3in/7.5cm pieces. Put them in a pan of boiling water with a little lemon juice to prevent discolouration. Add fines herbes and simmer for about ten minutes. Drain the scorzonera, but retain the water in which it has been cooked. Make a roux and add the vegetable stock and some milk to make a sauce. Pour it over the scorzonera, cover with grated cheese and brown it under the grill. Or it can be cooked plainly, in the same way as salsify.

Don't freeze the roots as they will discolour easily.

TURNIP
(Brassica campestris)

Unlike many of the other roots, turnips are both space- and time-efficient. Early varieties can be planted close together. There are new F$_1$ hybrids that will produce perfect small round turnips in six weeks and main-crop varieties will mature in three months. With these advances large, woody, unappetizing turnips should be a thing of the past, and though some may still creep into shops, you need never grow them yourself. Lift them when they are small and tender.

Furthermore, you can use the cut-and-grow-again technique to produce turnip-top spring greens. Sow main-crop varieties in late summer for cutting in spring. Frequent cutting encourages new growth: there should be several pickings. Container growing is possible, but best restricted to early varieties, in particular Tokyo Cross, which matures quickly. Roots should be harvested when about the size of a golf ball. At that stage they are tender and mild enough to be used raw in salads, grated or sliced – though they may not be to everyone's taste. You may prefer them cooked as a vegetable or made into a warming winter soup.

Varieties

Early These varieties are pulled when they are no bigger than a tennis-ball, and smaller if they are to be eaten raw. They are not stored, as main crops are, but pulled as they are needed. Snowball (or Early Snowball as it is sometimes described) has round white roots that mature quickly from a springtime sowing. Early White Stone (sometimes confusingly prefixed with the name Snowball) also has white globe-shaped roots. Purple Top Milan grows white flat-shaped roots with purple tops, while Milan White has totally white flat roots. The most useful variety for quickest results is the F$_1$ hybrid Tokyo Cross, which matures in around six weeks, producing small tasty white globes. For continuing supplies, sow successions of seed between late spring and early autumn.

Main-crop (For winter use.) Among this variety is Manchester Market. Green Top Stone produces globular mild-flavoured roots with green tops, which keep well when lifted. Golden Ball, with yellow-fleshed globes, is often considered the most superior for winter use. The flesh is tender and the roots keep well in storage.

Above, *Turnip, Purple Milan variety.*

Below, *Turnip, Tokyo Cross variety.*

The plant's needs

A firm, fertile and moisture-retentive soil is essential for successful turnip growing. This gives them a good start, especially the fast-maturing varieties. Don't sow early varieties in ground that has been freshly manured: choose a site that has been manured for a previous crop. Later varieties can be sown on ground that has been used for other early vegetables. As a brassica it needs a lime soil. Acid soil should be limed to achieve a pH level of 6.5 to 7. Dig over the ground thoroughly before sowing seed, breaking down any large lumps of soil until there is a fine tilth.

Sowing seed

Early varieties can be sown in late winter in mild areas, but they will need the protection of a cloche or frame. Take out drills ½in/1.25cm deep, 9in/22.5cm apart. Sow seed thinly. As soon as the seedlings can be handled easily thin to 2in/5cm and then to 4in/10cm for the smallest roots; for larger ones, thin to 3in/7.5cm and then to 6in/15cm. These sowings should be ready to pull in late spring or early summer.

The first unprotected sowings of early varieties can be made from spring onwards. Successional sowings can follow until the early part of summer. Sow seed at the distances already given.

In the later part of summer and through to late summer, main-crop varieties are sown. Take out drills ½in/1.25cm deep and 12in/30cm apart. Sow the seed thinly and thin the seedlings in stages until they are 12in/30cm apart.

Early varieties will be ready for lifting in late spring and early summer and main-crop varieties in autumn. In mild areas turnips can be left in the ground and lifted as required, but elsewhere should be dug up in late autumn. Twist off the leaves; do not cut into the root. Throw away any damaged or diseased roots. Store in boxes of peat or sand, making sure that the turnips are not touching each other.

Turnip tops with cut-and-grow-again technique

Choose a main-crop variety. In late summer or early autumn, take out drills ½in/1.25cm deep and 3in/7.5cm apart and sow the seed thinly. Seed can also be sown by broadcasting. Leave the seedlings to their own devices and do not thin. Start cutting them when they are about 4in/10cm high. Take a few leaves here and there among the plants and this will encourage fresh growth. Several pickings should be possible from a single sowing. When the crop is exhausted, dig the plants into the soil.

Growing turnips in containers

Containers should be at least 12in/30cm wide, 10in/25cm deep and about 2ft/60cm long. It is practical to grow only early varieties in containers, and a variety such as Tokyo Cross, with its small roots, is ideal. Fill the container with quality loam potting compost a few days before sowing the seed to allow the compost to settle. Fill up with more compost if necessary so that the surface is within 1in/2.5cm of the top of the container. Take out drills ½in/1.25cm deep, and 4in/10cm apart, starting 2in/5cm from the edge of the container, making three rows.

Sow the seed thinly. Thin the seedlings first to 2in/5cm and then to 4in/10cm. Containers will need frequent watering in warm weather, often twice a day. Lift the turnips when they are no bigger than a golf ball.

Turnip tops can also be grown in containers, using a main-crop variety. In late summer or early autumn, fill a container and broadcast sow the seed. Cover with a fine sifting of soil. Do not thin. Start cutting when the plants are about 4in/10cm tall, taking a leaf or two from each plant. New growth should appear.

PESTS AND DISEASES: TURNIP

Pests

Flea beetles attack the leaves of young seedlings, chewing holes in them. Spray with derris or pyrethrum.

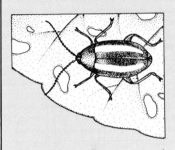

Diseases

Powdery mildew coats the leaves with a white deposit. Spray with benomyl, or the more organically acceptable Bordeaux mixture.

Club-root is the most likely disease to strike. The roots swell, the leaves

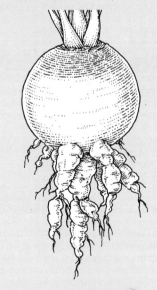

die and eventually the roots rot. Once infected, the plants cannot be saved: lift and burn them. Before sowing the following year take preventive measures. Practise crop rotation. Make sure the ground is adequately limed. Before sowing the seed apply calomel dust to the soil.

COOKING AND FREEZING TURNIPS

One of the most satisfying ways of using turnips in winter is in soup with mixed vegetables. Peel and cube turnips, carrots, potatoes and chop celery. Simmer them in a rich meat or chicken stock, with herbs and seasoning. Serve the mixture as it is or liquidize it to a purée.

Early turnips can be cooked whole if they are pulled when small. Trim the tops and peel. Boil in salted water (or chicken or meat stock for a better flavour) for about 20 minutes or until tender. When cooked, remove the turnips and use the stock for a sauce. Make a roux of equal amounts of butter and flour, add the stock and some milk, and cook, stirring all the time over a gentle heat, until it thickens. Season, add chopped parsley, and pour the sauce over the turnips.

Main-crop turnips should be trimmed, peeled and cubed. Cook for about 30 minutes. Drain and mash, adding butter, cream and seasoning to make a purée.

Only small turnips are worth freezing. Trim the tops and peel. Slice or dice and blanch for two minutes. Drain, cool and pack in rigid containers.

SWEDE
(Brassica napus)

Swedes have long been grown as animal fodder, but for many years gardeners have been reluctant to grow them, largely because the plants were prone to so many pests and diseases. Now dedicated work by plant breeders has made the unpleasant deposits of white mildew less common. They have not been able to eliminate it yet – some of the new varieties have greater resistance than others – so it is best to choose your variety with care. The unsightly swellings of club-root were another problem that is gradually being bred out with the latest introductions. All to the good, because today's gardeners can raise this mild, pleasantly sweet-flavoured vegetable with more confidence of success. It makes a perfect creamy purée, mashed and mixed with butter, milk or cream.

The large roots need room to develop, so swedes are not suitable for container growing.

Varieties

Top of the list is Marian, with high resistance to powdery mildew and club-root. The flesh is yellow, with a light-purple skin. Of the other varieties available, Acme is next in line, though it has less resistance to mildew. Attractive yellow flesh with a light-purple skin. Best of All is a yellow-fleshed variety that is hardy enough to stand in the ground all winter. Western Perfection, with light-purple skin, is one of the early-maturing varieties.

The plant's needs

Swedes, as members of the brassica family, need a lime soil. Before sowing, apply calcium carbonate or calcium hydroxide to the soil to produce a pH level of 6.5 to 7. The ideal soil is light and rich in humus, but don't grow the crop on newly manured ground; choose a part of the garden that has been manured for a previous crop. The ground should be well draining but water-retentive because if it dries out for any period of time, the swedes are likely to be woody and undersized. Dig in plenty of peat to help the soil retain moisture.

Prepare the bed by digging over in the autumn, leaving the frost to break down the larger lumps of soil during winter. All that should be needed in spring is to rake over the surface to get a fine tilth.

Sowing seed

Wait until late spring before sowing. That, coupled with growing a variety resistant to powdery mildew should keep the disease at bay. Take out drills ½in/1.25cm deep and 15in/37.5cm apart. Sow seed thinly or station sow in groups of three seeds at 5in/12.5cm intervals. Thin seedlings when they can easily be handled, to 10in/25cm apart. Hoe to keep weeds down or apply a mulch around the base of each plant, which will also help to keep the soil moist. Keep plants well watered to prevent the roots from becoming woody and splitting.

Roots of Western Perfection should be ready for lifting from early autumn; the other varieties from autumn. A few (as a treat) could be lifted earlier than this. The roots will not have reached their full size but they should be sweet and succulent.

In mild areas the roots can be left in the ground over winter and lifted as required. Elsewhere, lift all the crop in early winter and store in boxes of peat or sand in a cool but frost-free place. Twist off the top leaves and store in layers; the roots must not touch each other.

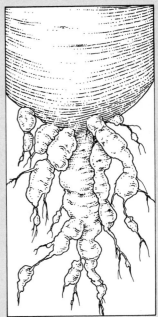

PESTS AND DISEASES: SWEDE

Pests
The flea beetle can be a nuisance at the seedling stage, nibbling at the tender young leaves. Dust with derris or pyrethrum.

Diseases
Powdery mildew covers the leaves with white powdery deposits. Spray with benomyl.

Club-root, the most common disease of brassicas, causes swellings on the roots, followed by rotting.

Leaves wilt and die. Nothing can be done at this stage except to lift the infected plants and burn them. Before sowing seed again, make sure the ground is adequately limed and rotate crops each year. Apply calomel dust to the soil before sowing seed.

Brown rot is a disease that indicates a boron deficiency in the soil. It shows as brown spots running through the flesh when the root is cut open. The current crop cannot be treated but before sowing seed for the next, water a borax solution into the soil at a strength of 1oz/30g of borax to 2gal/9l of water.

COOKING AND FREEZING SWEDES

Swedes, plain boiled and mashed, are unappetizing, but with a little something extra can easily be transformed. Prepare by cutting off the tops and peeling them, revealing the yellow flesh. Cut into cubes or lengths of thin sticks so that they don't take long to cook. Boil in salted water for about 20 minutes, or until tender. Drain and mash, adding butter, milk or cream, plus black pepper or ground nutmeg. If you find the flesh too sweet, add some lemon juice to sharpen the taste. Fo added flavour, cook the swedes in a good meat or chicken stock instead of water.

Instead of mashing the cooked swede you could also serve them cubed or in sticks, tossed in melted butter and lemon juice.

Freezing is not recommended.

Leek, Lyon Prizetaker variety.

ONIONS

Once again the East has solved a problem for the Western gardener. There need no longer be a gap between the last of the winter-stored onions and the first of the new season's crop. The solution has been the arrival of new early-maturing Japanese varieties. You can now be self-sufficient in onions all the year round.

The keeping quality of other varieties has also been improved, as have the sizes and shapes of the latest introductions. So now there are onion sizes available to suit every recipe.

Today's onion grower has better prospects of success too, with the latest trend of growing onions from sets (small partly grown bulbs). This helps reduce the risk of devastating onion pests and diseases.

Leeks also escape most of the onion pests even though they belong to the same family. If you enjoy their distinctive mellow flavour, you can now grow one of the newly introduced slender varieties. These are leeks at their very best.

LEEK
(Allium ampeloprasum)

If there is one vegetable that creates high feeling on the show bench more than any other, it is the leek. The rivalry has all to do with size and nothing to do with flavour. The larger the leek the less flavour it has, so if you are more interested in cooking than showing your leeks, aim to grow small and tasty ones. It is possible to buy leeks now that are no longer or thicker than a pencil, but that is going too far since they have not had enough time to acquire much flavour at all.

As a guide, reckon that mature leeks should be no longer than 10in/25cm in the shank and 3/4-1in/1.75-2.5cm in diameter. This is roughly the length that breeders have been aiming for. They have also been concentrating on the leeks' winter hardiness.

Leeks need a good depth of soil, so container growing is not suitable.

Varieties

By careful selection of varieties you can have leeks from early autumn to late spring. King Richard has the longest shanks (10-12in/25-30cm), and matures in early to late autumn. Maturing over the same period Gennevilliers Splendid has slender stems, up to 10in/25cm. Autumn Mammoth Snowstar has 6in/15cm shanks, maturing in late autumn for harvesting through the winter months. Autumn Mammoth Argenta is of similar size, matures in early winter and stands well in the ground until spring. Giant Winter Catalina produces long leeks maturing in winter through to spring. Blauwgroene Winter Kajak matures over winter for cropping in early to late spring.

The plant's needs

Leeks need a well-dug fertile soil, with an open, free-draining texture. In the autumn, dig in plenty of well-rotted manure or compost so that it has time to break down into rich humus before sowing seed in spring. Choose an open sunny part of the garden. An acid soil should be limed for a pH level of 6 to 6.5.

Sowing seed

An early start can be made in late winter by sowing seed indoors in gentle heat. Fill boxes or trays with loam seed compost and sow seed 1in/2.5cm apart each way.

Keep at a temperature of 55°F/13°C. Prick out seedlings when they can be handled easily, 2in/5cm apart. In spring or late spring, start to harden off the seedlings. Either place them in a garden frame or put them outdoors during the day in a propagating frame with the ventilators open. Remember to bring them in each night. They will be ready to plant out in late spring.

Outdoor sowings can be made in early spring or spring. Take out drills ½in/1.25cm deep and 6in/15cm apart. Sow seed thinly and cover with a fine sifting of soil. Gently firm down the surface. In early summer, another sowing can be made for a later crop.

In early summer, the seedlings can be planted out when they are about 6-8in/15-20cm tall. Water the bed the day before moving the seedlings. With a dibbler make holes 6in/15cm deep in the soil and 6in/15cm apart each way - the most economical use of space. Carefully lift the largest and strongest of the leek seedlings and lower one into each hole. Don't fill in the holes with soil; pour water into them instead. Do this gently; it will firm the roots without drowning the seedling.

Keep down weeds by hoeing. Make sure that the plants are well watered, especially in warm weather. A mulch applied round the base of each leek will help to keep down weeds and to retain moisture in the soil. To get white stems, the plants are blanched by earthing-up the soil around the plants a little at a time from

early autumn onwards. The soil should be fairly dry when you do this. Try not to let it fall between the leafy tops, otherwise you will have gritty leeks. Stop earthing-up in the autumn.

The leeks sown early indoors should be ready to eat in late autumn with the later sowings lasting through to the following spring. For the tastiest leeks, lift them when they are about ¾in/1.75cm in diameter. They are hardy and will stand in the ground until they are needed.

Pests and diseases: leek

Although leeks can be afflicted by the pests and diseases of onions (see page 93), they are seldom troubled.

COOKING AND FREEZING LEEKS

Leeks are a versatile vegetable. Use them in soups, as a hot vegetable on their own, or cooked, cooled and dressed in vinaigrette for salads.

A winter warmer is leek and potato soup, made with a rich chicken stock. Peel and roughly dice potatoes. Simmer in the stock until they are half cooked and then add sliced leeks. Cook until leeks and potatoes are tender. Liquidize to make a thick creamy soup.

To cook on their own as a vegetable, trim the green tops and rinse to remove any grit. Slice into 1in/2.5cm pieces and simmer in just enough boiling water to cover the leeks, for about five to eight minutes,

depending on the thickness of the leeks. They should remain complete rings and still have some crunch in them. Drain and toss in butter or cover with a cheese sauce.

Leeks can also be braised in chicken stock. Trim the top leaves and roots and place the stems whole in a heavy pan. Just cover with a chicken stock and simmer for about 45 minutes. Serve hot or allow to cool and pour a vinaigrette dressing over them.

To freeze leeks, trim the roots and tops, slice into 1in/2.5cm pieces. Blanch for two minutes. Drain, cool and dry before packing into polythene bags.

ONION
(Allium cepa)

No cook would want to be without onions and no gardener these days has an excuse not to provide them. Research has shown that closer planting increases the yield, so you can even grow them in containers if space if limited.

There does not need to be a gap in the supply of onions any more since new varieties mean that your crop can be ready during the summer, and other varieties now have improved keeping qualities so that the onions can be depended on for many weeks in store.

There is much to be said for growing onions from sets – small bulbs that were grown the previous year and harvested

while still immature. When planted again the following year, they produce a more reliable crop of onions than usually results from sowing seed. They are not so fussy about the soil they are grown in; their rate of maturity is quicker and they are less likely to fall prey to mildew and the major pest, the onion fly. This method may not suit the purists but for everyone else it is highly recommended, even though it costs a little more.

Varieties

For spring sowing Hyper is an F_1 that matures from early autumn, producing round uniform onions. It crops heavily and keeps well through the winter. Hygro, another F_1 hybrid, also has a uniform globe shape, with excellent keeping qualities. There are many strains of the Rijns-

Onion, Hygro F variety.

burger varieties, Balstora being one of the most reliable for keeping quality. The globes are uniform and large. There are red-skinned varieties, but the colour is usually either skin deep or restricted to the skin and the outer layers of the onion. Southport Red Globe has pink-tinged flesh that stores well through winter, as does North Holland Blood Red. Old-established varieties include Ailsa Craig, suitable for exhibition but not for keeping, and Bedfordshire Champion, which does keep well.

For autumn sowing Express Yellow O-X produces a semi-flat-shaped onion in early summer. Imai Early Yellow matures at about the same time, with globe-shaped yellow-skinned onions. Extra Early Kaizuka, with its flat bulbs, may beat the first two by a few days. Later to mature is Senshyu Semi-Globe Yellow, with round, golden straw-coloured bulbs.

Onion sets Varieties of onion sets are limited, but most seed catalogues offer one or two. Sturon has large straw-coloured bulbs that are resistant to bolting and keep well. Stuttgarter Giant, with flat bulbs, also keeps well.

The plant's needs

Onions need a sunny position in ground that has been well dug the previous autumn. Dig in plenty of well-rotted manure or compost that will have broken down to a rich moisture-retentive humus by spring. While onion sets will grow in less fertile soil than onions started straight from seed, it is still worth preparing the ground well to give them a good start. Lime acid soil for a pH level of 6 to 6.5. Before sowing, rake over the soil to break it down to a fine tilth.

Sowing seed

Seed can be started off indoors in late winter. Fill a seed tray with loam seed compost. Sow seed thinly and cover with a fine sifting of soil. Keep at a temperature of 60°F/16°C until the seed has germinated and then at 50°F/10°C. Remove the weakest seedlings, leaving the others about 2in/5cm apart.

Harden off in a cold frame or place the seedlings outdoors during the day in a propagator with the vents open. Bring them indoors each evening. They should be ready for planting out in the later part of spring, 4in/10cm apart in rows 9in/22.5cm apart.

Outdoor sowings can be made in spring. Take out drills ½in/1.25cm deep and 9in/22.5cm apart. Sow seed thinly. First thin the seedlings to 2in/5cm apart and then to 4in/10cm. Any further thinning will produce large onions of poorer keeping quality while reducing the overall crop yield. Hoe to keep down weeds, or apply a mulch, which will also help to retain moisture in the soil.

Sow the Japanese varieties in late summer or early autumn. Take out drills ½in/1.25cm deep and 9in/22.5cm apart. Sow the seeds about 1in/2.5cm apart. In spring, thin to 4in/10cm apart. Then treat in the same way as spring-sown onions.

When the bulbs show signs of ripening in summer and late autumn, stop watering. The foliage will begin to yellow, shrivel and flop over. This is the time to start lifting them. Choose a dry day and lift them carefully with a fork. Spread out the onions on sacking or in trays and, if the weather is fine, leave them to dry outdoors. If it is wet, dry them out in a greenhouse or bring them indoors. Store spread out in trays in a dry, cool but frost-free place. Examine them regularly, removing any that are soft or going rotten.

Autumn-sown Japanese onions will be ready from early summer onwards. They will have to be used as they ripen since they don't keep like spring-sown onions.

Growing from sets

In spring, plant the sets 4in/10cm apart, with 9in/22.5cm between the rows. Don't plant deeply – the tips should show just above the surface of the soil. Treat in the same way as onions grown from seed.

Growing in containers

The best results will be obtained by growing from sets, planting them in spring. Containers should be at least 12in/30cm wide, 10in/25cm deep and 24in/60cm long. Fill with quality loam potting compost two days before sowing to allow it to settle. Add further compost if necessary to bring the level to within 1in/2.5cm of the top of the container. Mark out rows 6in/15cm apart, starting 3in/7.5cm from the edge of the container – making two rows. Plant the sets 4in/10cm apart in the rows, with the tips just showing above the surface of the compost. Treat in the same way as sets grown in the open ground. However, compost in containers dries out quickly, so keep it well watered, especially during warm weather, when twice daily watering may be necessary.

SHALLOTS
(Allium ascalonicum)

Shallots are a smaller and milder type of onion, grown from sets. When planted they don't grow bigger but multiply, producing clusters of new bulbs, six or more from a single bulb. They are small enough to use whole in stews or casseroles, such as the French classic, boeuf bourguignon, or they can be pickled.

Varieties

There are limited named varieties, the most usual being Dutch Yellow, or variations on that name, such as Yellow Long Keeping. You may also find Giant Red listed.

The plant's needs

Shallots need the same growing conditions as onions, but will tolerate less fertile soil than onions grown from seed. But don't grow them on poor soil. Dig in manure or compost in autumn, or plant the sets in ground manured for a previous crop.

Growing from sets

In spring, mark out rows 9in/22.5cm apart and plant the sets 4in/10cm apart, with the tips showing just above the surface of the soil. Hoe to keep down weeds and keep the plants well watered. In summer, the foliage will begin to turn yellow. Lift the shallots and leave them to dry outside if the weather is good; if damp bring them indoors.

Store in trays in a dry, cool but frost-free place. Select some for planting next year. They should keep through the winter until the following spring. Look over the shallots regularly, removing any that are going bad.

Growing in containers

Follow the instructions for onion sets.

SPRING ONION
(Allium cepa)

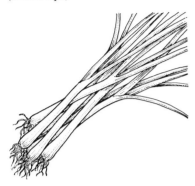

There have been few developments in the growing of spring onions. There is still only one variety to grow and that has been around for years. Not that this is a criticism; White Lisbon is a thoroughly reliable variety and hard to improve upon. However, there is now a versatile alternative to add to the salad onion repertoire – that is, the Japanese bunching onion (see *Oriental vegetables,* page 106).

Variety

White Lisbon, with small bulbs, is the old-established variety.

The plant's needs

The soil should be prepared as described for onions.

Sowing seed

In mild areas the first sowings can be made under cloches in late winter. Take out drills ½in/1.25cm deep and 6in/10cm apart. Sow seed thickly at ½-1in/1.25-2.5cm intervals. Unprotected sowings can be made from early spring or spring, with successional sowings every three weeks. The onions should be ready for pulling at about eight weeks after sowing the seed.

Growing in containers

A container should be at least 12in/30cm wide, 12in/30cm deep and 24in/60cm long. In spring, fill it with loam potting compost and take out three shallow drills, 4in/10cm apart, starting 2in/5cm from the edge of the container. Sow seed at ½-1in/1.25-2.5cm intervals and cover with a fine sifting of compost. Keep well watered at all times.

ONION PESTS AND DISEASES

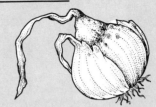

Pests

Onion fly is the biggest menace. It lays eggs in the soil. These develop into maggots that burrow into and eat the bulbs. The first sign of

trouble is when the foliage yellows and droops, and by then it is too late to do anything. Take preventive action before sowing by applying bromophos or calomel dust to the soil. A further dusting of calomel around the seedlings also helps.

Onion eel-worm distorts the bulbs and foliage and causes bloating. There is no cure. Lift the infected plants and burn them. Don't grow onions in that part of the garden for several years.

Diseases

Neck rot is a fungus that leaves a deposit on the neck of the onion, followed by rotting of the bulb. There is no cure. Destroy diseased onions. The disease usually emerges when damaged onions are stored, quickly spreading to healthy ones. Make sure that only sound onions are stored and look over them regularly, removing any diseased bulbs. Take preventive measures before sowing seed by dusting them with benomyl.

Downy mildew is another fungus that leaves brownish-purple velvety marks on the foliage. Cold and extremely wet conditions in the autumn are the usual cause. Infected plants can be sprayed with zineb or the more organically acceptable Bordeaux powder. These will not cure the disease, but should prevent it from spreading.

White rot is a fungus that attacks the bulbs and makes them rot. Take preventive measures before sowing by applying calomel dust to the soil. If there is an attack, lift and destroy any diseased onions and grow onions in a different part of the garden the following year.

COOKING AND FREEZING ONIONS

Onions often seem to have a secondary role in cooking – added to dishes such as stews, casseroles, soups and sauces – rather than as a vegetable in their own right. But try them sliced and fried in oil until they are crisp and golden brown or gently braised in an enclosed casserole dish. Remove the outer skin and braise them whole in oil or butter for 45 to 60 minutes.

Use shallots in boeuf bourguignon. Cube topside of beef and leave to marinate overnight in red wine and olive oil, with sliced onions, herbs and seasoning. Next day fry strips of bacon and whole shallots in oil until they are brown. Take the meat from the marinade, coat it with flour and brown it for a few minutes. Put the meat in a pan with the marinade and simmer gently for about two hours. Add the bacon and shallots and some small whole mushrooms and simmer for a further half hour.

Salad onions can be used raw, thinly sliced in mixed green salads, or with sliced tomatoes dressed with vinaigrette.

Onions are not worth freezing.

Aubergine, Slice Rite variety.

VEGETABLE FRUITS

Vegetable fruits all share a need for warmth and sunshine. In the past this has meant that gardeners living in cooler parts of the world had to have a greenhouse or frame in which to grow them. Now, thanks again to plant breeders, there are varieties of many vegetable fruits that are less demanding, and will grow outdoors in a moderately warm summer.

These varieties include the two traditional favourites, tomatoes and cucumbers. Both have been encouraged to come out of the greenhouse into the open air with dependable results. Now the home grower of tomatoes can enjoy an improved flavour at its best, that is when it is allowed to ripen on the plant; and cucumbers have been bred smaller with a much-improved flavour.

Aubergines and capsicums are tropical fruits that can be grown under glass and also outdoors against sunny, south-facing sheltered walls. They both grow well in containers. Today's F_1 hybrid capsicums are a great advance, quick to mature and high in yield.

The popularity of courgettes has grown in leaps as they have diminished in size. Once they were the immature fruits of marrow seeds, but now they have their own varieties producing small fruits.

Even marrows have improved, with far better flavour, compact bush varieties bearing manageable-sized fruits. Two unusual members of the marrow family are worth a try – squashes and pumpkins, much better if they are not allowed to grow enormous. With vegetable fruits, the maxim is always 'small is beautiful'.

AUBERGINE
(Solanum melongena)

The shiny, deep-purple egg-shaped fruit of the aubergine has been an everyday vegetable for centuries around the Mediterranean and in the warm climates of the East. Gardeners in more northerly parts have come to realize that it is not so difficult to grow aubergines in a greenhouse or under cloches or even outdoors in mild areas, against a sunny, south-facing wall. They are decorative plants with lavender flowers and make an attractive addition to a vegetable garden or to a patio when they are grown in pots.

White-fleshed aubergines are the latest import from the East. Grow both colours for an eye-catching contrast.

Varieties

The old-established variety is Long Purple, but there are new and better F_1 hybrids. Black Prince has almost black fruits, which mature early. Large Fruited Slice-Rite can produce weighty fruits, up to 1lb/600g, given a warm sunny summer. Compact varieties suitable for container growing include Bonica and Short Tom, with fruits that can either be harvested when they are 3-4in/7.5-10cm long or left to grow bigger. There are few white varieties, and they may be described as Oriental egg plant, but there is one named variety, Easter Egg.

The plant's needs

Plants grown outdoors need a rich fertile soil. Dig in well-rotted manure or compost in the autumn before sowing. Container plants should be grown in quality loam compost. In all but mild areas they will have to be grown in a greenhouse in pots, but they can be moved outdoors in summer.

Sowing seed

Sow seed for greenhouse plants in late winter. Fill 3in/7.5cm pots with loam seed compost, and sow two or three seeds to a pot. Keep at a minimum temperature of 60°F/16°C. Germination can take two weeks or longer. Remove the weakest seedling of each pair. Pot-on to larger pots

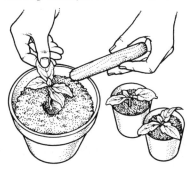

of loam potting compost until the plants are in 8in/20cm pots. Plants in pots can stay in the greenhouse throughout the summer or they can be put outside on a sunny sheltered patio from early summer.

For plants that are to grow in the open ground, raise them indoors, as described above. Pot-on and harden off in late spring and early summer, putting them outdoors in a propagator with open vents during the day and bringing them in at night.

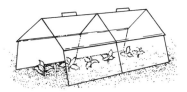

About a week before the plants are due to go into the ground, place cloches over the planting area. In early summer, plant out 18in/45cm apart each way and put the cloches back over them. Once the plants are well established, the cloches can be removed.

When the plants are 6in/15cm tall, pinch out the growing tips. After four fruits have developed, pinch out the side-shoots and remove all the flowers. This concentrates the plant's energies on swelling the fruit.

Keep well watered at all times and in summer, when the fruits start to develop, give a weekly liquid feed. Pick the aubergines while they are still shiny: if they have dulled, they are beyond their best and taste bitter.

COOKING AND FREEZING AUBERGINES

If aubergines have been picked at the right time before they have become bitter, they should not need to be salted and left to stand before cooking. (White Oriental egg plants are not bitter at all.)

For salads, put sliced aubergines in salted boiling water and simmer for about five minutes. Drain, cool and cover with vinaigrette,

Aubergines are an important ingredient of the classic Greek dish, moussaka. Briefly fry slices of aubergine in cooking oil, and put them on one side. Then fry sliced onion in the oil until soft. Add minced beef or lamb, cooking until brown. Stir in tomato purée and meat stock and simmer for about 20 minutes. Place a layer of aubergine in the bottom of a buttered dish, followed by a layer of meat mixture, and so on, ending with a layer of aubergine. Pour over a white sauce and bake in the oven for about 30 minutes.

Freezing is not advised.

PESTS AND DISEASES: AUBERGINE

Diseases

Diseases are seldom a problem, and pests are more likely to attack greenhouse and indoor plants than those grown outdoors.

Pests

Red spider mites will cause mottling on the leaves. In extreme cases, the whole leaves may yellow

and die, and thin webs will cover the plants. Spray with malathion or the more organically acceptable liquid derris. To keep this pest at bay, the greenhouse atmosphere should always be humid.

Aphids affect both indoor and outdoor plants, sucking the sap from young plants and stunting their growth. Spray with malathion, preparations containing the more acceptable pyrethrum, or one of the safer sprays prepared from fatty soaps.

SWEET PEPPER
(*Capsicum annuum*)

Sweet peppers were once thought to be exotic vegetables but nowadays they have become both familiar and popular. This, at least, is something for which we must thank supermarkets as peppers are available on their shelves for most of the year. This new-found popularity has encouraged plant breeders to develop F_1 hybrids and, to the benefit of gardeners, these varieties mature earlier and crop more heavily. It is now practical to grow them in containers; a new variety grows to only 15in/37.5cm, suitable for pots on a patio or even a sunny window-sill indoors.

Varieties

New Ace and Early Prolific mature early and produce a heavy crop. Canape has proved successful in colder climates, but it still has to be grown in a sunny sheltered spot. The yellow fruits go under various names – Golden Bell, Californian Golden Wonder, Yellow Bell and Luteus. (Red peppers are green peppers that have been allowed to ripen.) For container growing, Redskin is the very latest introduction.

The plant's needs

A medium, fairly fertile soil is ideal. It should not be too rich or the plants will produce too much foliage at the expense of fruit. Dig in a little compost or well-rotted manure before planting. In mild areas they can be grown outdoors in a sunny, sheltered position. Elsewhere, they will have to be grown under glass or indoors, bringing them outside during the summer months.

Sowing seed

In early spring, sow seed in trays of loam seed compost and keep at a temperature of 60°F/16°C. Prick out the seedlings into 3in/7.5cm pots of loam potting compost. If they are to be grown indoors or under glass, pot-on until the plant is in an 8in/20cm container. For the more compact Redskin, a 7in/17.5cm pot will be large enough. In early summer or summer, the pots can be placed outdoors on a sunny sheltered patio.

If plants are to be grown outside, prick out to 3in/7.5cm pots and in late spring start to harden off the seedlings. Place them outside during the day in a propagator with the vents left open. Remember to

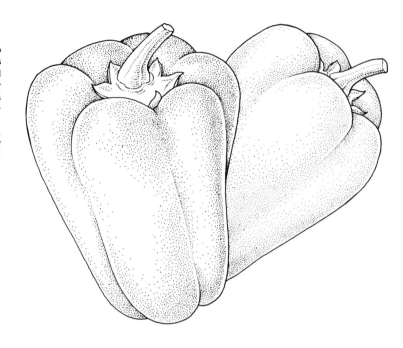

bring them indoors each evening. They should be ready for planting out in early summer.

A week before they are to go out, warm up the soil for them by covering the ground with cloches. Plant them 15in/37.5cm apart each way. Cover them with the cloches until the plants are well established. Keep the plants well watered, especially those grown in containers. Once the fruits start to swell, give them a weekly liquid feed.

Fruits should be ready from late summer onwards. They can be picked when they are green or left for a further two or three weeks, when they will turn red. Depending on the variety, yellow-skinned fruits will start green and turn yellow, or be yellow throughout their development.

Pests and diseases: sweet pepper

See *Pests and diseases: aubergine*, page 95.

COOKING AND FREEZING SWEET PEPPERS

Sliced green peppers bring a contrasting sweet flavour to a simple green salad; add red and yellow peppers to make it even more delicious. To prepare, cut off the top of the fruit. Cut away the pith and seeds and then thinly slice the pepper into rings. Serve with a mustard vinaigrette, as a contrast to the sweetness.

Cooked peppers are an essential ingredient to Southern European vegetable stews. For a ratatouille, cook onion slices gently in oil with seasoning until golden brown, then add sliced aubergine and peppers.

Cook for about ten minutes. Add sliced courgettes, cooking for a further eight to ten minutes. At the end drop in sliced tomato and cook for two minutes more. Cooking this way should ensure that the individual vegetables are still recognizable.

Peppers can be frozen, but it is unlikely that there will be any left over to freeze. If there are, remove the pith and seeds. Blanch the fruits whole or sliced, for two minutes. Drain, cool, dry and pack into rigid containers.

COURGETTE
(*Cucurbita pepo*)

The Italians and French have been eating courgettes for years and now they share the secret with the rest of Europe. Courgettes are only immature marrows, but whereas in the past you had to sow marrow seed and pick the marrows before they became too large, there are now varieties specifically bred to grow small fruits. They will grow to 6in/15cm long, but they are best picked when no more than 4in/10cm. The latest F_1 hybrids have been bred for uniformity of shape and size and, equally important, for a heavy crop.

The plants take up a lot of room, but they can be grown in large containers, one to a pot. The crop will not be large but it will look extremely decorative, especially if you grow a variety with yellow fruit.

Varieties

One of the earliest and best varieties is Ambassador, ready for picking in eight to nine weeks. Early Gem is another early heavy cropper, but pick the fruits small or they will grow to marrow size. Zucchini (which is also the name by which courgettes are known in Italy and the United States) has dark-green slender fruits, carried on bushy plants. Gold Rush produces bright golden-yellow fruits, on compact bushy growth.

The plant's needs

Choose a sheltered sunny part of the garden. The soil should be fertile and rich in humus. As bush courgettes are planted 24in/60cm apart each way, the usual way to prepare the soil in late spring is to dig holes 12in sq/30cm sq and the same depth, 24in/60cm apart. Put about 6in/15cm of well-rotted manure or compost into each hole. Mix some manure or compost with soil that has been removed and fill the holes with it. Mark with sticks where the holes are to aid planting. Lime acid soils to a pH level of about 6.

Sowing seed

Indoor sowings can be made in spring. Sow two seeds to a 3in/7.5cm pot of loam seed compost. If you use peat pots instead, the seedlings will not be disturbed when it comes to planting out. Keep at a temperature of 65°F/18°C. When the seedlings are large enough to be handled, remove the

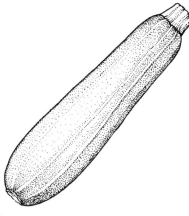

weaker of the two. Harden them off ready to plant out in early summer. Put them outside in a propagating tray with the vents open during the day. Remember to bring them in each evening. Plant out in the prepared areas.

Outdoor sowings can be made in the latter part of late spring. Warm up the soil by placing cloches over the marked sites a couple of weeks before sowing. Sow two seeds at the centre of each area, 1in/2.5cm deep and 4in/10cm apart. Cover them with the cloches to speed up germination. When the seedlings can be easily handled, remove the weaker of the pair. Once they are well established, the cloches can be removed. Lay down bait for slugs; they find the young leaves irresistible.

Keep plants well watered at all times, but do not water directly on to them. Spreading a mulch around the base of

each plant will help to retain moisture and keep down weeds. Black plastic sheeting can be used instead of a mulch.

When the fruits begin to show, feed weekly with a liquid fertilizer. The first fruits should be ready for picking in summer. Pick them when they are about 4in/10cm long, and do it regularly, to make the plant produce more fruits.

Growing in containers

Sow seed in spring as already described. Keep at a temperature of 65°F/18°C. Remove the weaker seedling of each pair and pot-on to a 6in/15cm pot. In late spring, start to harden off the seedlings. Put the pots outside during the day in a propagating tray with the vents open. Or cover them with plastic supported on wire hoops. For ventilation, punch a few holes in the plastic at the top. Bring the pots in at night, but the plants should be ready to stay out all the time from early summer. Choose a sheltered and sunny spot for them. Pot-on again to 10in/25cm pots.

Seed can also be sown outdoors directly into 10in/25cm pots in late spring or early summer. Sow two seeds, 1in/2.5cm deep, to a pot. Remove the weaker of the two seedlings. Container-grown plants will need frequent watering. Feed weekly with liquid fertilizer when the fruits have started to form.

Pests and diseases: courgette

See *Marrow, cucumber and courgette pests and diseases*, page 101.

COOKING AND FREEZING COURGETTES

Courgettes have more flavour if they are sautéd rather than boiled. Trim off both ends, then either slice lengthways or across into discs. Sauté in oil, butter or vegetable fat, five minutes if the courgettes have been sliced across and eight to ten minutes if lengthways. They should be crisp and golden on the outside and tender on the inside.

Bake them with lemon juice and herbs for a sharp tangy flavour. Top and tail the courgettes and slice lengthways. Arrange in a baking dish. To a chicken stock add chopped parsley, thyme, seasoning, grated lemon rind and the juice of half a lemon. Pour over the courgettes and

bake in the oven for about 30 minutes. Serve with the juices.

Courgettes are one of the essential ingredients of the vegetable stew ratatouille (see under *Cooking and freezing sweet peppers*).

Courgettes can also be eaten cold with salads. Slice into discs and simmer in salted water for two to three minutes so that they remain crunchy. Drain and leave to cool. Toss in a dressing of lemon juice, oil, seasoning and chopped parsley.

To freeze courgettes, cut into discs and blanch for one minute. Drain, cool and dry before packing into rigid containers.

CUCUMBER
(Cucumis sativus)

Today's cucumber varieties offer many different shapes and sizes. Some are small, bushy plants, perfect for containers or for the smaller garden, which produce highly flavoured fruits only 6in/15cm long. Other varieties – the latest coming from Japan – produce much longer, thinner cucumbers that grow up to 24in/60cm long. They need a strong wigwam cane structure to support them.

What is clear is that the snobbery of greenhouse cucumber growing is rapidly disappearing. The knobbly, outdoor ridge cucumbers are no longer considered inferior to the smoother greenhouse varieties. In fact, many gardeners have been converted to outdoor cultivation and now use the greenhouse for more exotic crops instead.

The breeders have managed to produce cucumbers of uniform shape and size, and, equally important for the cost-efficient gardener, plants that crop heavily. The Japanese breeders have even come to the rescue of people who find cucumbers indigestible by breeding a 'burpless' variety.

Varieties

Outdoor cucumbers Burpless Tasty Green is one of the most popular varieties, almost guaranteed to live up to its name. For the best flavour, cut the fruits when they are 9in/22.5cm long; leave them on the plants and they will grow into less appetizing giants. King of the Ridge has had most of the knobbles bred out of the uniform-sized fruits – 8-10in/20-25cm. Burpee Hybrid, with smooth-skinned fruits of similar sizes, is a heavy cropper. Japanese cucumber varieties include Tokyo Slicer, which stays a more compact 8-10in/20-25cm than its companions Kyoto and Chinese Long Green, both with fruits 12in/30cm or more long. The small bush varieties include Bush Crop, with small flavour-filled fruits, and Bush Champion.

Greenhouse cucumbers For those who insist on greenhouse cucumbers (and can afford the ruinous heating costs to raise them), the most reliable are Telegraph and Telegraph Improved. With all-female varieties, the gardener escapes the chore of removing male flowers that must be done; if they pollinate the female

Cucumber, Telegraph Improved variety.

plants, the fruit will be bitter. The all-female varieties include Pepinex 69, a heavy cropper; Petita, with small 8in/20cm fruits; Femspot; and any number of other varieties prefixed with 'Fem'.

The plant's needs

Choose a sunny sheltered part of the garden to get the best crops. The soil should be fertile and moisture-retentive. To make the most effective use of compost and manure, dig it into the ground only where the plants are to grow. In late spring, dig holes 12in sq/30cm sq, 12in/30cm deep and 18in/45cm apart or 15in/37.5cm apart for compact bush varieties. Put a 6in/15cm layer of manure or compost at the bottom of each hole. Fill the rest with the soil that has been removed, mixed with some manure or compost. Acid soils should be limed to reach a pH level of about 6.

Sowing seed

For the earliest crop, sow seed indoors or in a greenhouse in spring. Sow two or three seeds, on their edges, in pots of loam seed compost. Keep at a temperature of 65-70°F/18-21°C. When the seedlings can be easily handled, remove the weaker of each pair, leaving one in each pot.

In late spring, start to harden off the seedlings by placing them outdoors during the day in a propagator with the vents left open. Bring them in each night. They will be ready for planting out in early summer, in the prepared holes.

Outdoor sowings can be made from early summer when the soil has warmed up. Sow two or three seeds in each of the prepared holes. Cover with cloches; plastic sheeting supported on wire hoops; or large plastic bottles with the bottoms removed, until the seeds have germinated. Remove the weaker seedling of each pair. Lay down slug bait to protect the seedlings. When the plants have six or seven leaves, prick out the growing tip to make them bushy. The Japanese climbing varieties will need support. Construct a wigwam of canes or fix nylon mesh for them to climb up. Nip out the growing tips when the plants reach the top of the canes or mesh. Apply a mulch around each plant, or lay black plastic on the soil to keep down weeds and help conserve moisture. Plants with both male and female flowers will need pollinating; leave this to the insects.

After the fruits begin to form in summer give the plants a weekly liquid feed. Start

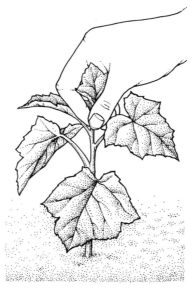

cutting the cucumbers when they are 6-8in/15-20cm long. Leave Japanese varieties until they are about 12in/30cm long, not letting them get too big. All plants should then produce a considerable number of reasonably sized fruits, rather than a few enormous ones.

Growing in containers

The best varieties to choose are the small bush plants such as Bush Crop and Bush Champion. Containers should be 12in/30cm in diameter. In spring, sow two or three seeds to a pot of loam seed compost. Keep at a temperature of 65-70°F/18-21°C. Remove the weakest seedling of each pair and pot-on to a 12in/30cm pot filled with loam potting compost. Keep the plants well watered at all times, es-

pecially in warm weather, then twice daily watering may be necessary.

Growing under glass

Sow seed in early spring in the same way as for outdoor cucumbers, but keep them at the top end of the temperature scale – 70°F/21°C – to germinate satisfactorily. When the seedlings have two or three true leaves, plant one seedling in a 10in/30cm pot or two or three into a growing bag. Maintain a temperature of 60-70°F/18-21°C. The all-female varieties prefer to be at the top end of the scale.

The plants will need staking with canes or to be trained up wires running vertically from the bottom to the top of the greenhouse. When the main stem reaches the roof, pinch out the tip and also the side-shoots two leaves beyond the developing fruit. Shoots without flowers should be pinched out when they are about 18in/45cm long. Any male flowers – those without a mini-fruit developing behind them – should be pinched out. If they manage to pollinate the female flowers, the fruits will be bitter. All-female varieties don't need this attention.

Keep plants well watered at all times and the atmosphere in the greenhouse should always be humid, but with adequate ventilation.

Give a weekly liquid feed as the plants develop. As with outdoor cucumbers, pick them from summer onwards when they are quite small and at their tastiest.

Pests and diseases: cucumber

See *Marrow, cucumber and courgette pests and diseases*, page 101.

COOKING AND FREEZING CUCUMBER

Raw cucumber slices should not be ruined by being doused in astringent malt vinegar. Use white wine vinegar, but even that is better used as a base for a dressing, rather than on its own. Thin down sour cream or yogurt with a little of the vinegar, add seasoning, and pour it over the cucumber. Liven up the taste even more by adding finely chopped fresh parsley, dill or mint.

Cooked cucumber is delicious. Melt an ounce or two of butter and add to it two teaspoonful of Dijon mustard. Sweat sliced cucumber in

the mixture for about five minutes until tender. Serve as it is with the mustardy butter, or add single cream or yogurt a minute or so before the cucumber is fully cooked.

Cucumber can also be used to make delicious soup. Simmer onions in a chicken stock until they are soft. Add sliced unpeeled cucumber and seasoning and cook very briefly to retain the full flavour. Liquidize and add a little lemon juice, cream or yogurt. The soup is better if it is a thickish purée. Serve either chilled or hot.

MARROW, SQUASH AND PUMPKIN
(Cucurbita family)

The old image of marrows – over-blown, watery, insipid to the point of being tasteless – is rapidly becoming out-of-date. Now plant breeders give us the chance to grow small, shapely marrows with a much better flavour. Moreover, instead of sprawling all over the place there are space-efficient new varieties, compact bushy plants, ideal for a small garden or for growing in containers.

Squashes and pumpkins, though grown and spoken of with reverence in the United States, have not been taken seriously in Europe where they have been seen as novelties rather than vegetables. However, vegetable growers are beginning to discover their excellent eating qualities and seedsmen have responded by offering greater choice in varieties.

Custard marrows, with their attractively coloured, scallop-edged fruits, make great talking points as patio potted plants, and great eating too. The giant pumpkins may leave you speechless.

Marrow varieties

Early Gem is a variety recommended for growing as courgettes, but the fruits can be left to grow to marrow size, and that should be little more than 12in/30cm long. Grow this variety for courgettes and leave some of them to grow into marrows. Green Bush, suitable for a small garden or for growing in a container, produces a crop of uniform, striped green fruits. White Bush has all-white fruits. Table Dainty is a trailer, with striped, light- and dark-green fruits, growing to about 12in/30cm. For those who must still grow whoppers, there are Long Green Trailing and Long White Trailing, taking up a large amount of garden space.

Squash varieties

Scallopini has dark-green top-shaped fruit with scalloped edges. Pick them when they are small, no bigger than the size of courgettes. Custard marrow goes under various names – Custard White, Custard Yellow and Sunburst. They all have unusual round, flat, white or yellow fruits with scalloped edges. Pick all of them when they are small, 4-6in/10-15cm across. Table Ace is an elongated egg-shaped fruit about 6in/15cm long. This stores well for

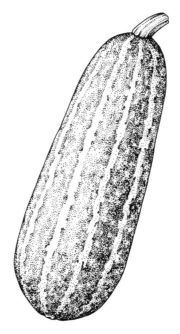

winter use. Vegetable spaghetti is a trailing plant with fat marrow-shaped fruits. When cooked, the flesh breaks into long spaghetti-like fibres.

Pumpkin varieties

Include Atlantic Giant and Mammoth, which are joke items, growing to enormous sizes. More sensible sizes are Spirit, up to 12in/30cm across, and Jackpot, 10in/25cm across.

The plant's needs

Choose a sheltered part of the garden where there will be a little shade in the summer months. The soil must be fertile and rich in humus. Because marrows need a lot of space between plants, there is no point in manuring the whole area, but instead, in late spring, just manure pockets of soil where the plants are to grow. Bush varieties are grown 24in/60cm apart, so for these dig holes 12in sq/30cm sq, 12in/30cm deep and 24in/60cm apart. Trailing varieties take up a lot of room and the holes for them should be 48in/120cm apart. Put a 6in/15cm layer of well-rotted manure or compost in the bottom of the hole and fill it with the soil that was removed, mixed with more manure or compost. Mark the holes to aid planting. Acid soils should be limed to reach a pH level of about 6.

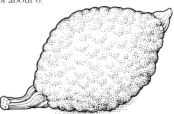

Sowing and growing

An early start can be made by sowing seed indoors in spring. Sow two seeds to a small pot of loam seed compost. If a peat pot is used, the seedlings will not be disturbed when they are planted out, pot and all. Keep at a temperature of 65°F/18°C. Remove the weaker of the two seedlings, without disturbing the other. Harden them off before planting out in early summer. Place them outdoors during the day in a propagator with the vents left open. Bring them in each night. After about two weeks, plant them out in the prepared holes.

Towards the end of late spring outdoor sowings can be made. Place cloches over the soil to warm it for a week or so before

sowing. Sow two seeds, 1in/2.5cm deep and 4in/10cm apart, at the centre of each planting area. To help germination, put the cloches back over them. Remove the weaker of the two seedlings when they can be easily handled. Once they are well established, remove the cloches. Tender young leaves make a delicious meal for slugs, so lay down slug bait to deter them.

Marrow plants need plenty of water and should never be allowed to get dry. Spread a mulch around the base of each plant to help retain moisture and keep down weeds. Black plastic sheeting laid between the plants has the same effect.

Pollination of female flowers can usually be left to insects, except perhaps in harsh weather, when a little human help may be needed. Remove a few male

flowers – those without a mini-fruit behind the flower – and strip away the petals to expose the pollen-bearing anthers. Push them into the centre of the

female flower and then move on to the next one.

As soon as the fruits begin to develop in summer, give a weekly liquid feed. Start cutting the marrows from late summer when they are 8-10in/20-30cm long.

Winter squashes and pumpkins should be harvested in early autumn and autumn, before the first frosts. They should store well for several weeks in a cool, frost-free place.

Growing in containers

Bush marrows are the varieties to grow in containers. Sow seed indooors in spring, as described under *sowing and growing*, and keep at 65°F/18°C. When the seedlings can be easily handled, remove the weaker of the two and pot-on to a 6in/15cm pot of loam potting compost. Begin to harden off the seedlings in late spring by placing the pots outdoors during the day in a propagator with the vents open; or each pot can be covered with a plastic bag supported on a hoop. Bring in the pots each night. In early summer, when they can be left outdoors all the time in a sheltered but sunny part of the garden, pot-on to 10in/25cm pots.

Sowing outdoors can be done in late spring, two seeds to a 10in/25cm pot. Remove the weaker of each pair of seedlings. Keep the plants well watered at all times - twice daily in periods of warm weather. Give a weekly liquid feed once the fruits have formed.

MARROW, CUCUMBER AND COURGETTE PESTS AND DISEASES

Pests
Slugs can be a great nuisance, feeding on the tender leaves of young plants. Lay down methiocarb baits or organic alternatives that will not harm other garden wildlife.

Aphids suck the sap of young plants and stunt their growth. Spray with derris, pyrethrum, or a safe spray prepared from fatty soaps.

Whiteflies in the greenhouse suck sap as aphids do, and excrete sticky honeydew on to the plants. Spray with malathion, the more acceptable pyrethrum, or go completely green and introduce the parasitic *Encarsia formosa* into the greenhouse to do the job for you.

Diseases
Cucumber mosaic virus is spread by greenfly. The leaves become mottled yellow, shrivel and die. More devastatingly, the fruits grow misshapen and never develop fully. There is no cure. Remove the affected plants and burn them. Take preventive measures with the next year's crop to control greenfly by spraying with derris or pyrethrum.

Mildew deposits white coatings on fruit and leaves, especially in very humid weather. Spray with benomyl.

Grey mould is another fungal disease, leaving grey deposits on fruit. In extreme cases, burn infected fruit and plants. In its early stages it can usually be treated with a benomyl spray.

COOKING AND FREEZING MARROWS

Never boil marrows; they are nearly all water already, and boiling makes them even more watery. Instead, braise them or bake them. Young marrows, the only kind to grow, should not need peeling. Cut lengthways and remove all the seeds and fibres. Slice the two halves crossways into 1in/2.5cm segments. Place in a shallow dish with melted butter, vegetable fat or oil and seasoning. Bake for about 30 minutes. Halved marrows can be packed with herb or meat stuffings and baked in the oven.

Vegetable spaghetti is boiled whole in water for about 30 minutes. Cut in half, remove the seeds and fibres, and the flesh can then be scooped out easily. Cover the spaghetti-like strings with a well-

seasoned tomato sauce or thin mayonnaise flavoured with herbs.

Slice custard marrows and cook gently in melted butter, vegetable fat or oil. Pumpkins that escape being made into Hallowe'en lanterns usually end up in pumpkin pie. Blind bake a short-crust pastry case. Cut the pumpkin into 1in/2.5cm pieces and simmer in water until soft. Reduce to a pulp in a food processor. Combine egg yolks, cream, sugar, cinnamon, nutmeg, ginger and lemon juice, and mix with the pumpkin. Whip egg whites until they stand in peaks, and fold into the pumpkin mixture. Pour into the pastry case and bake for about 45 minutes.

Freezing these members of the marrow family is not recommended.

TOMATO
(Lycopersicon esculentum)

The only way to discover the real taste of tomatoes is to grow them yourself. The reason is simple; the tastiest tomato is one that is ripened on the plant. Commercial practice does not allow for that. The fruit is picked when it is still green and often stored in cool chambers before it starts its journey to the supermarket. By the time it gets there some of the skin may still be green, or turning orange. A day or two in the light should turn it to an acceptable red colour, but it will have done nothing to give it the sweet, full flavour of a tomato ripened by nature in the sun. Moreover, it will probably have an unpalatable tough skin, which has been bred into it to help it withstand all its travelling.

On the other hand, breeders have certainly improved tomato quality in many ways. There are more reliable croppers than there were only a few years ago, especially among the outdoor varieties. They are more resistant to the devastating diseases that once plagued tomatoes too; for example, the once-ruinous leaf mould and tomato mosaic virus.

Shape and colour have improved; the reds are darker and richer and there are attractive yellow-fruited varieties. Plenty of space-, cost- and time-efficient bush varieties, yielding heavy crops are now available, many suitable for growing in containers. Fruit sizes vary between the large beefsteak tomatoes and the tiny cocktail tomatoes that you can grow on a window-sill.

Varieties

For growing outdoors Bush varieties are less trouble than the taller varieties that need staking or training. They all produce uniform small fruits that are of high quality and good flavour. Bush varieties include Sleaford Abundance, Alfresco and Red Alert. All these can be grown in containers, but there are varieties even more suited to this method – Pixie, with medium-sized fruits, and Tiny Tim with cherry-sized fruits. Totem is the latest bush variety for the small garden or container, and it is thought by many to have the best flavour among the dwarf tomatoes. In spite of its heavy cropping, it should not need staking unless it is planted in growing bags or light peat compost.

Outdoor varieties that need support include the ever-popular Gardener's

Delight, which has a very sweet flavour; Sweet 100, exceptionally sweet cherry-size fruits; Outdoor Girl, an early ripener; and Ronaclave, another early ripener with good disease resistance.

Among the beefsteak varieties Marmande produces large fruits, ideal for slicing. Yellow-fruiting varieties include the very sweet Golden Sunrise and Yellow Perfection.

For glasshouse growing Old favourites include Ailsa Craig, Alicante (which is far superior to the ubiquitous insipid Moneymaker) and Best of All. F_1 hybrids bred for good disease resistance under greenhouse conditions include Abunda, Danny and Shirley, all heavy croppers. Dombito and Big Boy are beefsteak varieties for growing under glass. Minibel is a windowsill cherry tomato, which can be grown in a 6in/15cm pot.

The plant's needs

Choose a sunny sheltered part of the garden. The soil must be well draining and fertile. Prepare the site in advance of planting by digging in plenty of well-rotted manure or compost in winter. Fresh manure should not be dug in just before planting but if the soil is acid, liming can be done then to bring the soil to the ideal pH level for tomatoes of 6.5.

Sowing and growing

Sow seed indoors or under glass in early spring. Sow in trays of loam seed compost, or sow two seeds to a soil block or peat pot. Cover the seed with a thin layer of sifted soil. Keep at a temperature of 65°F/18°C. Seedlings in trays will have to be pricked out into individual peat pots of loam potting compost when the first pair of true leaves have developed. Remove the weaker of the pair of seedlings grown in soil blocks or peat pots.

Seedlings will be ready for planting out in the latter part of spring when they are about 8in/20cm tall, but first they must be hardened off. For a week or two, place them outdoors during the day in a propagator with the vents left open. Bring them in each evening. Plant out in rows 30in/75cm apart with 18in/45cm between plants. Bush varieties can be planted more closely, at 18in/45cm each way. This not only saves space, but also increases the overall yield.

As an alternative to the conventional mulch round the base of the plants, it makes sense before planting out to lay

black plastic over the ground, making slits in the plastic through which the young plants can be planted. This not only keeps down weeds and conserves moisture, but also keeps low-growing fruit off the soil. This is essential with bush varieties.

All varieties, apart from bush tomatoes, will need staking at an early stage. Tie them loosely to a stake alongside them and continue to secure them as they grow. This chore is avoided with bush tomatoes, which need little attention other than watering and liquid feeding.

For all other varieties, remove any sideshoots that develop when they are 1-2in/2.5-5cm long and pinch out the growing tips in summer. This concentrates the plants' energy on producing fruit. Leave three or four fruit trusses and pinch out, leaving a pair of leaves above the highest truss.

Keep plants well watered at all times and give a weekly liquid tomato feed after the pinching out. Tomatoes should be ready for picking from late summer. Leave them on the plant until they are fully ripe. Towards early autumn they may be reluctant to ripen. To speed the process, place the bush varieties under cloches. However, tall varieties will have to be cut down and the plants laid on straw under the cloches.

Growing in containers

The best varieties for containers are bush plants. Sow seed in early spring, as already described, either in a tray or in 3in/7.5cm peat pots, two seeds to a pot. Prick out tray-raised seedlings to 3in/7.5cm peat pots. As the plants grow, pot-on until they are in a 10in/25cm diameter container. Harden off before leaving them outside all the time on a warm, sunny, sheltered patio. Instead of pots growing bags can be used, three plants to a bag.

Keep plants well watered at all times. Growing bags and containers may need watering twice a day in warm weather.

Once the trusses have started to develop, give the plants a weekly liquid tomato feed.

Growing in a greenhouse

Sowing is carried out as described under *Sowing and growing*, but in a heated greenhouse sowing can start in late winter. The temperature must be kept constant at around 65°F/18°C, day and night, until the seeds germinate; then it can safely be dropped to 60°F/16°C. When the seedlings are 8in/20cm tall, they can be planted out to individual 10in/25cm pots, or growing bags, three plants to a bag. If the greenhouse has a border at ground level, the tomatoes could be planted directly into the soil, 18in/45cm apart. But there may well be pests and diseases lurking in the soil ready to attack the young plants. Pots or bags standing on the greenhouse floor are safer.

The plants will need support. The easiest method is to run two wires along the length of the greenhouse – one just above the level of the pots or bags, and another at eaves level. Soft twine is tied to bottom and top wires behind each plant to give it something to climb up. As the stems grow, gently wind them round the string.

Nip out any side-shoots that grow from the leaf axils – the point at which the leaf meets the main stem. Pinch out the main stem before it reaches the roof of the greenhouse. Each plant should then have about eight trusses.

The greenhouse should be warm but well ventilated and the plants well watered at all times. A fine mist spray when the plants are in flower helps pollination. After three or four trusses have developed on the plants, give them a weekly liquid tomato feed.

Tomato, Sweet 100 variety.

From a late-winter sowing the first tomatoes should be ready in early summer. The main crop will follow from summer onwards.

PESTS AND DISEASES: TOMATO

Pests

Major pests, especially in the greenhouse are:

Aphids, which suck the sap, stunting growth. Spray with derris, pyrethrum or one of the safe fatty soap sprays.

Whiteflies, which also suck the sap and leave sticky honeydew on the plants. Spray with malathion or the

more organically acceptable pyrethrum. Introducing the parasitic *Encarsia formosa* will eliminate whitefly and the need to use a spray.

Diseases

The latest varieties are largely immune to the worst diseases, but tomato growers should have some idea of the worst that could befall their plants.

Tomato mosaic virus causes yellow mottling to leaves and stunts growth. There is no cure. Burn all affected plants. One preventive measure is to keep aphids at bay – they are the usual carriers of viral diseases. (See *Pests*.)

Leaf mould, a fungal disease, is recognizable by yellow markings on the surface of the leaves and brown patches on the undersides. Spray with maneb or zineb.

Grey mould, another fungal disease, appears as a grey deposit, often on damaged parts of the plant. Always cut away shoots cleanly with a knife and clear away dead leaves still on the plant and any that have fallen on to the soil. Spray with benomyl.

Potato blight causes leaves to brown at the edges, and brown areas may appear on the skins of the tomatoes. Destroy all fruits and plants. If caught at an early stage, spray with maneb or zineb.

COOKING AND FREEZING TOMATOES

The flavour of a tomato ripened on the plant and freshly picked needs nothing to enhance it, except perhaps a little salt. If you don't think it is sweet enough, you could cheat by slicing it and sprinkling a little caster sugar over it, but it should not be necessary. A salad can be made by slicing tomatoes and dressing them with vinaigrette, sprinkling with chopped spring onion, parsley or mint if you wish.

If there is a glut of tomatoes, make them into a sauce to serve with pasta. The sauce can be frozen and this is the only practical and satisfactory way of freezing tomatoes. Cook sliced onion gently in olive oil with a clove of finely chopped garlic and sliced celery. Add chopped tomatoes, basil and marjoram and simmer for about 45 minutes, stirring now and again.

Liquidize the mixture to make a thick purée and add some sugar if necessary. Any tomatoes that refuse to ripen can be made into chutney.

MUSHROOM
(Agaricus bisporus)

The number of varieties of mushroom growing wild is staggering. Many are edible, but it is not always easy to identify them. The home grower of mushrooms has no such problems, largely because only a handful of seed catalogues offer spawn, and then it will usually be just the familiar white button mushrooms. But even with this lack of choice it is still well worth trying to grow mushrooms. Not only do freshly picked mushrooms taste much better than shop-bought ones, but also you will be able to enjoy the novelty and fascination of watching these mysterious things grow. You will not have long to wait for results if all goes well. The time from starting into growth to harvesting is no more than eight weeks, and often less in ideal conditions.

To grow mushrooms you need a few deep boxes, manure, mushroom spawn and a corner of a greenhouse, shed, cellar or a cupboard at the right temperature (55-65°F/13-18°C). Or you could make it easy for yourself and buy one of the complete kits available with the spawn already sown in prepared compost.

Varieties

Grain spawn is becoming more popular than manure spawn because the mushrooms mature much more quickly. It may be identified only as grain spawn, but is sometimes called Darlington's Grain Spawn. Spawn is now also available as pellets, which are not as fussy about growing conditions as grain spawn. The grain spawn and mushroom kits with ready planted spawn will produce white mushrooms, a form of *Agaricus bisporus*.

The plant's needs

The best medium for growing is a rich horse manure with straw if you can find enough of it. A bucket or two is no good: a block 3-4ft sq/90-120cm sq is needed, and before it can be used it has to break down into a rich brown compost. If the manure is not moist, dampen it and pile it into a heap in a corner so that it heats up and starts the process of breaking down. Turn it every week, forking the cold outside of the heap into the warm centre. Eventually, the manure will have broken down to a sweet-smelling compost with no astringent farmyard smell. That is the point at which it is ready to use.

(If you find the thought of all this ex-

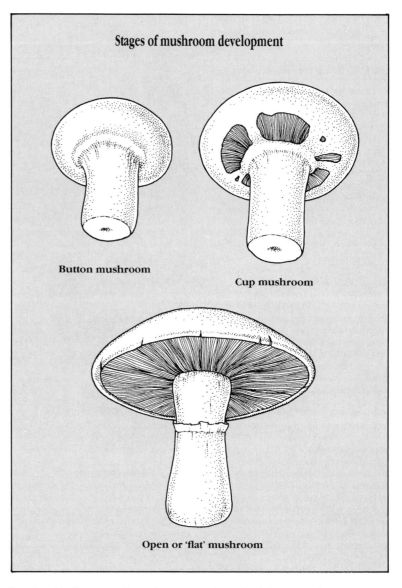

Stages of mushroom development

Button mushroom

Cup mushroom

Open or 'flat' mushroom

hausting, skip the next section and turn to *Raising mushrooms from kits*. Otherwise read on.)

Planting spawn in manure compost

Fill boxes with the compost to a minimum depth of 9in/22.5cm. Firm it down thoroughly so that the surface of the compost is 4in/10cm below the top of the box. Wait until the temperature of the compost has dropped to 75°F/24°C before planting the spawn.

Manure spawn is in blocks that you break off in 1in/2.5cm pieces. Push them

about 1in/2.5cm into the compost at 10in/25cm intervals. Grain spawn is scattered over the surface of the compost.

Cover the tops of the boxes with a sheet of black polythene to retain moisture. Keep at a controlled temperature of 55-65°F/13-18°C. After a week or so, the spawn will start to spread over the surface of the compost as fine white threads. Now cover the spawn with a 2in/5cm layer of freshly sterilized moist soil or peat. Make sure this top layer is moist at all times, but the compost below must not become wet: that is the quickest way to kill the spawn. Maintain the same controlled temperature

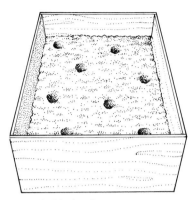

Plant the blocks of spawn at 10in/25cm intervals, pushing them in to about 1in/2.5cm.

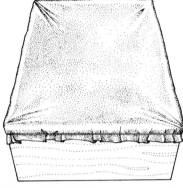

Cover in black polythene and secure to retain moisture.

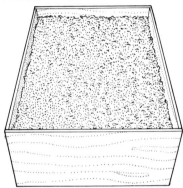

When the spawn spreads over the surface as white threads, cover with the 'casing' of soil or peat.

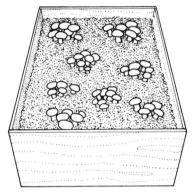

Pick after six weeks or so.

PESTS AND DISEASES

Pests

Mushroom fly is the major pest, and hovers over the surface of the compost. The flies lay eggs, developing into larvae that tunnel into the mushrooms, rendering them inedible. Spray with malathion, or the more organically acceptable pyrethrum. A regular dusting of the compost surface every ten days should keep the fly at bay.

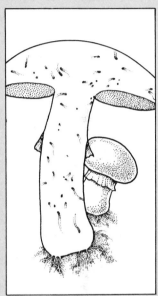

Diseases

Diseases usually only affect commercially grown crops and should not be a problem with mushroom kits.

throughout the growing period and keep the boxes out of direct sunlight.

After a further six weeks the first mushrooms should appear. Wait until the tight buttons have opened up before picking them – their flavour will then be far superior. Give a twist to the stalk when harvesting the mushrooms. Don't wrench them out of the compost.

Fresh crops should appear every two weeks over an eight-week period. After the last crop, use the compost in the garden. Fresh manure will have to be used to start a new lot of spawn.

Raising mushrooms from kits

The kit consists of a box ready planted with spawn. Water the compost and place the box somewhere where there will always be a temperature of 55-65°F/13-18°C, either in a shady corner of a room or in a cupboard. Keep the box out of direct sunlight.

After a week or so when the spawn has spread over the surface of the compost, cover it with the top dressing known as the casing (which is also provided with the kit). Maintain the same temperatures.

Start picking the mushrooms after about four weeks and carry on for six weeks. Use the spent mushroom compost in the garden.

COOKING AND FREEZING MUSHROOMS

Pick mushrooms just before cooking for the best flavour.

Cook them whole in butter or vegetable fat with a little lemon juice and seasoning. Fry gently for just a few minutes.

Mushroom soup is delicious, and it can be made entirely or partly with the stalks. First fry some sliced onion in butter and then add the mushrooms with a little lemon juice.

Sprinkle a little flour over the mushrooms and add a rich chicken stock. Simmer gently for ten minutes. Liquidize and stir in cream.

Mushrooms make an excellent salad too. Cook them in a mixture of chicken stock, lemon juice, wine vinegar, and olive oil, with either fines herbes or thyme on its own. Serve cool in the rich oily liquor.

Mushrooms should not be frozen.

ORIENTAL VEGETABLES

Oriental vegetables have only recently started to make an impact in the West. Once restricted to the 'China Towns' of large cities they have now begun to appear in ordinary supermarkets. They are not just a novelty either, but a genuine alternative to familiar Western vegetables, served raw, cooked in Western style, or cooked with an Eastern flourish. Seed can be tracked down easily in seed catalogues; some even have sections devoted exclusively to them.

The attractive pale-green Chinese cabbage, either short and dumpy or long and willowy, is the one Oriental vegetable that everyone must have seen. In fact, it almost seems to have become naturalized, since the names of new varieties introduced by Western seedsmen pay scant homage to the plant's Chinese ancestry.

The leafy mustards, such as mizuna, Chinese mustard and mustard spinach, can be grown as seedling leaves, using the cut-and-grow-again technique and eaten when they are no more than 3in/7.5cm tall. Alternatively, they can be grown towards maturity but picked before they become too hot. Chinese chives, with their onion-garlic flavour, make a change from the usual milder-flavoured chives.

As well as leaves and stems the Chinese have contributed some delicious flower tastes to our diet. The flower-heads of varieties of flowering pak choi and of Chinese broccoli are delicious, and the petals of garland chrysanthemum make an exotic addition to any clear soup.

Before long you will wonder how you ever cooked without them.

Chinese cabbage, Kasumi variety.

CHINESE CABBAGE
(Brassica pekinensis)

Of all Oriental vegetables the most widely known and popular is Chinese cabbage. It has even overcome the prejudice often associated with the very name of cabbage. This is fortunate for *Brassica pekinensis* has an altogether more delicate taste, whether eaten crispy raw or crispy cooked, than any variety of the common or garden cabbage. The original varieties of Chinese cabbage had a tendency to bolt, that is, running to flower and seed instead of producing leaves. Now breeding has had a fair amount of success in overcoming this failing. Some varieties have been bred for even earlier-maturing crops.

Varieties

There are two types of Chinese cabbage – the short barrel type, known as Wong Bok, and those with taller heads, known as Michihili. Nagaoka is a barrel type that matures slightly earlier than other varieties. Tip Top is another popular barrel type, but it has only medium resistance to bolting, while Kasumi has probably the greatest resistance. Tall-growing varieties include Green Pagoda and Green Rocket.

The plant's needs

Grow Chinese cabbage in rich well-draining soil as for other cabbage. Prepare the ground in autumn, digging in plenty of well-rotted manure or compost in a sunny shelterd part of the garden. By spring it will have broken down into humus. Lime acid soil for a pH level of 6.5 to 7.

Sowing and growing

In late spring, take out drills ½in/1.25cm deep and 12in/30cm apart. Sow the seed thinly, about 4in/10cm apart, and gradually thin to 12in/30cm apart. Seed can also be sown in soil blocks, one to a block, and transplanted when they have four or five true leaves, at 12in/30cm apart each way. Keep seedlings and plants always well watered or the plants may bolt in dry weather. As the heads develop quickly, further sowings can be made every three weeks until the beginning of late summer. When hearts begin to develop, wrap raffia around the leaves to keep the heads tightly closed.

COOKING AND FREEZING CHINESE CABBAGE

Those who dislike the usual cabbage taste should try Chinese cabbage either raw or slightly cooked. It has a unique delicate flavour. Slice or shred it and dress with oil or mayonnaise for salad dishes. Or add an Oriental taste to coleslaw, mixing shredded cabbage, carrot, finely diced ginger, a little soy sauce and mayonnaise.

Chinese cabbage needs a minimum of cooking; stir-frying is the only way to retain its crisp texture. Put a little salt and sunflower or sesame oil in a wok or frying pan, and quickly stir-fry the shredded leaves for no more than two minutes. If you want a contrasting flavour, cook a little ginger or some finely sliced salad onions in the wok for 30 seconds before starting to cook the cabbage.

Freezing is not recommended for Chinese cabbage.

BURDOCK
(Arctium lappa)

Edible burdock is a fairly new taste in the West, but relished by the Chinese and Japanese for its bitter-sweet sharpness. The young stems and leaves can be gathered in spring and eaten raw in salads or gently cooked; but the root is the most popular part of the vegetable. Long and slender, similar in appearance to scorzonera, the roots grow to 24in/60cm, so they need a deep and rich soil. The young roots can be peeled and eaten raw, but mature roots have to be cooked.

The plant is very hardy, so seed can be sown in autumn for a crop of stalks and shoots in spring, followed by the root. Or sowing can be delayed until spring to produce roots for storing over winter.

Varieties

Seed catalogues may describe it simply as burdock, but a few named varieties include Takinogawa Long and Watanabe.

The plant's needs

Edible burdock must have a rich deep soil that has been deeply cultivated. The ideal soil is a sandy loam, but clay, if well prepared, gives reasonable results. Make it more open and workable by digging in well-rotted manure or compost. Soil should be neutral. Choose a sunny and sheltered part of the garden – especially important for autumn sowings.

Sowing and growing

Sow seed in early autumn or spring. Take out drills ½in/1.25cm deep and 12in/30cm apart. Before sowing soak the seed in warm water for 24 hours to encourage germination. Sow groups of three seeds at 6in/15cm intervals and thin to the strongest seedling in each group. Apply a mulch round the base of the plant to keep weeds down and to retain moisture. As flower-heads appear pick them off to prevent seeds from developing, ruining the root crop.

Cut the leaves and young stalks from autumn-sown seed in early spring, and roots should be ready from late spring to early summer. A spring sowing will produce roots ready for lifting from late summer to early autumn, when the top foliage begins to die down. Lift the roots by loosening the soil round them with a fork until they can be pulled up easily. Try not to damage them because then rot will set

in and spread. Roots can be left in the ground, but they may become difficult to lift if the ground becomes frozen. In areas of frequent hard frost lift the roots and store in boxes of sand or dry peat. Keep in a frost-free place.

Growing in containers

Roots grown in containers will be nowhere near as long as those grown in the open ground. Containers must be at least 12in/30cm wide and deep, but the deeper the better. In early autumn or spring, fill the container with loam compost a day or two before sowing in order to allow it time to settle. Add more compost if neces-

sary to bring it to within 1in/1.25cm of the top of the container.

Take out two drills 1in/2.5cm deep and 6in/15cm apart, and 3in/7.5cm from the side of the container: a 12in/30cm wide container will therefore have two rows of plants. Soak the seeds in warm water for 24 hours before sowing. Sow three seeds at 6in/15cm intervals, starting 3in/7.5cm from the end of the container. Thin to the strongest seedling in each group. Feed monthly with a high potash fertilizer to stimulate root growth.

Pests and diseases

Seldom a problem.

CHINESE MUSTARD
(Brassica juncea)

As well as mizuna or Japanese greens there are other mustard leaves with a pleasantly mild peppery flavour. The secret of that mildness is to cut them when the leaves are young, 6-8in/15-20cm tall. If taller, the taste can become too hot.

The 'mustards' can be treated as cut-and-grow-again vegetables. Make the first cut when the leaves are about 3in/7.5cm tall and very mild in flavour so that they can be used raw in salads. Further growth will appear, making two or three cuts possible. Other plants can be left to grow to their full size.

The 'mustards' are hardy plants. They will survive periods of cold with a degree or two of occasional frost. If winters are more severe, the protection of cloches or frames will be needed.

Varieties

Green in Snow (or Green in the Snow) is a variety of Chinese mustard. As its name suggests, this is a hardy variety. Tendergreen is a variety of mustard spinach for late summer, autumn and winter cropping. This variety should not be sown in the height of summer since heat makes it run to seed quickly.

The plant's needs

All mustards do best in rich well-draining soil. Dig in well-rotted manure or compost. Remove all weeds from the soil and keep weeding as the crop grows.

Sowing and growing as a cut-and-grow-again vegetable

In early spring and spring, take out drills ½in/1.25cm deep and 3in/7.5cm apart. Sow seed thinly and thin further if necessary so that there is about 1in/2.5cm between seedlings. Keep them well watered. Start cutting the leaves when they are 3in/7.5cm tall, but leave about 1in/2.5cm of stem showing above the ground from which new growth will develop. Two or three cuts should be possible before the plants begin to deteriorate. At that stage dig them up. If there is room, successional sowings can be made since the crops mature very quickly.

Sowing and growing for winter use

In late summer, sow seed in ½in/1.25cm drills with 9in/22.5cm between rows. When the seedlings are about 2in/5cm tall, thin to 9in/22.5cm apart. From autumn onwards cover plants with cloches if frequent hard frosts are expected, though plants should be able to cope with the occasional light frost, especially if they have a mulch around them. Start cutting the leaves when they are 6-8in/15-20cm tall. If you harvest them beyond that stage, the flavour will be strong and hot.

Growing in containers

A seedling crop using the cut-and-grow-again technique is the best method for raising mustards in containers. Containers should be about 10in/25cm deep and at least 12in/30cm wide. In early spring or spring, fill the container with loam compost a day or two before sowing to allow the compost to settle. Fill up with more compost if necessary to within 1in/2.5cm of the top of the container. Take out drills 3in/7.5cm apart, starting 2in/5cm from the side of the container. Thin seedlings to leave about 1in/2.5cm between them.

Keep containers well watered at all times; twice daily watering may be necessary in warm weather. Make successional sowings if you have enough containers, but stop in late spring as crops will not do well in hot weather. Start sowing again from late summer for another seedling crop before the first frosts.

Pests and diseases

Seldom a problem.

MIZUNA
or JAPANESE GREENS
(Brassica juncea 'Japonica')

Most of the Oriental leaf vegetables come from China but mizuna greens are widely grown in Japan, particularly as a winter crop. They are hardy enough to survive a few degrees of occasional short frosts, but with some protection they will do much better; the crop will be heavier and the leaves and stalks more tender. They are ideal for growing in containers as a cut-and-grow-again vegetable.

Plants can be treated in two ways – the leaves can be cut when young, about 3in/7.5cm tall, or grown to maturity for winter leaves about 8in/20cm tall.

The advantage of cutting the young leaves is that they will be tender with a delicate flavour and the leaves will then grow again. It may be possible to cut leaves from each plant two or three times. At this stage the leaves have delicate, deeply cut fernlike foliage, which becomes coarser with age. The younger tender leaves are highly nutritious and make an excellent addition raw to salads. Although this type of leaf is often referred to generally as mustard greens, it does not taste hot. Young cut-and-grow again leaves have a mixed sweet-and-sour flavour which becomes stronger in mature plants.

Varieties

Usually described as mizuna, mizuna early or just plain Japanese greens.

The plant's needs

The bed should be prepared well in

Japanese greens add zest to a salad.

advance by digging in plenty of well-rotted manure or compost. It should be as weed-free as possible; a combination of mizuna greens and weeds is not the tastiest of dishes. Choose a slightly shaded spot for a summer-sown crop to try to prevent the plants from running to seed in hot weather.

Sowing and growing as a cut-and-grow-again vegetable

An early start can be made by sowing seed indoors in trays of loam seed potting compost in late winter or early spring. Sprinkle the seed thinly over the compost and press it into the surface. Thin seedlings to about 2in/5cm when they can be handled easily. Harden them off and plant out in a prepared bed in spring. Space plants about 2in/5cm apart in a block formation.

From spring onwards it is easier to sow seed straight into the ground. Take out rows 2-3in/5-7.5cm apart and ½in/1.25cm deep, and sow the seed thinly. If necessary, thin to give the seedlings room to develop, allowing at least 1in/2.5cm between seedlings. Keep the soil well watered so that it is moist at all times; lack of water is one of the most frequent causes of failure. When the leaves are 2-3in/5-7.5cm tall cut them, leaving behind 1in/2.5cm of stem to grow again. Whole heads can be cut, leaving behind the same length of stem, and they too should grow again. When the

plants are past their best, dig them up and sow fresh seed, but preferably not in the height of summer. Very warm, sunny weather tends to bring the seedlings on quickly, making them run to seed. The leaves then loose their tenderness and delicate flavour.

Mature mizuna greens for winter use

Sow seed outdoors from summer to early autumn in a square bed with rows about 9in/22.5cm apart. When the time comes to thin the seedlings, thin them also to 9in/22cm apart. This block planting makes it easier to protect the plants under a frame in winter.

In late autumn in all but mild areas, cover the plants with cloches or a frame. A frame can be as simple or as elaborate as you want, from a custom-built type to one of your own construction. Flexible plastic sheeting can be pushed into the ground around the bed to create a framelike shape – slightly higher at the back than the front with gently sloping sides. The frame must be tall enough to accommodate the mature plants, which will be about 8in/20cm tall. Stretch strong plastic sheeting over the top weighted down at the side

with bricks. Or the frame can be covered with rigid transparent plastic.

An alternative is to use the Chinese method of extending crops into the winter, but the snag is that this involves borrowing soil from another part of the garden. The soil is mixed with water to the consistency of thick mud, which is used to create the walls of a frame, including the sloping sides. The walls will dry hard and should survive the winter if nothing heavy is placed on them. Stretch strong plastic sheeting over the top and weight it down with bricks on the outside of the walls.

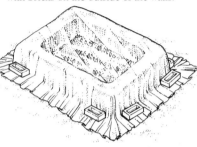

If using cloches, the simplest and cheapest are plastic tunnel cloches. Semi-circular wire supports are pushed into the ground and covered with strong plastic sheeting. If using cloches, it is better to plant in longer rows, with spacing appropriate to the width of the cloches, rather than in blocks.

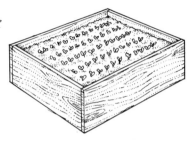

Growing in containers

Containers should be 12in/30cm or more wide and 8-10in/20-25cm deep. Use quality loam potting compost and not garden soil, which may harbour pests and diseases. Fill the container a week or so before it is to be planted up to allow the compost to settle. Add more if necessary before planting, leaving a gap of 1in/2.5cm between the surface of the soil and the top of the container.

Seed can be sown indoors for an early crop (see *Sowing and growing as a cut-and-grow-again vegetable*) or it can be sown in the container. The rows in the container should be 2-3in/5-7.5cm apart, starting about 2in/2.5cm from the edge to make the most use of the limited space available. Thin seedlings as necessary so that there is 1in/2.5cm between them. It is essential, as with all container growing, that the soil is kept moist at all times. Daily or twice daily waterings may be necessary in warm weather. Cut leaves or whole plants as required, making successional sowings when plants are no longer productive.

It is not worth growing mizuna greens to maturity because of the limited number of plants that can be grown in a container.

Pests and diseases:mizura greens

Seldom a problem.

CHINESE BROCCOLI or CHINESE KALE
(Brassica alboglabra)

Chinese broccoli is also known as Chinese kale, though it resembles the broccoli grown in Western gardens. While Western cooks usually throw away the tall stems that carry the flowering heads, the Chinese eat everything, stem and all. Young stems can be eaten without any special preparation, but more mature stems have to be peeled or at least split along their length so that they cook all the way through in a reasonable time. The joy of this Oriental vegetable is that it takes about only ten weeks to grow to harvesting. Seed can be sown in succession from late spring onwards for continuous supplies.

Another plus for this vegetable: it is highly nutritious, rich in vitamins A and C, and various minerals.

Varieties

The usual variety offered is the F₁ hybrid Green Lance.

The plant's needs

Chinese broccoli needs a rich, fertile and firm soil. Improve sandy soil by adding even more well-rotted manure and compost than you would to other types of soil. Do this in autumn so that it breaks down into humus before sowing seed the following late spring. Lime acid soils for a pH level of 6.5 to 7.

Sowing and growing

In late spring, take out drills ½in/1.25cm deep and 12in/30cm apart. Thin seedlings to 6-8in/15-20cm apart when they are about 3in/7.5cm tall. Water well throughout the growing period – this vegetable is very thirsty. Successional sowings can be made every three to four weeks until late summer.

Cut the stems when the flower-heads have formed but are still tightly closed. Treat as a cut-and-grow-again vegetable by cutting the flower-heads with 6-8in/15-20cm of stalk, leaving behind a long stump that still has side-shoots. New flowering growth should appear from the cut stems to give another cutting.

Growing in containers

Because Chinese broccoli takes up less room than conventional broccoli, con-

tainer growing is possible. Containers should be at least 10in/25cm deep, 12in/30cm wide and about 24in/60cm long. In late spring, fill the container with loam compost a day or two before you intend to sow, to allow the compost to settle. Fill up with more compost if necessary to within 1in/2.5cm of the top of the container. Take out two drills ½in/1.25cm deep and 6in/15cm apart, starting 3in/7.5cm from the edge of the container. Sow seed thinly and cover with a sifting of compost. Thin seedlings to 6in/15cm apart when they are 3in/7.5cm tall. Leave a gap of 3in/7.5cm between the end of the container and the first seedling so that the two planted rows of a 24in/60cm container will have eight plants.

Keep the compost moist at all times; twice daily watering may be necessary in periods of warm weather. Harvest as already described under *Sowing and growing*.

PESTS AND DISEASES

Pests

Cabbage butterflies or moths lay eggs on the undersides of leaves. Pick off any caterpillars that emerge and spray the plants with liquid derris or pyrethrum.

Flea beetles eat holes in young seedlings, stunting their growth or killing them. Dust with derris powder or pyrethrum.

Aphids suck the sap and stunt growth. Spray the plants with liquid derris, pyrethrum, soft soap or a solution of fatty-acid soaps.

Diseases

Club-root can be avoided by ensuring the ground is adequately limed and by observing strict rotation of crops. Dust seedlings with calomel dust.

Downy mildew's white furry deposits appear on the undersides of leaves. Spray with zineb.

Powdery mildew appears on the upper surfaces of leaves. Spray with benomyl.

COOKING AND FREEZING CHINESE BROCCOLI

Unless the stems are young, split them along their length before cooking or the heads will have overcooked before the stems are soft. One way of preventing the flower-heads from collapsing is to arrange them in a large pan with all the heads facing the same way. Just-cover with water and place the pan so that the stems are boiling over the hottest part of the ring while the flower-heads are barely simmering. With a little experience, stems and heads will be cooked to perfection at the same time.

To stir-fry Chinese broccoli, cut

the stem into 2in/5cm pieces and cook in sunflower or sesame oil for about four minutes. Alternatively, stir-fry for two minutes, then add a good chicken stock with a little soy sauce and simmer for a further two or three minutes. Serve with the stock. Plainly simmered or stir-fried stems can be served with mayonnaise or left to cool and covered with an oil and vinegar dressing.

Before freezing remove the leaves, blanch for a minute and then pack in rigid containers.

CHINESE or GARLIC CHIVES
(Allium tuberosum)

Chives, with their mild onion flavour, are familiar to all herb gardeners and to these can now be added a new taste – of onion-garlic chives. These also make highly decorative plants. Instead of the small, rounded hollow leaves of *Allium schoenoprasum* Chinese chives have flattened leaves about 12in/30cm long. In late summer and early autumn, tall flower spikes (up to 24in/60cm) carry clusters of white star-shaped flowers. They are very fragrant, with a roselike smell, and they can be eaten fresh or dried. Use the leaves in the same way as the more common chives, either raw or cooked.

Chinese chives are perennial. They can be bought as young plants, but at that stage it is hard to distinguish between the leaves of the two species and you may finish up with the wrong one. It is better to start with seed and keep a supply going in future years by division.

Varieties

Chinese or garlic chives areill usually sold by that name, perhaps with the botanical (Latin) name added for identification.

The plant's needs

Chinese chives will grow well in all types of well-draining fertile soil. Prepare the ground by digging in manure or compost.

Neutral to slightly alkaline soils usually give best results. Grow in full sun or partial shade, and keep them well watered in the growing season.

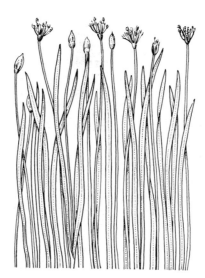

Sowing and growing

In early spring, take out a drill ½in/1.25cm deep and sow the seed thinly. Cover with a fine sifting of soil. Both germination and growth from the seedling stage are slow; patience is needed. When they first appear above ground, leave them to grow to about 2in/5cm tall before attempting to thin them. Make the first thinning to 3in/7.5cm and finally to 6in/15cm apart.

In the first year very few leaves should be cut and then only when they are 6in/15cm or more tall. If flower stems develop in the first year, pinch them out. In the second season you can cut more frequently, but still only leaves that are more than 6in/15cm tall and take a few from each plant, leaving behind about 2in/5cm of stem. Never cut all the leaves from a single plant. Allow some plants to flower each year, first to admire them and then to eat. Pinch out the flowering stems of the remainder so that they produce a substantial crop of leaves.

With the onset of winter the leaves die down to reappear the following spring. When there are several large clumps, lift and divide them in autumn before they begin to die down. Pot-up one or two pots to bring indoors to the kitchen window-sill for winter use.

Growing in containers

In spring sow seed thinly, ½in/1.25cm deep in a 12in/30cm container of loam compost. Thin the seedlings in stages until

you are left with the strongest six evenly spaced in the container. Keep well watered and apply a liquid feed monthly from late spring to late summer each year. For generous supplies of leaves, pinch out the flowering stems, but one or two plants can be left to produce white fragrant flowers. When the clumps fill the pot completely, they can be divided in autumn before dying down. Separate one clump each year in autumn to pot in a container for indoor growing in winter. As a result you can have Chinese chives all the year round.

Pests and diseases

Seldom a problem.

COOKING AND FREEZING CHINESE CHIVES

As it is possible to have fresh Chinese chives all year round there is no need to freeze them.

Combine chopped leaves with cottage cheese, cream cheese or yogurt for dressings. Add them to tomato salad and mixed green salads. Add chopped Chinese garlic during the last 30 seconds of stir-frying bean sprouts, stirring all the time. In fact, where you might use onions or garlic for flavouring, you can use Chinese chives instead.

Use the fresh buds and flower-heads in salads and as a garnish. They look pretty and smell and taste delicious. Flower-heads can be dried and the dried flowers crushed into soups and stews.

Sowing and growing

In early spring, take out drills ½in/1.25 cm deep and 3in/7.5cm apart. Sow seed thinly and cover with a fine sifting of soil. Thin the seedlings to about 2in/5cm apart. Make successional sowings every two to three weeks until late spring or early summer if the weather is not already too warm. Sow again from the end of late summer to early autumn, growing those plants for flowers.

For a seedling crop, start cutting them at about six weeks when they are 2-3in/5-7.5cm tall, leaving about 1in/2.5cm of stem, which will produce further growth. For larger leaves, best cut at not much more than 6in/15cm, thin seedlings to 6in/15cm apart.

Growing in containers

Containers should be a minimum of 12in/30cm wide, 8-10in/20-25cm deep and at least 24in/60cm long. Fill the container a day or so before sowing to allow the compost to settle. If necessary, fill up with more compost to within 1in/2.5cm of the top of the container. Take out drills 2-3in/5-7.5cm apart, starting 2in/5cm from the side of the container. Thin seedlings 1in/2.5cm apart and start cutting when they are 2-3in/5-7.5cm tall.

Keep the compost moist at all times and place the container out of direct sunlight. In periods of warm weather it may be necessary to water twice a day.

CHOP SUEY GREENS
(Chrysanthemum coronarium)

Above, Shungika or Chop Suey Greens.

Not all chrysanthemums can be eaten, as you could learn by bitter experience. The variety that can be cooked and eaten is one of the annual flowering chrysanthemums, sold as shungiku or garland chrysanthemum or as chop suey greens.

These can be grown as a seedling crop, using the cut-and-grow-again technique, cutting the seedlings when they are 2-3in/5-7.5cm tall. At this stage they can be eaten raw in salads, but the flavour may be too strong for some tastes. If so, cook them briefly instead. If they are allowed to grow to maturity (2ft/60cm tall), they will be too coarse and bitter. Instead cook them when they are about 6in/15cm long.

The plant's needs

Chop suey greens will grow in any type of soil, but they prefer cool and moist conditions so choose a somewhat shady part of the garden. If grown in full sun, especially in summer, the leaves will be coarse and bitter, so restrict sowings to the spring months and then again in autumn for a late crop. Dig in well-rotted manure or compost before sowing.

PESTS AND DISEASES:

Aphids can be a nuisance. Spray with derris, pyrethrum or a solution of fatty-acid soaps.

COOKING AND FREEZING CHOP SUEY GREENS

Use only the smallest leaves raw in mixed green salads, tossed in an oil dressing; the flavour and aroma of larger leaves can be a little overpowering. Cook chop suey greens with other ingredients rather than on their own. Stir-fry briefly with diced salad onion or garlic chives, bean sprouts and a little ginger. Cook spinach leaves and chop suey greens in a pan with a little water. Steam for eight to ten minutes. Press out the water. Chop finely and mix with butter.

Fresh and dried flower petals can be added to clear soups. To dry, separate the petals individually. Briefly dip in boiling salted water. Blot dry on paper towelling and then dry in the sun or in the coolest oven, with the door open, for about 20 minutes. Store in screw-top jars.

Chop suey greens are not worth freezing.

JAPANESE PARSLEY
(Cryptotaenia japonica)

The closest thing to Japanese parsley is the increasingly popular plain-leaved parsley, and Japanese parsley or mitsuba seems destined to become just as popular. It is an evergreen perennial, best treated as an annual, and as it easily self-seeds there will be new seedlings popping up each year. The tall stems carry groups of three heart-shaped leaves. Both leaves and stems can be cut and used as needed, or the whole plant can be pulled up and the root eaten as well.

As with many new vegetables the flavour is not easy to describe. For some it tastes just like plain-leaved parsley; for others it is a mixture of parsley and celery. It has an attractive delicate taste and can be eaten as a vegetable on its own or added to other dishes.

Varieties

This plant is usually described as Japanese parsley or mitsuba.

The plant's needs

Japanese parsley will grow in any type of fertile, well-draining but moisture-retentive soil. Dig in well-rotted manure or compost to make it more fertile, and peat to make it hold water better. This is a plant that prefers to be in a partly shaded position. If grown in full sun, the leaves are likely to yellow and the plant look unhealthy.

Sowing and growing

Seed can be sown as soon as the ground has warmed up in spring. Take out drills ½in/1.25cm deep and 6in/15cm apart. Sow seed thinly and cover with a little fine soil. When seedlings are large enough to handle, thin to 6in/15cm apart.

Plants reach maturity in about 60 days, so several sowings can be made throughout the summer. Seed sown in early autumn with cloche protection should produce leaves for winter use. Keep the plants well watered. If they are allowed to dry out the crop is likely to fail. Cut a few stems and leaves from each plant, leaving about 2in/5cm to produce further growth. Pull up whole plants if you want to cook the roots.

Growing in containers

Containers should be at least 12in/30cm

wide and deep, and at least 24in/60cm long. Fill with loam compost a day or two before sowing in order to give it time to settle. Add more compost if necessary to bring it to within 1in/2.5cm of the top of the container. In spring, take out three drills 4in/10cm apart, starting 2in/5cm from the side of the container. Sow the seed thinly and cover with a little sifted compost. Thin seedlings to 4in/10cm, or 6in/15cm if you want larger plants. Either cut leaves as required or clear the whole container when the plants reach maturity and sow another crop.

Pests and diseases

Neither should be a problem.

COOKING AND FREEZING JAPANESE PARSLEY

Chop the leaves and stems and mix with other salad leaves for a green salad, tossing all the leaves in vinaigrette. Try a combination of chopped Japanese parsley and shredded Chinese cabbage, either dressed in oil, or hot, stir-fried.

Sprinkle chopped leaves and stems over soups, vegetables and tomatoes.

Slice the roots and quickly stir-fry them in sunflower oil, or simmer them gently in water until tender.

Drain, cover with melted butter and sprinkle with the finely chopped leaves.

Before freezing, wash and dry leaves and stems. Pack into plastic bags and freeze. Leaves can be finely chopped, packed into ice-cube trays, topped up with water and frozen. Turn out the frozen cubes, place them in plastic bags and return to the freezer.

PAK CHOI
(Brassica chinensis)

Pak choi is becoming almost as popular as Chinese cabbage among Western gardeners and most catalogues list at least one variety. It is a leafy vegetable with thick white succulent stalks, and both stalks and leaves can be eaten; they have a mild subtle taste.

Like many Oriental vegetables, pak choi has a tendency to bolt in warm weather, so restrict sowings to spring and autumn. In autumn, sow one of the hardier varieties with some protection – frame, cloche or unheated greenhouse – and you can have winter greens. All varieties can be grown as seedling crops, using the cut-and-grow-again technique, but this method involves sowing much more seed. A more economical way is to start off treating the crop as cut-and-grow-again and then leaving some of the plants to mature.

Varieties

Pak choi is also known as Japanese white celery mustard, and may be so described in seed catalogues. It is also called Chinese pak choi. Both are slow to bolt and quite hardy for winter crops. Newer varieties include the F_1 varieties Joi Choi and Mei Quing Choi, Japro and Lei-Choi. All produce white stems topped with spoon-shaped green leaves, used raw in salads when young and small or cooked when mature.

The plant's needs

Plants will come to maturity after as little as six to eight weeks, so the ground must be moisture-retentive and reasonably fertile to sustain this rapid growth. Prepare the soil in advance by digging in plenty of well-rotted manure or compost. Dig peat into soil that does not hold water well. A mulch round the plants also helps to retain moisture. Acid soils should be limed for a pH level of 6.5 to 7.

Sowing and growing

Make a first sowing in spring, taking out drills ½in/1.25cm deep and 3in/7.5cm for a seedling crop, and 9in/22.5cm apart if the plants are to be grown to full size. Thin seedling crops to about 2in/5cm apart. When they are about 4in/10cm tall, start picking the leaves or cut the whole plants but leave about 1in/2.5cm of stem to grow again. Allow some seedlings to grow to

full size, thinning to 9in/22.5cm each way.

If the whole crop is to be grown to full size, thin to 6in/15cm, and then to 9in/22.5cm, using the thinnings as excellent salad leaves.

Another sowing can be made in late spring and again in late summer and early autumn. The life of late-sown crops can be extended by covering them with cloches or growing in a frame. Keep well watered - if the plants dry out the crop will fail. As plants come to maturity start picking the outside leaves. Take a few from each plant, leaving the hearts undisturbed to go on growing. When the plants are about 12in/30cm tall, cut them completely.

Growing in containers

Since mature pak choi are large it is not economical to grow them to that size in containers. Seedling crops are a different matter. Containers should be a minimum of 12in/30cm wide, 8-10in/20-25cm deep, and at least 24in/60cm long. Fill with loam compost a day or two before sowing in order to allow it to settle. Fill up with more compost if necessary to within 1in/2.5cm of the top of the container.

Sow seed from spring to late spring and then again from late summer to early autumn. Take out drills ½in/1.25cm deep and 3in/7.5cm apart, starting 3in/7.5cm from the edge of the container, so that a 12in/30cm wide container has three rows. Sow seed thinly and cover with a fine sifting of soil. Thin to 1-2in/2.5-5cm between seedlings. Seed can also be broadcast, thinning to the same distances.

When seedlings are about 4in/10cm tall, start picking a few leaves from each one, or cut whole seedlings. Leave about 1in/2.5cm of the stem behind and this will grow again. Two or three cuttings should be possible before they become totally unproductive. Keep container plants well watered; it may be necessary to water twice a day in warm weather.

Pests and diseases: pak choi

See *Pak choi pests and diseases,*
page 117.

COOKING AND FREEZING PAK CHOI

Use the leaves of seedling crop raw in salads to get the most of their high vitamin C and mineral content. Some is lost in cooking, but pak choi still makes a nutritious meal.

To cook the mature leaves of pak choi, chop the thick stems into 1in/2.5cm pieces and then shred the leaves. Stir-fry the stems first in oil with some salt and, as they start to soften, add the leaves, stirring for about a minute.

To make a complete meal combine pak choi with mushrooms, Chinese for preference. Lightly fry sliced ginger in sunflower or sesame oil. Add mushrooms and soy sauce and simmer for about ten minutes. Add chopped pak choi stems and leaves and a little water and simmer for ten minutes more.

To freeze, blanch stems and leaf complete for two minutes. Pat dry, pack in plastic bags and freeze.

FLOWERING PAK CHOI
(Brassica chinensis)

FLOWERING PURPLE PAK CHOI
(Brassica campestris)

These pak choi varieties are grown for their edible flower stalks rather than for their leaves. The flower stems are picked when they are about 8in/20cm tall, which is usually about eight weeks after sowing. If you cut individual flowering stems leave some of the leaves behind, rather than cutting whole plants; new flowering stems should grow.

Flowering purple pak choi is delicious to eat and highly decorative as well. Leaves and flowering stems are dark green flushed with purple and the flowers are yellow.

Varieties

Flowering pak choi is known as Chinese tsai shim and flowering purple pak choi as hon tsai tai. They will be described in seed catalogues by the English or Chinese names, sometimes by both.

The plant's needs

Like the leafy pak choi, plants will mature quite quickly, between six and nine weeks, so they must have moisture-retentive soil. Dig in plenty of peat to help the soil retain moisture, and spread a mulch around the plants. The soil should also be rich, so dig in well-rotted manure or compost, preferably a few months before sowing to give it time to break down to fertile humus. Lime acid soils for a pH level of 6.5 to 7.

Flowering pak choi does better in cool summers and in such a climate crops should be possible from spring through to autumn. In warmer conditions spring and late summer sowings will be the most successful.

Sowing and growing

In spring, take out drills ½in/1.25cm deep and 10in/25cm apart for flowering pak choi and 16in/40cm apart for flowering purple pak choi. When seedlings can be handled easily, thin to 6in/15cm apart and then to 10in/25cm apart for flowering pak choi and 16in/40cm apart for flowering purple pak choi – equally spaced in block formation.

Spring-sown crops should be ready in

early summer. If summers are cool, it is possible to make later sowings and pick flowering stems throughout the summer months. Another sowing of flowering pak choi can be made in late summer for cropping in autumn, but no later because the first frosts usually cut it down. Flowering purple pak choi will survive occasional light frosts and can go on cropping until early winter. With protection under cloches, stems may well continue to flower until spring.

Flowering pak choi takes up too much room for container growing.

Pests and diseases:

See *Pak choi pests and diseases*, this page.

COOKING AND FREEZING FLOWERING PAK CHOI

Young tender flowering shoots can be cut into short lengths and tossed in vinaigrette for salads. They can become tough quite quickly so pick them young to be eaten raw. Mix with other Oriental leaves, such as mizuna, Japanese parsley, and chop suey greens, and dress with vinaigrette for a sharp spicy salad.

The best way to cook flowering pak choi is by stir-frying in sunflower or sesame oil. That way the flower-heads don't collapse into mush as they do if the stems are boiled. Cut the stems into small pieces and stir-fry them for about three minutes with some salad onions or garlic chives. Add the flowering heads last of all and stir-fry for a further one or two minutes.

Freezing is not recommended.

HERBS

Herbs are among the oldest of plants known – used for centuries for culinary and medicinal purposes. They were long associated with the Church; and the herb gardens of the monasteries are legendary. Interest in herbs has waxed and waned over the years, but at the moment their popularity is definitely on the increase.

The natural food movement of the past decade has brought about a new awareness of herbs. Synthetic flavourings are out; natural flavours are in. The numerous different herbs available make the perfect source of healthy natural flavouring.

The curious fact is that not only are herbs health-giving, but most of them manage to keep very healthy themselves. They are virtually untroubled by pests and diseases. If all vegetables and fruits were like herbs life, for the gardener, would be far simpler.

There is a surprisingly large range of herbs used in our daily food, both sweet and savoury. There are spicy herbs, like coriander used in curries, or sweetly spicy ones like cinnamon, often used with cooked fruit. Other herbs such as rosemary play a dual role, going equally well with sweet or savoury dishes.

ANGELICA
(Angelica archangelica)

The majestic stems of angelica, growing to 6ft/1.8m, are a decorative backdrop for the herb garden. It is a biennial, so its natural life cycle is over two years, but it can be made to last longer if it is prevented from flowering. However, that destroys one of the main attractions of the herb, the spherical heads of greenish-white flowers that appear in the summer months.

The plant's needs

Angelica will grow in most types of rich, moist but well-draining soil, either in full sun or part shade.

Sowing and growing

In late summer or early autumn, sow seed in drills ½in/1.25cm deep. If there is any likelihood of frost, cover with cloches. In the following early spring, thin to 12in/30cm apart and in autumn, transplant to their final positions, 3ft/90cm apart. Sowings can also be made in early spring, thinning out in autumn and transplanting finally in early spring the following year. If you want the plant to last for several years, cut off any developing flower-heads. In late spring, cut the stems if they are to be candied; if left longer, the stems become too hard for candying.

Growing in containers

As in the open ground, seed can be sown in late summer or early spring, a few seeds to a container that must be at least 12in/30cm wide and a similar depth. Use loam compost. Thin to the strongest seedling.

Pests and diseases: angelica

Seldom a problem, but if aphids appear spray with derris or a solution of fatty-acid soaps.

> ### USING ANGELICA
> To candy the stalks, boil them in water. Peel off the outer skin and boil again until transparent and green. Boil again in thick sugar syrup until the stalks lose their colour. Dry and sprinkle with sugar leaving them to dry.
> Peeled stems and leaves can be stewed with rhubarb and other fruits for an interesting contrasting flavour similar to juniper berry.

ANISE
(Pimpinella anisum)

Anise is an attractive compact annual (about 12in/30cm) with loose umbels of white star-shaped flowers. The leaves are used as flavouring, but with discretion since aniseed flavour can easily overwhelm a dish. Small brown fruits follow the flowers, and extracts from these are used in making liqueurs and flavouring cakes.

The plant's needs

Anise will grow in any type of soil. For best results choose a warm and sunny site.

Sowing and growing

In spring, sow seed thinly in drills ½in/1.25cm deep. Cover lightly with soil. Thin to 12in/30cm apart. Seed can also be sown in trays of loam seed compost. Thin and transplant with plenty of compost round the roots to 12in/30cm apart. In

summer and late summer, when the seeds on the flower-heads have turned brown, cut off complete heads and leave them to dry out in a warm place. When the seeds are dry, rub them to remove the chaff and store in a paper bag in a dry place.

Growing in containers

In spring, sow three seeds in 8in/20cm containers of loam compost. Remove the weaker seedlings, keeping one to a pot.

Pests and diseases: anise

Seldom a problem, except for aphids. Spray with derris or a solution of fatty-acid soaps.

> ### USING ANISE
> Freeze or dry the leaves. Chop the leaves finely and add a little to mixed green salads. Or sprinkle over sliced tomatoes along with a little sugar. Crush the seed with a pestle and mortar and add a small amount to plain cakes.

BALM
(Melissa officinalis)

Balm, or lemon balm, is a perennial growing to 2½ft/75cm, suitable for the middle or back of the herb garden. Bees find the lemon scent irresistible and crowd round the small white flowers in the summer months collecting nectar and pollinating. This is an easily grown herb and its attractive lemon-mint flavour deserves much wider use.

The plant's needs

Balm is not fussy about the type of soil it is grown in, but it should be fertile and moist. Prepare the soil by digging in well-rotted manure or compost, and adding peat will make it more moisture-retentive. Best in full sun, but partial shade is tolerated.

Sowing and growing

In spring or late spring, sow seed thinly in drills ½in/1.25cm deep. Thin to 4in/10cm apart and in late summer or early autumn, transplant to final growing positions, 12in/30cm apart. In the first year cut only a few leaves, leaving the plant to become well established. For the strongest-flavoured leaves, pick them when the plant is about to come into flower in early summer. Cut again in summer and then in early autumn for leaves to dry. In between, some leaves can be cut to use fresh. In autumn, cut back all the stems to just above ground level. In areas prone to frost cover the ground with straw or leaf mould for protection during winter. For new plants, divide roots in autumn.

Balm – sometimes mistaken for mint.

Growing in containers

In spring, sow four seeds in an 8in/20cm pot of loam compost. Thin to the strongest seedling, leaving one to a pot.

Pests and diseases: balm

Seldom give trouble.

> ### *USING BALM*
>
> Freeze or dry the leaves. Add them chopped – fresh or dried – to soups, sauces or salads to give a lemon-mint tang. Balm goes especially well with sauces to accompany fish. Add sprigs to cold fruit drinks and tea, both iced and hot.

BASIL
(Ocimum basilicum)

In warm countries basil is treated as a hardy perennial, but in cold climates it dies at the first hint of frost and has to be treated as an annual. To make it last longer, one or two plants can be lifted before the first frosts, planted in pots and overwintered in a greenhouse or a warm spot indoors.

The bright-green oval leaves are carried on stems up to 18in/45cm. Their clove-like flavour spices up the taste of many dishes, including curries. *Ocimum minimum* is smaller, making a bushy plant up to 12in/30cm. The leaves are not so heavily scented or flavoured as sweet basil.

The plant's needs

Choose a sheltered part of the garden that gets full sun. Basil will grow in any type of well-draining fertile soil and dry conditions don't bother it. Dig in well-rotted compost before sowing or planting.

Sowing and growing

In early spring, sow seed in boxes or pots of loam seed compost. Keep at a temperature of 55-60°F/13-16°C. Thin to 2in/5cm apart when the first true leaves have developed. Harden off before planting out by placing the seed trays or pots outdoors in a propagator with the vents open or enclosed in a plastic bag with holes punched in them. Bring the plants indoors each evening. Continue this daily routine for about two weeks before planting out in late spring, 8in/20cm apart.

Seed can be sown directly into the open ground in late spring. Thin to 2in/5cm and then to 8in/20cm.

Pinch out flower spikes as they develop to force the plant to concentrate on producing leaves. In early autumn, lift a few plants and move them into pots of loam compost. Cut back the stems to within 2in/5cm of the soil. This will encourage new growth for use during the winter months. Keep the pots in a warm greenhouse or in a kitchen on a window-sill.

Growing in containers

The smaller *Ocimum minimum* is the best choice for containers. Sow seed as already described. Transplant five seedlings to an 8in/20cm pot and harden off.

Pests and diseases: basil

Seldom give trouble.

> ### *USING BASIL*
>
> Freeze or dry the leaves.
>
> Basil is the perfect complementary herb to tomatoes, both raw and cooked. Slice tomatoes, sprinkle with a little sugar and finely chopped basil. Italians would be lost without this herb – it is an essential part of thick tomato sauce to go with pasta. (See *Tomatoes*, page 103.) Add to tomato soup, made by simmering onions and tomatoes in a chicken stock. Give a lift to plain omelettes by sprinkling with finely chopped basil before folding over for serving.

BORAGE
(Borago officinalis)

The appealing star-shaped sky-blue flowers of borage make it a particularly decorative plant in the herb garden. It is a hardy annual and the flowers appear in summer or late summer and last until the first frosts; a great attraction for bees. The cucumber-flavoured oval grey-green leaves are carried on stems that grow 18-36in/45-90cm long.

The plant's needs

All types of soil are suitable, with best results on light sandy soils. Choose a sunny sheltered part of the garden.

Sowing and growing

In spring, sow seed ½in/1.25cm deep in small groups 6in/15cm apart. Thin the plants to 12in/30cm apart. When the plants start to flower they will self-seed readily, providing new plants the following spring. Transplant these to where they are to grow when the first true leaves appear; if left later they may suffer a check in growth.

Growing in containers

In spring, plant four seeds to an 8in/20cm pot of loam compost. Thin, leaving the strongest seedling to grow on.

Pests and diseases

Aphids can sometimes be a nuisance. Spray with a solution of fatty-acid soaps or derris.

> ### *USING BORAGE*
>
> Freeze or dry the leaves, but freezing is more successful. Chop the leaves finely and add to mixed green salads. The leaves will also give a refreshing clean flavour to fruit cups and alcoholic drinks. If you add some flowers to clear drinks they will tinge the liquid blue, perhaps not to everyone's liking. Add chopped leaves to soups and stews and try cooking a little with cabbage, the result is pleasantly surprising.

CARAWAY
(Carum carvi)

Caraway is grown for its seeds, an essential ingredient of seed-cake. It is a biennial, coming to the flowering stage in the year after sowing. When flowering is over the plant dies. The finely dissected feathery foliage is carried on hollow stems, growing to 2ft/60cm. The loose clusters of white flowers are allowed to ripen to produce seeds in the second summer.

The plant's needs

Any type of soil is suitable. Choose a sunny sheltered part of the garden.

Sowing and growing

In late summer, take out a drill ½in/1.25cm deep. Sow thinly, aiming at 3in/7.5cm apart. Thin to 8in/20cm and finally to 12in/30cm apart. In the following summer, the flowers develop and at this stage the plants may need to be supported by canes. Leave the seeds to ripen on the plants, but cut off the heads before they start to fall. Leave the heads to dry out thoroughly in a warm sunny place indoors. Rub the heads between your hands and very gently blow away the chaff. Store the seeds in a screw-top jar.

Growing in containers

In late summer, plant four seeds in an 8in/20cm pot of loam compost. When the seedlings are large enough to decide which is the most promising, remove all but that one. As the plant comes into flower the following year apply a liquid feed every two weeks.

Pests and diseases: caraway

Seldom give trouble.

USING CARAWAY

Mix two teaspoonsful of the seeds into a basic Victoria sponge mixture and bake for 50 minutes to give an aniseed flavour. Fresh young leaves can be finely chopped and added to soups, stews and salads.

CHERVIL
(Anthriscus cerefolium)

Chervil is another aniseed-flavoured herb with a sweetish taste, but that brief description does not do it justice. It can be used on its own or as an ingredient of fines herbes. Chervil grows to 18in/45cm and the lacy fernlike leaves look rather like parsley. Loose umbels of white flowers appear in the summer months, but the plants should not be allowed to flower, or they will rapidly run to seed and die.

It is a biennial but best treated as an annual with two sowings, one in early spring and another in late summer for winter use. The second sowing can be made outdoors in a sheltered part of the garden or indoors in pots.

The plant's needs

Chervil will grow in any type of soil, apart from heavy poor-draining soil such as clay. It will grow in full sun or partial shade, but summer sowings are best done in some shade so that the soil does not dry out too quickly. Hot dry summers produce poor crops of chervil.

Sowing and growing

In early spring, take out shallow drills ¼in/0.6cm deep. Sow seed thinly and cover with a fine sifting of soil. When the seedlings are about 2in/5cm tall thin to 6in/15cm. Never let the plants dry out. Successional sowings can be made as plants come to maturity in eight to ten weeks. For winter use, make a final sowing in late summer. Pinch out flowering stems as soon as they appear so that the plant produces more leaves instead.

Growing in containers

In early spring, plant three seeds to a 6in/15cm pot of loam compost. Keep only the strongest seedling. Chervil has such a delicate flavour that you may need more than one plant. Ten seeds in a 12in/30cm pot can be thinned to five well-spaced seedlings. Also succesional sowings can be made every six weeks.

Pests and diseases: chervil

Seldom give trouble.

USING CHERVIL

Leaves should be frozen as the flavour is quickly lost in drying. To have any impact, large quantities of this delicate-flavoured herb have to be used. Never cook it or all the flavour will be lost; always add it to cooked dishes. Add chopped leaves to cold soups, such as cucumber. Use it in salads and as a garnish, or make a sauce with it to serve with fish. Season fresh cream with salt and pepper and mix in a generous quantity of finely chopped chervil.

CHIVES
(Allium schoenoprasum)

For those who find the flavour of spring onions too strong, chives are the ideal milder alternative. Small though they are, growing in clumps about 8in/20cm high, they are a highly productive perennial. The best way to enjoy a continuous supply for much of the year is to keep on cutting them down to within 2in/5cm of the soil. The more you cut them the more they send up new grasslike stems. They are cut down by the first hard frosts but sprout again in spring.

The plant's needs

Chives are not fussy about the type of soil, but it must be fertile. Before sowing, dig in plenty of well-rotted manure or compost. Light slightly alkaline soils tend to give the best results. Chives grow well in full sun or partial shade, but they must be moist at all times.

Sowing and growing

In early spring, take out drills ½in/1.25cm deep and sow the seed thinly. Cover with a sifting of soil. Thin the seedlings when they can be handled easily to 6in/15cm apart. Let the plants become well established before taking the first cutting. Pinch out any flowers that develop. They may be pretty but they reduce the output of leaves. Cut the individual leaves to within 2in/5cm of the soil. When clumps have started to spread, they can be divided and replanted in autumn every two to three years. One or two clumps can be moved to pots and kept on the kitchen window-sill for winter use.

Growing in containers

In spring, sow seed thinly in a 12in/30cm pot of loam compost. Thin the seedlings, removing the weaker and leaving six evenly spaced out. Give them a liquid feed every month from late spring to late summer. Divide the clumps every two to three years.

Pests and diseases: chives

Seldom give trouble.

USING CHIVES

As fresh chives can be available all year round there is no need to freeze them. Finely chopped chives can be used in many dishes for subtle flavouring. Sprinkle them over sliced dressed tomatoes and mixed green salads. Combine with yogurt or cream for dressings. Mix them with mashed potato, cream cheese and cottage cheese spread. Serve grilled fish with blended butter and chives. Add to white sauces, combine with omelettes and scrambled egg – the possibilities are endless.

CORIANDER
(Coriandrum sativum)

Coriander, staple curry spice.

Ground coriander is an essential ingredient of curry powder. The powder comes from the seed (or more correctly the fruit) of the plant, which in its raw unroasted state has a mild, sweet orangey taste. The mild flavour means that large quantities have to be used to make any impact. Roast the seed, as they do in India, and the flavour is no longer so subtle, but has a more familiar curry flavour. Coriander leaves are often neglected in the West, but they add a distinctive flavour to curries if chopped up and used in large quantities.

Coriander is an annual with fernlike foliage carried on stems up to 2ft/60cm tall. Heads of white or pink flowers appear about three months after sowing, followed by the seed, which is left on the plant to ripen.

The plant's needs

Grow coriander in any type of well-draining, rich soil. Dig in well-rotted manure or compost before sowing seed. Choose a sheltered sunny part of the garden.

Sowing and growing

In early spring, take out a drill ½in/1.25cm deep and sow the seed thinly. Cover with a sifting of soil. Thin to 6in/15cm apart. Grow some plants for leaves, cutting off the flower-heads as they appear. (Make successional sowings throughout the summer to ensure a constant supply of leaves.) Allow other plants to flower to provide seeds for ripening. Let the seeds turn brown on the plants; green unripe seeds have a very unpleasant taste. When they have turned brown, cut off the heads and leave them to dry in the sun. Rub the seeds between your hands, and carefully blow away the chaff. Store in screw-top jars in a dark place.

Growing in containers

In early spring, sow seeds thinly in loam compost in a window-box 18-24in/45-60cm long. Thin seedlings to 6in/15cm apart each way. Keep well watered.

Pests and diseases: coriander

Seldom give trouble.

USING CORIANDER

Freeze the leaves rather than drying them.

Use the ground seeds in curries or add them to soups, stews and pickles. Rub the powdered seed over the skin of pork and lamb joints for a spicy roast. The seed can also be added to bread and cakes. Chop the leaves for curries, chutneys, soups, stews and salads.

DILL
(Anethum graveolens)

The Scandinavians make great use of dill in their cooking, and this is how many people first taste the delicious herb. It has a mild aniseed taste, as many herbs have, but the overall flavour is unique. Both leaves and seeds are used in cooking, the leaves being milder than the seeds. Dill is a tall-growing annual – up to 3ft/90cm – with feathery foliage, and is best grown at the back of the herb garden. Loose heads of yellow flowers appear in summer and late summer, followed by the seed that is left to ripen on the plant.

The plant's needs

Dill will grow in any type of soil, but it must have a sunny sheltered position. Pre-

Dill, a Scandinavian favourite.

pare the soil in advance by digging in well-rotted manure or compost.

Sowing and growing

The method of growing depends on whether you want leaves or seeds. For continuous supplies of leaves, sow seed in early spring and every month until late summer. Remove any flower-heads as they appear. To grow for seed make a sowing in spring, allowing the plants to flower and the seed to ripen.

Sow seed in ½in/1.25cm drills and thin plants being grown for leaves to 6in/15cm. Thin those being grown for seed to 9in/22.5cm. Keep well watered at all times or leaf development will be poor.

When the seed heads on the plants being cultivated for seed are turning brown, cut them off and leave them to dry in the sun. Roll the seeds between your hands to remove the chaff. Store in a screw-top jar.

Growing in containers

Choose a container at least 10in/25cm deep to allow plenty of room for roots to grow. In spring, sow seed thinly in loam compost and thin to 6in/15cm apart each way (for leaf crops) and 9in/22.5cm (for seed crops). Keep well watered always, especially in warm weather.

Pests and diseases: dill

Seldom give trouble.

USING DILL

Dill is more successful frozen than dried. To use the leaves, fresh or frozen, chop them finely and add to mixed green salads, soups and stews. Dill sauce is made by adding chopped leaves to cream seasoned with salt and pepper. Combine a little Dijon mustard with mayonnaise, lemon juice and chopped dill for a dressing to go with cold salmon.

Dill is indispensable in the dish called gravlax, raw pickled salmon. If salmon fillets are too expensive, use trout fillets instead. Rub two fillets with a mixture of sea salt, sugar and ground peppercorns. Place one fillet in a dish, skin side down, and cover with sprigs of dill. Place the other fillet, skin side up, on top of the first. Cover with a plate and weight it down. Place in a refrigerator and keep it there for at least 24 hours, turning the sandwiched fillets twice. The results are better if left for 36 to 48 hours. Remove the dill before serving with the mayonnaise, mustard and dill dressing described above.

FENNEL
(Foeniculum vulgare)

Fennel is a very handsome perennial herb, but it grows 5ft/1.5m tall and has a wide spread, so avoid planting too many. The feathery bright-green leaves have a distinctive flavour, a cross between aniseed and liquorice, and they are used to flavour soups and sauces. The ground seeds have a stronger flavour. The heads of yellow flowers, which appear in early autumn, should be removed before they develop fully if you want large quantities of leaves. There is another form that has handsome bronze-red leaves.

The plant's needs

Fennel will grow in any type of well-draining fertile soil. Before sowing the seed, dig in well-rotted manure or compost. Choose a warm, sheltered part of the garden that gets full sun.

Sowing and growing

If you want the plants to produce seeds, make a sowing in early spring; to crop leaves only, sow in spring or late spring. Sow thinly in a drill ½in/1.25cm deep. Thin the seedlings when well established to 12in/30cm apart. If growing for leaves, cut out flowering stems as they appear. If seeds are wanted they will take a long time to develop and are gathered when they are still light-green. Leave them to dry out thoroughly in a cool place, out of the sun. Store in screw-top jars.

In autumn, plants can be divided before they begin to die down. Or one or two plants can be lifted and planted in pots and kept indoors or in a greenhouse to give supplies of leaves in winter. The remaining fennel plants should be cut down to within some 4in/10cm of the ground. After three to five years' growth, pull up the plants and start again with fresh seed.

Growing in containers

Containers should be at least 10in/25cm deep and of the same diameter. If you intend to crop the plants for their leaves, sow in early spring, six seeds to a container of loam compost. Thin to the strongest seedling. Cut out flower stems. If the plants are wanted to seed, sow in spring and let the plants flower. Keep fennel well watered at all times.

USING FENNEL

Fennel can be dried, but freezing is more successful.

Place lengths of fennel in the bottom of a dish and bake fish such as mackerel, trout and sea bass on top. Or place lengths of fennel inside gutted fish or underneath them when they are being grilled.

Add chopped leaves to soups, stews, salads and dressings. A combination of sour cream, yogurt and chopped fennel makes an excellent dressing for cucumber.

Whole seeds are used for cooking with shellfish and ground seeds can be rubbed into the skin of pork.

GARLIC
(Allium sativum)

Garlic is an abused herb, at least by those who use far too much of it. Used in small quantities it is one of the most helpful of herbs, enhancing the flavours of many foods. Garlic is simple to grow. It is a bulb that is divided into cloves. When these are planted new bulbs develop underground, with narrow leaves showing above ground.

The plant's needs

Garlic will grow in most types of soil but it does best in rich light soil. Choose a sunny sheltered part of the garden and dig in well-rotted manure or compost before planting the cloves.

Growing

To get supplies of garlic for most of the year, make two sowings – one in autumn or late autumn, and the other in early spring the following year. Remove the papery skin from the bulb to reveal the cloves. Divide the bulb into the separate cloves and plant them pointed end upwards at a depth of about 1in/2.5cm and 6in/15cm apart: the tip of each clove should be just below the surface of the soil.

The new bulbs are ready to lift when the top foliage starts to die down. Autumn plantings will be ready the following summer and early spring plantings will be ready in autumn. Lift them carefully to avoid damaging the bulbs and leave them

---

to dry, in the sun if possible but indoors if there is any danger of their getting wet. Store in a cool dry place where air can circulate round them.

Save some bulbs for planting in late autumn and the following early spring for next year's crop.

Growing in containers

Containers should be at least 10in/25cm deep and 12in/30cm wide. In late autumn or early spring, plant cloves in loam compost in the container, 1in/2.5cm deep and 6in/15cm apart; the top of the cloves should be just below the surface of the compost. Keep containers well watered at all times. Harvest as described under *Growing*.

PESTS AND DISEASES: GARLIC

Pest
Onion eel-worm can be a problem, distorting the bulbs and bloating the foliage. Lift and destroy all infected plants; there is no cure.

Diseases
White rot, a fungal disease, attacks and rots the bulbs. Lift and destroy diseased plants. Take preventive measures, dusting cloves and soil with calomel dust before planting.

USING GARLIC

Dried garlic bulbs will last for many weeks.

Garlic can be used to flavour many dishes, but should always be used with discretion. Peel the cloves and use them chopped or crushed in salad dressings, or in butter. To give a mild flavouring to food, cut a clove and rub it over fish or chops before grilling. Small slivers can be inserted in cuts in the skin of meat before roasting.

HORSE-RADISH
(Cochlearia armoracia)

The long roots of this ancient herb are grated to make horse-radish sauce. It is usually partnered with roast beef, but goes extremely well with smoked fish, such as trout and mackerel. It can also be used with more delicately flavoured fresh fish as long as you are restrained in the amount of hot horse-radish you put in the sauce.

Plants are usually grown from root cuttings, about 6in/15cm long. If left to themselves they will rapidly spread, becoming weeds. To prevent the spreading, dig up the bed every year and save some of the healthiest roots, or thongs, for planting the following year. Above ground the large oval dock-shaped leaves grow to 18in/45cm; as long as they are young they can be used in mixed green salads.

The plant's needs

The only soil in which horse-radish will not grow well is compacted clay, which drains badly. Horse-radish must have fertile well-draining soil, so before planting, dig in well-rotted manure or compost.

Don't consign the bed to a shady part of the garden; growing horse-radish in full sun greatly improves the quality and flavour of the roots.

Growing horse-radish

Either buy roots (thongs) for planting or use root sections lifted and stored from the previous year's crop. In early spring, use a dibbler to make holes in the soil, 8in/20cm deep and 2ft/60cm apart. Drop in a piece of root 6in/15cm long, with the tapering part of the root towards the bottom of the hole. Fill in the holes with soil. Cut a few of the young leaves that sprout from each root to use with salads. In autumn, lift all the plants, storing the roots in boxes of sand in a cool but frost-free place.

Because of the depth of its roots, horse-radish is not for container growing.

Pests and diseases: horse radish

Seldom give trouble.

USING HORSE-RADISH

The impact of horse-radish comes from the essential oils it gives off when it is grated. Place some freshly grated horse-radish under your nose and the effect is similar to smelling salts. Cook it and all that is lost, so horse-radish must be used raw.

To make horse-radish sauce, grate a root – the outer part has more flavour than the central core. Mix it with sour or fresh single cream, seasoned with salt and pepper. A few drops of white wine vinegar can also be added.

Horse-radish can be preserved by cutting the root into slices and drying them in the oven at the lowest possible setting for about 20 minutes.

HYSSOP
(Hyssopus officinalis)

The rather bitter mint taste of the perennial hyssop may account for its culinary unpopularity, but on appearance alone it is worth a place in the herb garden or a perennial border. It forms a small dense shrub, growing to 18in/45cm, the stems covered their whole length with small strap-shaped dark-green semi-evergreen leaves. From early to late summer there are successions of bright-blue flowers, which attract bees in profusion. There are also forms with pink and white flowers. Plants can be kept under control by pruning, or clipped to form a low hedge around the herb garden.

The plant's needs

Hyssop will grow in any type of soil but does best in light chalky soil. It must be fertile and well draining, so dig in well-rotted manure before planting out. Replace plants every three to four years.

Sowing and growing

In spring, sow seed in drills ½in/1.25cm deep. Thin to 3in/7.5cm when seedlings can be handled easily and then to 6in/15cm. Plant out to their final positions 12in/30cm apart in autumn or the following spring, depending how advanced the plants are.

Cut the leaves as they are needed or take a major crop just before the plants come into flower. A second cutting should be possible in late summer. In spring each year, cut back hard to promote bushy growth and pinch out growing tips.

New plants can be raised from seed or from cuttings in spring or in autumn after flowering is over. Take 2in/5cm cuttings of side-shoots, strip away the lower leaves and plant in pots of half sand and half peat.

If taken in spring, plant out in early autumn. Overwinter autumn cuttings in a frame amd plant out in spring.

Growing in containers

In spring, sow four seeds in a 10in/25cm pot of loam compost. Thin to the strongest seedling, leaving one to a pot. Keep well watered always and give a liquid feed every month from early summer to early autumn.

Pests and diseases: hyssop

Seldom give trouble.

USING HYSSOP

Leaves can be dried or frozen. Hyssop can be used in a similar way to mint, but the bitter flavour may not be to everyone's taste. The chopped leaves can be used in salads, soups and stews. They can also be added to stewed fruit, such as apricots.

LOVAGE
(Levisticum officinale)

The yeasty celery flavour of the perennial lovage gives body to soups and stews. The hollow stems can also be candied in the same way as angelica. It is a neglected herb, but it is well worth finding room for a plant or two. Plant at the rear of the herb garden for the hollow stems bearing the dark-green serrated celery-like leaves grow to 4ft/1.2m. Large heads of small green-yellow flowers appear in summer. Pinch them out before they flower if you want plenty of leaves for cutting.

The plant's needs

Lovage will grow in any type of well-draining fertile soil; the deeper it is the better for the large root structure. Dig in plenty of well-rotted manure or compost before planting. A sunny spot would be preferable, although lovage will grow in a slightly shaded position.

Sowing and growing

In early spring, take out a drill ½in/1.25cm deep and sow the seed thinly, covering with a fine sifting of soil. When seedlings can be handled easily, thin to 12in/30cm apart. Plant out to growing positions in autumn or the following spring, spacing plants 24in/60cm apart. If you are growing several plants, they will have to be further thinned to 4ft/1.2m apart, because of their eventual spread. To obtain a copious supply of leaves, remove developing flower stalks.

Alternatively, the plant can be allowed to flower and seed. Gather the seeds when they are still yellow and leave them to dry in the sun for several days.

Pick leaves as required. Cut young stems for candying in late spring, and in autumn cut the stems down to 10in/25cm. To raise new plants, divide the roots in spring. Plant the separated pieces 24in/60cm apart.

Growing in containers

Containers must be at least 12in/30cm across and as deep. In early spring, sow four seeds to a pot and thin to the single strongest. Keep well watered and feed monthly from early summer to autumn. Cut down to 10in/25cm in autumn.

Pests and diseases: lovage

Seldom give trouble.

Marjoram, much used in bouquet garni.

MARJORAM
(Origanum majorana)

Sweet marjoram is a perennial in warm climates but elsewhere is treated as an annual. If treated as an annual, winter supplies can be obtained by taking cuttings in late summer and growing them indoors.

Sweet marjoram grows no more than 12in/30cm tall, making a bushy plant covered with small oval greyish leaves. White to pink flowers appear from early summer to early autumn. Leaves can be gathered as needed or the whole plant cut away at the base after flowering, the stems tied together and dried in a bunch. The leaves are an essential part of bouquet garni.

Pot marjoram, *Origanum onites*, is a hardy perennial with a less subtle flavour than sweet marjoram. Dark-green oval leaves are carried in layers along the length of the stems, 9-12in/22.5-30cm long. Purple-pink flowers appear from summer to late summer. Oregano, or wild marjoram (*Origanum vulgare*) grows to 18in/45cm.

The plant's needs

Marjoram will grow in any type of fertile well-draining soil, preferring quite alkaline soil. All marjorams need to be grown in full sun, and sweet marjoram needs a sheltered position and full sun to bring out the full peppery flavour.

Sowing and growing

Plant sweet marjoram in trays of loam seed

compost in early spring and keep at a temperature of 55°F/13°C. Prick out the seedlings to small pots when they can be handled easily. Harden off, placing them outdoors in a propagator with the vents left open. or covered in plastic bags with holes punched in them. Bring the seedlings in each evening. Plant out in late spring 8in/20cm apart.

Leaves can be picked throughout the summer but they are thought to be at their best just before the flowers open. For winter supplies of leaves, take 2in/5cm cuttings in late summer. Strip off the lower leaves and plant several cuttings in a pot of half peat and half sand. Keep in a warm and sunny place indoors, such as a kitchen window-sill.

In spring, sow seed of wild and pot marjoram in drills ½in/1.25cm deep. Thin to 8in/20cm apart. Plants die back in autumn but if one plant is cut back in late summer it can be potted up and brought indoors. New growth will appear for use in winter months if the plant is kept in a warm sunny spot indoors.

Raise new plants by taking 2in/5cm cuttings in late spring. Plant them in pots of half peat and half sand and keep in a cold frame until rooted. Plant out 8in/20cm apart.

Growing in containers

Sow seed of sweet marjoram as described under *Sowing and growing*, and plant out in late spring in containers of loam compost, spacing plants 6in/15cm apart.

Seeds of wild and pot marjoram can be

> ### *USING LOVAGE*
>
> Leaves can be dried or frozen.
> Candy the stems as for angelica (see page 119). Add the chopped leaves to stews and soups. Try lovage in potato and onion soup. Simmer diced potato and sliced onion in a chicken stock and add a generous helping of chopped fresh or dried lovage leaves. Liquidize and add a little cream.
> Try sprinkling a few lovage seeds over cheese straws before cooking.

sown directly into a container in spring, eight seeds to a 10in/25cm pot. Thin, leaving four of the strongest seedlings evenly spaced. Keep well watered and give a liquid feed to wild and pot marjoram once a month from early summer to early autumn.

Pests and diseases: marjoram

Seldom give trouble.

USING MARJORAM

Leaves can be dried or frozen, but drying preserves and releases a fuller flavour.

Few Italian dishes are complete without marjoram. Sprinkle over pizza, pasta and vegetable stews of courgettes, peppers and tomatoes. Rub over the skin of joints of meat before roasting and insert sprigs of marjoram inside fish before baking. Don't be too heavy-handed with wild and pot marjoram – it can be overpowering.

MINT
(Mentha spicata)

The difficulty with mint is to decide which type to grow and then how to keep it in check as it makes its rampant way across the garden. Spearmint has a strong distinctive flavour, with its narrow, toothed leaves carried on stems up to 18in/45cm. Bowles variety (*Mentha rotundifolia*), growing to 3ft/90cm, looks the most attractive, the rounded leaves covered with a woolly down. Apple mint is smaller-growing, to 18in/45cm, with a mint-apple flavour. For low-growing clumps choose pineapple mint, which has striking, yellow-variegated leaves.

The plant's needs

Mint will grow almost anywhere and in any type of soil. For best results, grow in a fertile and reasonably deep soil for the roots to roam in, and in a slightly shaded part of the garden. Dig in well-rotted manure or compost before planting.

Growing

It is hardly worth the effort of growing mint from seed. Rooted plants are readily available from nurseries and even more from friends eager to press roots on you.

In spring, plant roots 6in/15cm apart and watch the gaps between readily fill as the plants put out underground runners. Stems will be ready for cutting from late spring onwards.

An attractive variegated mint.

As flower-heads develop pinch them out or the quality of the leaves will go downhill rapidly. By early autumn mint is usually looking very sorry for itself. Cut it back to ground level, if it has not died down already.

Growing in containers

Growing mint in a container is an ideal method, as there is no chance of its getting out of control. A deep window box filled with loam compost is a good container. How long the window box should be depends on how much mint you use, but a box 18-24in/45-60cm long with roots planted 4in/10cm apart should provide reasonable supplies.

PESTS AND DISEASES: MINT

Rust, a fungal disease, is likely to be the only problem. Orange or brown markings, the spores of the fungus, appear on the leaves and stems. If the whole bed is riddled with the disease, dig it up and start another bed somewhere else.

USING MINT

Freeze or dry the leaves for use when the bed has died down.

Mint has numerous uses, giving a lift to so many dishes. Cook new potatoes and peas with sprigs of mint, not only for the flavour they impart to the vegetables but for the aroma in the kitchen as they cook. Lamb and mint sauce are inseparable. Chop the mint finely, add a little sugar, moisten with boiling water and then add white wine vinegar – never malt vinegar, which totally destroys the mint flavour.

Add chopped mint leaves to salads, soups, soft cheeses and cool summer drinks.

PARSLEY
(Petroselinum crispum)

There is curly parsley and there is plain-leaved parsley. Northern Europe is the stronghold of curly parsley, but the plain has long been popular in Mediterranean countries and now it is catching on elsewhere. It may not look as attractive as the curly type, but it has one great advantage – a stronger flavour.

Parsley is a biennial, best treated as an annual.

Varieties

The most popular curled varieties are Moss Curled, growing to 8in/20cm, and the smaller Curlina, a compact and bushy plant. Plain-leaved parsley is known as just that; it grows to 18in/45cm.

The plant's needs

Parsley needs a rich moisture-retentive soil. Dig in well-rotted manure or compost before planting. Choose a slightly shaded spot so that there is no danger of the plants drying out, a common cause of failure.

Sowing and growing

An early start can be made by sowing seed in early spring in trays of loam seed compost. Keep in a cool greenhouse, frame or somewhere cool indoors. Seed can take up to five weeks to germinate, so be patient. Thin the seedlings to 3in/7.5cm and then plant out in spring or late spring 6in/15cm apart. Keep picking the leaves one or two from each plant at a time to encourage new growth; never pick a plant bare.

Outdoor sowings can be made from spring onwards in drills ½in/1.25cm deep. Thin seedlings to 3in/7.5cm and finally to 6in/15cm apart. Successional sowings can be made with a final sowing in late summer, but this will have to be protected with cloches. A few plants of curly-leaved varieties can be lifted in late summer and planted in pots to keep indoors over winter.

Growing in containers

Curly-leaved parsley can be grown in parsley pots – tall clay pots with the sides peppered with holes through which the parsley plants grow. They are tricky to plant but can look attractive. Ordinary plant pots are a simpler alternative.

Start the seeds off in trays of loam seed compost, as described under *Sowing and growing*. To transplant to a parsley pot, fill it with loam compost to just below the first layer of holes and carefully insert the roots of one plant through each hole along that layer. Put more compost in the pot, up to the next layer, gently firming the roots of the first layer of plants in the compost. Carry on until the top of the pot is reached with all the holes filled. Plant two or three

seedlings in the soil at the top of the pot.

If you are using ordinary pots transplant five seedlings, equally spaced, to a 10in/25cm pot. Pot-grown parsley must be kept moist at all times; it dries out rapidly.

Pests and diseases: parsley

Seldom give trouble.

> ### USING PARSLEY
>
> Parsley can be dried or frozen. Chopped parsley adds that little bit of extra interest to cooked dishes and vegetables. Sprinkle over soups, sliced tomatoes and vegetables. Coat boiled new potatoes in butter mixed with chopped parsley, or add it to sauté potatoes in the last minute of cooking.
>
> Sprigs of parsley can garnish many dishes to add colour. And don't just leave it on the side of the plate – eat it for its high content of vitamin C and its trace elements. It is one of the healthiest herbs around.

ROSEMARY
(Rosmarinus officinalis)

No herb garden is complete without rosemary. It is a bushy, evergreen perennial shrub that looks and smells attractive in the garden, and smells and tastes good in the dining-room. The stems are covered with narrow lance-shaped grey-green leaves, with clusters

of blue flowers in late spring. Once established, the shrub grows to about 4ft/1.2m with a spread of about 2ft/60m. One named variety 'Severn Sea', which you may be able to track down, stays a more compact 18in/45cm.

The plant's needs

Rosemary will grow in any type of well-draining soil, but does best in a light chalk soil. Lime acid soils to a pH level of about 7. Choose a sunny sheltered part of the garden. Don't plant in frost pockets as rosemary is quite a tender shrub and can be killed off by cold winds and severe frosts.

Sowing and growing

You can buy small plants from a nursery, but it is easy to grow rosemary from seed, even though germination is slow. In spring, take out a drill ½in/1.25cm deep and sow seed thinly. Cover with a fine sifting of soil. Thin seedlings to 2in/5cm when they can be handled easily. Transplant when they are 4in/10cm tall, spacing them 6in/15cm apart. Finally in summer move to their final positions, 3ft/90cm apart. Let the plants become established in their first year, taking no cuttings of leaves at all. A few sprigs can be taken the following year. In later years if you want to dry a fair amount of rosemary, wait until late summer to make a major cut.

New plants can easily be raised from 6in/15cm cuttings taken in early spring or early summer after flowering. Strip off the bottom leaves of the cuttings and insert several in a pot of half peat and half sand. Keep in a cold frame or under a cloche and plant out the following spring. Hardwood cuttings, 8in/20cm long, can be taken in autumn and planted where they are to grow, covered by a cloche during the winter.

Growing in containers

In early spring, sow seed in a pot of loam seed compost. Cover the pot with a plastic bag and keep at a temperature of 60°F/16°C. When the seedlings can be handled easily, prick out to individual 3in/7.5cm pots. As the roots fill the pot, move the plant each spring to a pot 1in/2.5cm larger each time. Keep well watered and feed with a liquid fertilizer monthly from late spring to early autumn.

Growing rosemary in a container may be the only way in areas where there are hard frosts and the plant has to be brought inside in winter. Trim back the stems in late summer, when you take the major cutting for drying, to keep the plant a good shape and size for indoor growing.

Pests and diseases: rosemary

Seldom give trouble.

USING ROSEMARY

Rosemary is better dried than frozen.
It is a herb with a pungent smell and strong taste, so don't be heavy-handed with it. Before roasting lamb, make slits in the skin and insert small sprigs of the herb. Use it to flavour soups and stews.

For a sweet dish, heat but don't boil half a pint of cream and half a pint of milk with sprigs of bruised rosemary. Leave to infuse for about an hour. Remove the rosemary and add 2oz/60g of sugar and two eggs, beating well. Divide the mixture into the necessary number of ramekins. Place them in a baking tray of boiling water to half-way up their sides. Cook them in a cool oven for 45 minutes, until set.

SAGE
(Salvia officinalis)

Many people only use sage in sage and onion stuffing to go with pork. It can be used in other ways, but always with moderation, for the flavour can be overpowering. It grows from 12-24in/30-60cm, and the stems are covered with oval, woolly grey-green leaves. It is perennial and as it grows it tends to sprawl; after about four years, the plants pass their best. Dig them up and replace them.

The plant's needs

Sage grows in any type of well-draining soil, but prefers chalky soils. Lime acid soils to a pH level of about 7. Choose a sunny part of the garden.

Sowing and growing

In early spring, sow seed in trays of loam seed compost and cover lightly with sifted compost. Keep in a cold frame, greenhouse, or cool part of the house. When seedlings can be handled easily, prick out to small individual pots of loam compost. Harden off for a few days before planting out in late spring when all danger of frost is over. Plant out 12in/30cm apart.

Outdoor sowings can be made in spring or late spring, thinning first to 6in/15cm, and finally 12in/30cm. Pick the leaves as required, making a major cutting for drying just before plants come into flower. After flowering, give the plants a light trim to encourage new growth, and trim regularly to keep their shape.

Growing in containers

Start off plants from seed as already described. Transplant three small plants, equally apart, to a 10in/25cm pot of loam compost. Keep well watered and give a liquid feed once a month from late spring to early autumn. Trim regularly for new growth and shape.

Pests and diseases: sage

Seldom give trouble.

USING SAGE

The leaves of sage should be dried.
Make sage and onion stuffing, combining one chopped onion, two chopped sage leaves, breadcrumbs, seasoning and butter to hold it all together. Stuff the meat with it or bake it separately in the oven for about 30 minutes. Sage can also be added to onion sauce to serve with pork or goose. Combine a little sage with cottage or cream cheese, or add small quantities to soups (tomato in particular) or stews.

SALAD BURNET
(Sanguisorba minor)

This is a cucumber-flavoured herb much favoured for use in salads and cold drinks, such as claret cup. It makes a compact bushy plant, growing to 12in/30cm, with serrated leaflets and small rounded heads of green flowers, turning reddish-brown, from early to late summer. It is perennial but does not die down completely in winter.

The plant's needs

Salad burnet will grow in any type of well-draining soil, but does better in light soils, including chalk. Choose a sunny part .

Sowing and growing

In early spring or spring, sow the seed thinly in ½in/1.25cm drills. Cover with a light sifting of soil. When seedlings are well established with several true leaves and can be handled easily, transplant to their final growing positions, 12in/30cm apart. Pick a few leaves as they are needed or make major cuts periodically to freeze the leaves. When the first flower-heads appear, pinch them out so that the plant concentrates its energy on producing leaves. This is the time to take the first major crop of the leaves, cutting the stems back by about ½-6in/1.25-15cm. Make two further cuts, reducing the stems to 6in/15cm each time.

Growing in containers

In early spring or spring, plant four seeds to an 8in/20cm pot of loam compost. Thin, leaving only the strongest single seedling.

Pests and diseases: salad burnet

Seldom give trouble.

USING SALAD BURNET

Freeze the leaves — drying is not always successful.
The cucumber-flavoured leaves, with a nutty aftertaste, are an excellent addition to cold drinks, such as claret cup. Bruise the leaves to release the flavour. Use them chopped finely in salads or add them to mayonnaise or oil dressings. Soups are improved with the addition of a few leaves while they are being cooked.

SORREL
(Rumex acetosa)

French sorrel is almost a weed, a relative of the dock, but its lemon-flavoured, bitter leaves can be used to make excellent soup as well as to flavour other dishes. It is perennial, grows to 2ft/60cm, has arrow-shaped leaves and bears reddish-green flowers from late spring to summer. However, the flowering stems should be removed to prevent the leaves from becoming tough.

The plant's needs

Sorrel grows in any type of soil, and particularly well in light acid soils. It will grow in full sun or part shade in a sheltered part of the garden.

Sowing and growing

In spring, take out a drill ½in/1.25cm deep and sow seed thinly. When the seedlings can be handled easily, thin them to 6in/15cm and then to 10in/25cm apart. Cut out flower stems as they develop in order to encourage new leaf growth. In the first year, take cuttings of leaves from summer onwards, but in following years the best-flavoured leaves will be those gathered early in spring. Clumps can be divided in spring or autumn for new plants.

Growing in containers

In spring, sow a few seeds in a 10in/25cm container of loam compost. Thin seedlings to 6in/15cm apart, removing the weakest. Keep well watered and apply a liquid feed every month from late spring to early autumn. Replace plants after three years.

USING SORREL

Leaves can be dried or frozen.
  Serve sorrel purée with veal or fish. Cook 4oz/125g of finely chopped sorrel leaves gently in a little melted butter for about two minutes. Add salt, pepper, a little nutmeg and cream or milk if wished. Liquidize.
  To make sorrel soup, simmer sliced onion and diced potato in chicken stock until soft. Add 4oz/125g of sorrel and liquidize. Add cream before serving.
  Roughly slice young and tender leaves and add them to green salad.

Winter Savory, a distinctive taste.

SUMMER SAVORY
(Satureia hortensis)
WINTER SAVORY
(Satureia montana)

Summer savory is a hardy annual with a peppery taste. It is a rather sprawling plant, the 12in/30cm stems sparsely covered with narrow lance-shaped leaves. The pink-mauve flowers that open in summer are very attractive to bees.
  The leaves of winter savory have an even stronger peppery taste. This is a perennial that makes a more compact shrubby plant, growing to 12in/30cm, with lance-shaped grey-green leaves. Pink to violet flowers open from summer to early autumn.

The plant's needs

Summer savory grows in any type of soil, but best in light sandy soil. Winter savory grows well in alkaline soils, so acid soils should be limed for a pH level of about 7. Both need full sun.

Sowing and growing

In spring or late spring, take out a drill ½in/1.25cm deep. Sow the seed of both types thinly and cover lightly with soil. When seedlings are about 2in/5cm tall thin to 6in/15cm. Pick the leaves as they are needed. Cut back stems of winter savory to 4in/10cm in spring each year. Make another sowing of summer savory in late summer in a tray of loam seed compost. Prick out into 3in/7.5cm pots when they can be handled easily, and bring indoors for winter use.
  Plants of winter savory can be divided in early spring or 3in/7.5cm cuttings can be taken in late spring and planted where they are to grow.

Growing in containers

In spring, sow seeds of both types in a tray of loam seed compost. Prick out seedlings to individual 3in/7.5cm pots. In early summer, transplant summer savory to 10in/25cm containers of loam compost, spacing five plants at equal distances. Transplant three plants of winter savory to a similar-sized container of loam compost.

Pests and diseases: summer and winter savory

Seldom give trouble.

USING SAVORY

Leaves can be dried or frozen.
  Sprigs of savory can be used like mint when cooking peas and beans, but be sparing, especially when using winter savory. A little can be added to stuffings for meat, or to soups, especially bean or lentil ones.

SWEET BAY
(Laurus nobilis)

Sweet bay is one of the herbs that makes a good decorative shrub as well as a provider of strongly aromatic – almost bitter – leaves for cooking. The shrubs grow to 12ft/3.6m if allowed to, but they are best trained to a rather formal shape, a pyramid or a rounded head, and kept at a more manageable 6ft/1.8m. The oval dark-green glossy leaves have grey-green undersides. To release the pungent aroma and flavour for cooking, tear round the edges of the leaves.

The plant's needs

Sweet bay will grow in all types of well-draining soil. Plant in a sheltered sunny spot. It will survive the occasional light frost, but anything more will damage it or even kill it. In areas prone to frost grow a bay tree in a container so that it can be taken inside in winter.

Growing bay

Start with a young bush bought from a

Sweet Bay – useful and attractive.

nursery or a garden centre. The best time of the year to plant is early spring or spring so that it has the summer to become established. The natural shape of the bay is a pyramid and it is easy to retain that outline. In late summer, simply cut back new shoots to the desired shape.

If you want to train a standard bay – a ball of foliage perched on a tall stem – start with a shrub 4ft/1.2m high. In early summer, pinch out the leaves at the top of the main stem. Shoots growing from the main stem should be pruned back to three leaves – the beginning of the ball shape. The following year, in early summer, prune to 6in/15cm the shoots covering the top 18-24in/36-60cm of the stem. Any shoots below these should be pruned back to three leaves. In the following early summer, prune the top growth to five leaves and remove completely all the lower shoots. In later years, prune lightly to keep the ball shape.

New shrubs can be raised by taking 4in/10cm cuttings with a heel in early autumn. Dip cuttings in hormone rooting powder and plant them in a cold frame in a mixture of half peat and half sand. In the

following spring, transplant rooted cuttings to individual pots of loam compost. Plant out to final positions in autumn.

Growing in containers

Transfer a newly bought shrub to a pot 2in/5cm larger in diameter than the one in which it was growing originally, using loam compost. Pot-on every other year, or when the roots have filled the pot, increasing the diameter of the pot by 2in/5cm each time until 18in/45cm is reached. You can pot-on to a larger container – a wooden tub, for example – if you are training the bay to a ball shape and want to underplant with small herbs.

PESTS AND DISEASES: SWEET BAY

Diseases are seldom a problem.

Pests
Scale insects can be a nuisance. They are small, brown semi-circular, hard-coated insects that cling to the undersides of leaves and stems, often difficult to spot until they are well established. They suck sap, reducing the vigour of the shrub. Spray with malathion, or for bad infestations the systemic insecticide dimethoate. A spray of fatty-acid soaps is more organically acceptable, but regular treatment will be needed for these determined and persistent insects.

USING BAY

Dry the leaves. They are often used in marinades with meat – boeuf bourguignon is a prime example. See *Onions*, page 91.

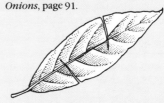

Before adding bay leaves to the liquid, tear the leaves to release the aroma and flavour. Bay is an essential ingredient of bouquet garni – a mixture of parsley, thyme, marjoram and bay. Add the leaves to stock when poaching fish or when French roasting chicken in stock.

SWEET CICELY
(Myrrhis odorata)

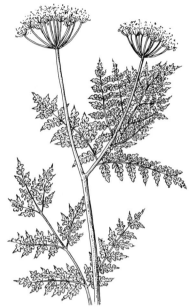

Sweet cicely is one of the decorative perennial herbs that can be grown either in the working herb garden or a flower border. The large fernlike light-green leaves are carried on hollow stems that eventually grow to 5ft/1.5m, but not for several years. The clustered heads of white flowers are borne in profusion from early summer to summer, but you will have to sacrifice the flower-heads if you want a plentiful supply of leaves.

The plant's needs

Any type of soil is suitable, but there are particularly good results on chalk. Grow in partial shade if possible. Keep moist at all times, especially if the plant is grown in full sun.

Sowing and growing

In early spring or spring, take out a drill ½in/1.25cm deep and sow seed thinly. (But seed sown in autumn often germinate more efficiently after a winter freezing.) Thin seedlings to 6in/15cm apart and transplant to final positions 18in/45cm apart. Plants die down in late autumn but by late winter or early spring they should reappear. Pick the leaves as required and remove flower-heads. This limits the spread of self-sown seed that can become a nuisance. Plants can be divided in autumn, spacing them 18in/45cm apart.

Growing in containers

In spring or late autumn, sow six seeds to an 8in/20cm pot of loam compost. Remove the weakest seedlings, leaving one seedling to a pot. Keep well watered and give a liquid feed every month from late spring to early autumn. Pot-on to a larger container in spring as the roots fill the pot.

Pests and diseases: sweet cicely

Seldom give trouble.

USING SWEET CICELY

The large leaves of sweet cicely are difficult to dry, so try freezing instead. Use this herb to flavour fruit and alcoholic drinks – it gives a delicate sweet aniseed flavour – and to enhance the flavours of soups and stews. Add a leaf or two to such fruits as rhubarb, gooseberries and currants to reduce the acidity and help to sweeten them.

TARRAGON
(Artemisia dracunculus)

Seed of French tarragon is rarely available because plants seldom produce fertile seed. Instead, plants are obtained from cuttings or division. Beware of being palmed off with Russian tarragon, (*Artemisia dracunculoides*), which has an inferior flavour. Check carefully. This perennial herb grows to about 2ft/60cm, the stems bearing narrow, pointed dark-green leaves. The green-white flowers cluster on the end of the stems, but rarely open fully.

The plant's needs

Grow tarragon in light well-draining soil in a sheltered place in full sun.

Growing

Buy nursery-raised plants in early spring. One or two should be enough to make a start, planted 2ft/60cm apart. (In later years, raise new plants by dividing the underground runners in spring – pulling them apart, not cutting them.) Remove flowering stems as they appear. Pick leaves from late spring to autumn – they have more intense flavour just before the plants come into flower. If most of the leaves begin to fall from late autumn onwards, cut down the stems just above ground level and protect with a mulch of leaf mould or straw.

Growing in containers

Pot-on a newly bought tarragon plant to a container 2in/5cm larger, using loam compost. Move to a larger container in spring as necessary. Cut back the stems to about 2in/5cm above compost level each year in late autumn, and cover with leaf mould or straw. Tarragon thrives in relatively poor soil so restrict liquid feeding to once every two months from late spring to early autumn.

Pests and diseases: tarragon

Seldom give trouble.

USING TARRAGON

Tarragon can be dried, but is more successful frozen.

To the French, tarragon goes naturally with chicken. Add chopped tarragon to some water and poach chicken pieces in it. When the chicken is tender, thicken the juices with two egg yolks, cream and a little more chopped tarragon. Serve the sauce hot or cold with the chicken.

Make your own tarragon vinegar by adding a few sprigs to white wine vinegar and leaving it to stand for about two weeks.

THYME
(Thymus vulgaris)

Thyme is a must for the kitchen garden. It takes up little room but provides distinctive flavouring for all types of soups, stews, sauces and stuffings.

It is an evergreen perennial that forms a bushy low-growing plant, up to 12in/30cm, with closely packed grey-

PRESERVING HERBS

Drying leaves

In general, the younger the shoots of herbs when picked the better, but each entry advises which is the best time. Pick the stems when they are completely dry, remove damaged parts, tie into bunches and wash them in hot water. Spread the stems out on absorbent kitchen paper to dry out but keep them out of the sun.

The herbs can then be spread out on a tray and kept in a warm dark place, such as an airing cupboard, and left there for two or three days, turning twice a day. Alternatively, the herbs can be tied into small bunches again and hung in a darkened but airy room for about a week.

The quickest, but trickiest, way is to dry them in an oven, but the oven must not get too hot. Place a muslin cloth loosely on a baking tray and spread the herbs over it. Heat the oven to no more than 70-90°F/21-33°C and leave the oven door open while the herbs are drying. Leave them in the oven for an hour, turning once. This way, though the quickest, often reduces the strength of the flavour.

After drying, crumble the leaves between your fingers and store in screw-top jars in the dark.

Freezing leaves

This method preserves flavour and colour, but leaves herbs limp after defrosting. To freeze, wash and dry the herbs; put them into plastic bags and label clearly before placing them in the freezer. Herbs that are used finely chopped can be chopped before freezing. Wash, dry and chop them and pack them in ice-cube trays. Fill up with water and freeze. When the cubes are frozen, turn them out into plastic bags and return to the freezer. They can be added to soups and stews without defrosting.

In fact, no herb requires defrosting if it is being added to a hot cooked dish. You will also find it easier to chop many herbs in their frozen state.

green leaves covering the length of the stems. In early summer, there are small pink to mauve flowers which, though attractive, should be removed to encourage leaf growth.

Lemon thyme, *Thymus × citriodorus*, has a more subtle lemon flavour, generally considered superior to that of common thyme.

The plant's needs

Thyme grows in any type of well-draining soil but a neutral soil suits it best.

Sowing and growing

In spring or late spring, take out drills ½in/1.25cm deep. Sow the seeds thinly and cover with a fine sifting of soil. When the seedlings are large enough to handle, thin to 2in/5cm. Plant to final growing positions in early autumn, spacing 12in/30cm apart. Pick some leaves as required, but wait until the following spring before making the first cutting for drying, which is best done just before the plant comes into flower. (But there will probably always be some fresh thyme available.) Cut back stems to 4in/10cm each autumn.

After three or four years plants are past their best and should be replaced. In late spring, take 2in/5cm cuttings of lateral shoots with a heel. Insert the cuttings in pots of half sand and half loam. Transplant to their final positions in early autumn, 12in/30cm apart. Plants can also be divided in spring or late spring.

Growing in containers

In spring or late spring, sow seed in trays of loam seed compost. Thin to 2in/5cm when the seedlings can be handled easily. Transplant four plants to a 10in/25cm container, spacing them equally. Keep them well watered and apply a liquid feed monthly during the summer months.

Pests and diseases: thyme

Seldom give trouble.

USING THYME

Thyme, together with parsley and bay, is one of the essential ingredients of bouquet garni, used as flavouring in so many dishes. Common thyme is used in stuffings to go with pork and poultry and countless soups and stews. Simmer diced carrot, parsnip, sliced onion, pearl barley and thyme to make a delicious winter soup.

Use sprigs of lemon thyme to stuff gutted trout before baking.

SOFT FRUIT

Commerce has been the greatest influence on soft-fruit growing in recent years. Plant breeders have succeeded in improving the flavour, appearance and size of the fruits, but commercial growers have been looking for fruit that travels well, and as a result have often neglected the flavour. Strawberries, in particular, have suffered.

Raspberries have been less affected, probably because they are nowhere near as popular, and profitable, as strawberries. However, there are many people who think that raspberries are far superior to strawberries, especially since their reliability and quality have been greatly improved. Certainly flavour rarely disappoints. Yields have increased dramatically, with larger crops from smaller canes, ideal for restricted gardens.

The development of spineless blackberry varieties, which make commercial harvesting so much simpler, is also welcome for the home grower. The blackberry's sprawling habit has also been curbed, so even small gardens can find room for the new compact bushes.

There have been great advances with new black currant varieties. They are far less likely to be killed off by late frosts, having been bred to flower later and to have greater frost resistance.

Gooseberries have been left alone for decades, neglected even, and therefore have suffered less from dubious improvements than other soft fruits. Fortunately, recent efforts have been aimed at improving the size and taste of the berries, and the health of the plants rather than their travelling qualities.

BLUEBERRY
(Vaccinium corymbosum)

Blueberries, Blue Crop variety.

The blueberry has long been enjoyed in America – hence the expression 'as American as blueberry pie' – but until recently gardeners elsewhere who wanted to grow this delicious fruit could count the varieties available on the fingers of one hand. Now, just as the fruit's popularity has spread outside America, the choice of varieties has increased.

The bushes, which may grow to 6ft/1.8m with a spread of about 3ft/90cm, are decorative as well as productive and look equally at home in a shrub border as in a vegetable garden. The dark-green leaves, with lighter shading on the upper surface, change in autumn to beautiful reds and golds. In spring, there is a good show of clusters of white, bell-shaped flowers tinged with pink. The fruits are blue-black with a waxy bloom.

Bushes are usually sold in containers and they are as easy to grow that way as in the garden. Varieties are said to be self-fertile so that a single bush should produce a strong crop. However, for the best results plant two different varieties that will pollinate each other.

Varieties

Reliable, old-established varieties include Jersey with large, almost black fruit, cropping towards the latter part of late summer; Coville, which ripens a little earlier; and Herbert, a variety with exceptional flavour, fruiting at the same time.

Some of the newer varieties are Patriot, which ripens towards the end of summer, the earliest of all; Grover, fruiting in the early part of late summer; Heerma 1, with crops of small berries and reckoned to have strong resistance to disease; Dixi, which crops late in the season; Blue Crop, with yields of sweet berries; and Berkley, with large, full-flavoured fruits.

The plant's needs

For best results, blueberries must be grown in an acid soil. If your soil is not acid, the easiest solution is to prepare pockets of slightly acid soil where the bushes are to be planted. Choosing a sunny but sheltered spot, dig holes 18-24in sq/45-60cm sq to a depth of 18in/45cm and 5ft/1.5m apart. Mix half the soil taken out with an equal amount of peat and fill the holes with the mixture. The soil left over can be moved to another part of the garden.

Growing

Remove the young bushes from their containers and plant them 5ft/1.5m apart at any time between autumn and early spring when the weather is suitable and the ground not frozen. Each year in spring apply a mulch of peat round the base of each bush and feed with an all-purpose fertilizer. Make sure the ground is moist all through the summer or else the crop may be disappointing.

Berries should be ready for picking from summer onwards. When the berries have turned blue, leave them for a further week before picking so that they ripen fully to their rich sweet flavour. It may be necessary to net the bushes: birds find the fruit very tempting.

Young bushes will probably not need pruning for two or three years after planting. After that, they should have a little pruning, but only to remove old wood. Cut off this old wood just above ground level, leaving the new young shoots.

Growing in containers

Newly bought containerized bushes should be potted-on in early spring to a pot 2in/5cm larger in diameter, using an acid rhododendron compost. Thereafter, potting-on will only be necessary every two or three years. Each time this is carried out, in spring, increase the diameter of the container by 2in/5cm until it has reached 15in/37.5cm. After that, remove the top 4in/10cm of compost each year in early spring and replace it with fresh compost. Every year in early spring also apply fertilizer. Prune in winter as required. Keep the bushes well watered at all times, especially in periods of warm weather.

Pests and diseases: blueberry

Seldom a problem.

COOKING AND FREEZING BLUEBERRIES

It is not mandatory to eat blueberries in a pie. They can be gently stewed in just enough water to cover them, with sugar and a little lemon juice. Serve with cream.

For blueberry pie, place the fruit in a pie dish, sprinkle with sugar and cover with short-crust pastry. Bake for about 30 minutes.

Blueberries make an excellent contrast to a sweet/sour cheesecake base. Simmer the berries in a little water (even less than for stewed berries), with sugar and lemon juice. Make a base for the cheesecake with crushed wholemeal biscuits and melted butter and line a flan dish with it. Blend cottage cheese and cream cheese together and work in a mixture of egg yolks, sugar and gelatine dissolved in water. Fold in beaten egg whites and spoon into the flan dish. Leave in the refrigerator for two hours and then cover with the thick blueberry mixture. Alternatively, blend the cottage cheese and cream cheese and work in sugar and egg yolks only. Cook for about 30 minutes. Leave to cool and then spread on the blueberry topping.

BLACKBERRY
(Rubus ulmifolius)

LOGANBERRY
(Rubus loganobaccus)

Blackberries used to have one big disadvantage – the spines that made picking them so hazardous. That has become a thing of the past with the arrival of spineless varieties. (However, for those who believe that blackberries and spines are inseparable, there are still plenty of spiny varieties around and many of them produce excellent fruits.)

There have been other important changes. You no longer need to have plants that sprawl in all directions (though you still can if you want) for there are new varieties that are erect and compact. These space-saving plants are excellent for small gardens and for growing in containers. Varieties have been bred for disease resistance, and most of the new hybrids should be largely virus-free.

Loganberries, a cross between blackberry and raspberry, were also originally plagued with spines but new spineless varieties have been developed. They have deep-red juicy fruits with a sharp flavour, and are virus-free.

One of the newest fruits is the tayberry, another blackberry-raspberry cross, with deep-purple fruit and a distinctive flavour.

Varieties

Blackberry Bedford Giant is one of the old-established varieties, full of spines, but producing large sweet berries in late summer. Even spinier, and recommended only for very large gardens, Himalayan Giant crops very heavily from late summer to autumn. Ashton Cross, developed from wild blackberries, has possibly the best flavour, fruiting in late summer and early autumn.

Of the many thornless varieties the most popular are Oregon Thornless, with attractive foliage and large berries from early autumn, and Merton Thornless, which crops at the same time. Merton Thornless is a compact grower, suitable for small gardens or for container growing. Smoothstem needs a sunny spot to grow the best crops of its early autumn berries. Thornfree should crop heavily in the latter part of early autumn and into autumn.

Loganberry LY 59 is a thorny strain, cropping well with large conical-shaped fruit. LY 654 is spineless. Both are developed from a virus-free strain.

Tayberry The virus-free Medana Tayberry has large fruits ripening in summer.

The plant's needs

Although blackberries will ripen without much sun, crops will be better if there is a reasonable amount. Choose a sheltered part of the garden, especially for loganberries and tayberries. Blackberries seem capable of surviving in the poorest soils, but give them the best possible start by digging in plenty of well-rotted manure or compost. Acid soils should be limed before planting to a pH level of 6.

Growing

Plant thornless blackberries, loganberries and tayberries 8ft/2.4m apart and spiny blackberries 10ft/3m apart, except Himalayan Giant which needs 15ft/4.5m between plants. Although planting can be done at any time between late autumn and early spring – as long as the ground is not frozen – the best time is late autumn. Dig a hole for each plant a few inches larger than the root ball so that the roots can be spread out. Plant at the same level as they were growing originally (the soil mark will show it). Firm down the soil around the plant and prune all canes back to 9in/22.5cm.

The canes must be supported as they grow, otherwise they will trail along the ground, making the fruit dirty and difficult to pick. If the canes are to be trained against a wall, attach plastic netting or rows of galvanized wire to the wall to a height of 6ft/1.8m, for the canes to ramble over.

If grown in the open, a strong wire fence is needed. It must be able to support the fruiting canes (those that grew the previous year) and the new canes, which will be the following year's canes. Drive stout posts into the ground at intervals of about 6-8ft/1.8-2.4m along the row where the canes are being planted, so that they stand 6ft/1.8m above soil level. Starting half-way up the posts, run wires between them at 12in/30cm intervals.

To make life easier when picking and to make an attractive display, train the fruiting canes in the form of a fan. This can be done whether the canes are grown against a wall or alongside a fence. First train them upwards and then to the left and right, along the wires or through the netting.

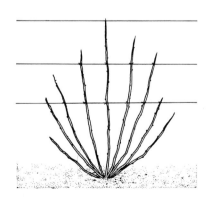

During the summer the plant will also be growing new canes from the centre of the plant for the next year's fruiting. Don't fan these out but tie them together and secure them vertically to the wires. Once the fan-

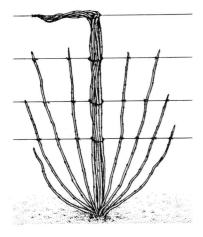

trained canes have fruited, they are cut down and the new canes are untied and trained in their place.

Instead of being fan-trained, the canes can be woven up and down between the wires.

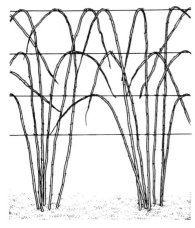

In spring, feed the plants with all-purpose general fertilizer and apply a mulch of well-rotted manure or compost around the base of each plant. This will provide valuable food and help to conserve moisture. Lack of water not only affects the current crop but also the development of new canes.

Tayberries are the first to fruit – in summer – and blackberries and loganberries fruit from late summer. Loganberries will crop for two to three weeks, but blackberries will fruit for up to six weeks. Pick the berries when they are dry.

After stripping all the canes of fruit, prune the plants at ground level, leaving behind all the year's new growth. Train the new canes against the supporting framework, but in cold areas it is better to leave them tied together and fan them out the following late winter or early spring. Any cane tips that have died back should be pruned to the first dormant bud.

Propagating

It is easy to raise new plants by layering. In late summer, select a cane of that year's growth and bury 6in/15cm of the tip in a hole, resting on a mixture of sand and

peat. Cover with soil and weight down the cane with a stone to prevent the tip from springing out of the ground. By spring the

tip should have rooted. Sever it from the cane at about 8in/20cm above the point where it enters the soil. Lift and plant out.

Growing in containers

The new compact varieties are suitable for container growing. Plant the newly bought cane in a pot 2in/5cm larger in diameter than the root ball, using quality loam potting compost. Pot on every two or three years increasing the size of the container by 2in/5cm each time until you reach the maximum manageable size of 18in/45cm. After that remove the top 4in/10cm of compost each year and replace it with fresh. Give a feed of general fertilizer each year in early spring. Train and care for the canes as already described. Keep the compost well watered at all times, especially in warm weather. Container plants are vulnerable, because shortage of water will reduce fruit yield and growth of new canes.

PESTS AND DISEASES

Diseases are seldom a problem.

Pests
Raspberry beetle may attack blackberries. The eggs, laid in the centre of the flowers, develop into grubs that burrow into the developing fruit, rendering it inedible. When the flowers first open, spray blackberries with malathion or the more organically acceptable derris. Spray loganberries and tayberries when flowering is well advanced and again as the fruit colours.

Aphids can also be a nuisance, spreading viral diseases among the canes. Spray with derris.

COOKING AND FREEZING

Round off late-summer Sunday lunches with blackberry-and-apple pie. Rinse the blackberries and peel, core and slice the apple. Fill a pie dish with the fruit; sprinkle with sugar and add a little water. Cover with short crust or puff pastry and bake for 30 minutes.

Blackberries poached in a little water for about five minutes are delicious on their own. Serve with cream.

Loganberries and tayberries are ruined by cooking. Serve them as they are, sprinkled with sugar if necessary.

All can be frozen just as they are off the cane. Don't wash them first or they will be mushy when thawed.

GOOSEBERRY
(Rubus grossularia)

The 1800s were the big time for gooseberries, with new varieties coming thick and fast. Then the decline set in and the poor gooseberry has never fully recovered its popularity. Compared with other soft fruits gooseberry varieties were reasonably disease-resistant, so there was no great urge to make them more immune through the development of new varieties.

However, the gooseberry is now on the up again and the plant breeders are at work producing bigger, tastier and even healthier gooseberries. Not that anyone can guarantee absolute freedom from disease as long as aphids exist. They are the major carriers of disease from plant to plant, and there is always a chance that they will introduce viral and other diseases (mildew especially) from other non disease-free stock.

As well as being more resistant to disease, new varieties will ripen earlier and produce larger berries of a better colour and improved flavour. The gooseberry deserves its comeback.

For the smaller garden, space-saving cordon gooseberries can be grown against a sunny wall. Some varieties are available as half standards, which can be grown in containers.

Varieties

The oldest varieties include Lancashire Lad, with red fruits; Whitesmith, with large white well-flavoured fruits; Whinhams Industry, with sweet dark-red fruits; Leveller, the sweet dessert gooseberry with large yellow berries; and May Duke, another dark-red berry that can be eaten raw when fully ripened.

Invicta is a new variety resistant to mildew, with well-shaped and well-flavoured berries. It makes an excellent shape when grown as a bush, and is equally good as a cordon. Jubilee is another disease-free variety with early-maturing, large yellow fruits. Pick them at that stage for cooking, or leave them on the bush to ripen and eat as dessert berries. Achilles can also be grown for cooking or eating raw later. Black Velvet is a hybrid gooseberry with rich dark-red fruits. Grow it as a bush, cordon or half standard in a container.

The plant's needs

Choose a sunny site with some shelter from battering winds and frost. Prepare

Gooseberry, Whinhams Industry variety.

the soil by digging in well-rotted manure or compost in early autumn. Gooseberries will grow in all types of well-draining soil, but loam gives the most successful results. They prefer a somewhat acid soil, with a pH level of 6 to 6.5.

Growing

Bushes can be planted between late autumn and early spring, but planting is best done at the start of this period in order to give them time to settle down before starting into growth in spring. Make holes a little larger than the root ball so that there is room to spread the roots when planting. Plant bushes 5ft/1.5m apart; single cordons 1ft/30cm apart; double cordons 2ft/60cm apart; and triple cordons 3ft/90cm apart.

Cordons can be planted and secured either against sunny walls or in the open if given support. Drive two stout posts into the soil so that they stand 4ft/1.2m above ground. Fix wires horizontally between the posts, one 2ft/60cm from the ground and the other near the top of the posts. Secure canes vertically to the wires at the recommended planting distances for the cordons to grow up.

Make sure that bushes and cordons are

planted at the same level as they were previously. Each year apply a mulch of well-rotted manure or compost round the base of the plant to provide nourishment and to help to keep down weeds. Avoid hoeing round bushes as this can damage roots near the surface. In each spring apply a high potash fertilizer around each bush or cordon.

Early varieties will be ready for picking in summer, and the season lasts until late summer.

Pruning bushes

The aim in pruning a gooseberry bush is to achieve open growth in the centre of the plant. The berries will then ripen more readily, be easier to pick, and the bush will be more open to the sun and air. Pruning is usually done in early winter unless birds start to eat the young buds, in which case pruning can be delayed until spring.

The stems of young bushes should be cut back by half or up to three-quarters to an upward-growing bud. This encourages an upward, cup-shaped growth instead of a sprawling, spreading growth. By pruning time the following year, the bushes should have about eight prominent stems. Prune the main stems by half, again to upward-facing buds. Any shoots growing near the base of the bush should be cut away completely.

Each year after that, prune back any side-shoots to within about 1in/2.5cm of the main branches, leaving a bud. Take care to remove growths from the centre of the plant to keep it open.

Pruning cordons and standards

Cordons need different pruning and at different times of the year. In early summer, prune all the side-shoots back to five leaves. The leading stem is left until it is the height you want. In early winter, again

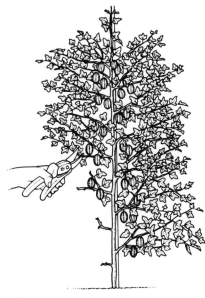

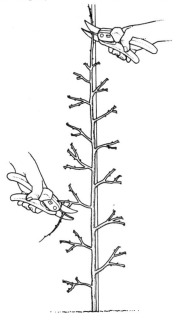

prune the side-shoots back to three buds and remove growth on the leading stem by a third – leaving 6-10in/15-25cm of that

year's growth. When the leading stem has finally reached the required height, prune the side-shoots back to four leaves in summer and one bud in winter.

Gooseberries grown as standards need the same treatment as the bushes, but it is more important to keep the cup shape if they are to continue looking attractive.

Propagating

New plants can be raised from cuttings in early autumn or autumn. Take 12in/30cm cuttings of the current year's growth, preferably with a heel. Remove all but the top four buds, and plant the cuttings 6in/15cm deep in a shallow trench. Leave them there all through the following year and they will be ready to plant out in spring.

Single cordons are trained by cutting back all but the strongest branches to the main stem. For double cordons, select the two strongest branches, cutting back all the rest. Train each branch along a cane pushed into the soil at a 30° angle. When each branch is between 3-6in/7.5-15cm long, start training it upwards.

Growing in containers

The best plants for containers are those grown as standard bushes. Pot-on newly purchased bushes to a container 2in/5cm larger in diameter, using loam potting compost. Thereafter pot-on every two or three years in spring when roots can be seen near the surface of the compost, until a 15in/37.5cm container has been reached. Then each spring remove the top 4in/10cm of compost and replace with fresh, taking care not to damage the roots. Also each spring feed with a high potash fertilizer and give monthly liquid feeds of general fertilizer. Keep the plants well watered at all times, especially in warm weather. Prune to shape as with bush plants. In all but mild areas protect the roots from frost by wrapping the container in plastic bubble sheeting. It may look ugly, but it should save the bush.

PESTS AND DISEASES: GOOSEBERRY

Pests
Aphids are the biggest nuisance, stunting the growth of bushes. Spray with malathion, or the more organically acceptable pyrethrum.

Caterpillars usually appear in late spring or early summer, after the gooseberries have flowered. They can strip the plants of new leaves. Spray with malathion or derris.

Diseases
Gooseberry mildew is the worst disease, and is spread by aphids. White powdery deposits appear on the leaves and berries, turning brown and felty. Cut out and burn badly affected branches. Spray regularly with benomyl or dinocap. Instead of a chemical spray, a solution of washing soda sprayed at regular intervals should keep the disease at bay. Spray first in spring and then at monthly intervals.

COOKING AND FREEZING GOOSEBERRIES

Fully ripened gooseberries are sweet enough to eat as they come off the bush. Just top, tail and wash them. Green gooseberries have to be cooked. Sprinkle them with sugar and just cover with water. Simmer gently for five to ten minutes. Watch them carefully as they quickly disintegrate.

Gooseberry fool has a delicious sharp taste, an ideal pudding for summer. Cook the gooseberries, as

above, liquidize the fruit and juice, chill and stir in thick cream.

Or make a gooseberry sauce to serve with smoked mackerel. Sprinkle sugar over the fruit and add a little water. Simmer until soft and liquidize with a little butter, salt and nutmeg.

To freeze gooseberries top, tail and wash them. Thoroughly dry them before freezing in rigid containers.

CURRANTS
(Ribes family)

Black currants are far more popular than the red and white types, especially since they became an almost legendary source of vitamin C. Probably because of their commercial importance, plant breeders have devoted more time to improving black currants than they have to the reds and whites. The list of improvements is long.

In the past black currants were regarded as tricky to grow in colder areas because flowers were often destroyed by late spring frosts, which drastically reduced the crop. This risk can now be avoided by choosing new varieties that are far more frost-resistant or by planting new varieties that flower later and so avoid the hardest frosts. They are now sold certified free from diseases such as mildew. The fruits are larger and tastier. The bushes crop for longer in the fruiting season and the yields are higher. The bushes of some of the new varieties are more compact, around 3ft/90cm tall, ideal for the labour-saving garden.

Red and white currants, alas, have not been given the same attention as black currants. Commercially they are more difficult to harvest and by the time they get to the shops they are likely to have disintegrated to pulp. These are problems that home growers don't have, of course; they can harvest the currants at their peak, still firm, and enjoy their distinctive tart flavour.

Both red and white currants are sold as cordons as well as bushes, a great advantage for gardeners with little space. Black currants grow in a different way, not from a single stem but from many stems that emerge at ground level, so cannot be trained as cordons.

Varieties

Black currants Of the new varieties, Ben Sarek has been shown to be thoroughly reliable with thick clusters of large full-flavoured berries that ripen early, cropping in summer. The laden branches may need support. It has high frost and disease resistance. Since it stays a compact 3ft/90cm tall, the bushes can be planted closer together, and it is ideal for container growing. Ben More is equally good for frost and disease resistance, with heavy, high quality crops. Ben Lomond has compact growth, crops summer to late summer with sharp acidic berries. Good frost and disease resistance. Malling Jet

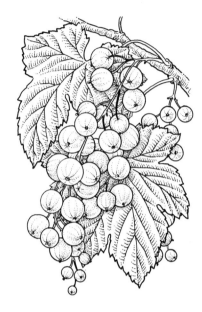

crops late in the season, in late summer. It flowers later as well, thus escaping the worst of the spring frosts. The flavour is not as acidic as other varieties.

Older varieties include Boskoop Giant with large fruits, but fewer to each cluster than the newer varieties. It has a spreading habit, needing plenty of room. Blackdown has large fruits and the bushes have a high resistance to mildew.

Red currants Stanza is the latest red currant success story, with rich dark-red fruits. Late to flower, it avoids the worst of the spring frosts. Ready to pick from the middle of summer. Red Lake crops around the same time, with large sweet fruits. Laxton No. 1 is a heavy early cropper, from the beginning of summer.

White currants White Versailles is one of the most popular and old-established whites. It can be relied upon to produce a heavy crop of sweet berries. White Grape is a later-maturing variety.

The plant's needs

Grow currants in an open but sheltered part of the garden. Although some varieties do have frost resistance, don't tempt providence – avoid any parts of the garden that you know are prone to frost. Currants grow in any type of soil, but the richer the better. In early autumn, dig in manure or compost. Currants prefer a slightly acid soil. The ideal pH level is 6 to 6.5.

Growing

Plant currant bushes in autumn or late autumn so that they have a chance to establish themselves before starting to grow the following spring. Allow 5ft/1.5m between bushes and 6ft/1.8m between rows. The black currant variety Ben Sarek needs less room and can be grown at 3ft/90cm intervals.

Make a hole larger than the soil ball so that the roots can be spread out in the hole. Plant black currants about 1in/2.5cm below the original planting level, and red and white currants at the same level at which they had previously been growing. (You can easily tell the original soil level from the soil mark on the stems.)

Plant cordon red and white currants against a wall or in the open, where they will need support. Single cordons need to be 18in/45cm apart, double cordons 3ft/90cm, and triple cordons 4ft/1.2m apart. Provide support by driving posts firmly into the ground at 6ft/1.8m intervals. The posts must be long enough to leave 6ft/1.8m above the level of the soil. Stretch and fix a wire between the posts 2ft/60cm above the ground, and then at intervals of 2ft/60cm up to the top of the posts. Behind each cordon, tie a cane vertically to the wires for the cordon to grow against.

Immediately after planting, prune the stems of black currant bushes to within 2in/5cm of the soil level. There will be no fruit the following summer, and the bush will concentrate its energies on producing fresh-fruiting stems for the next year. Apply a mulch of compost or well-rotted manure around the base of all currant plants after planting, and then each year in early spring. Avoid hoeing round the plants as this damages the shallow-growing roots. Also in early spring apply a high potash fertilizer.

Pruning

In autumn of the second year, prune any weak shoots of black currants to just above ground level: this should leave most of the shoots intact. Then each year in autumn remove the old dark wood that has just borne fruit, cutting it down to within a few inches of ground level. Leave the lighter-shaded new wood to fruit the following year.

Red and white currant bushes are pruned in early winter, but pruning can be delayed until spring if birds are a nuisance eating the buds. Cut stems by a half to an outward-facing bud. Do this each year, removing half the length of the shoots each

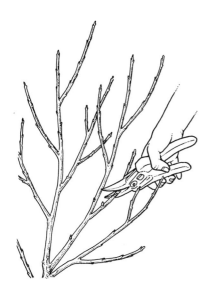

time. Any lateral side growths should be pruned to about 2in/5cm, leaving two buds. Pruning in this way should ensure an open centre to the bush.

Prune cordons of red and white currants in early summer. All the side-shoots should be cut back to four leaves. In early winter, prune back side-shoots to three buds, leaving about 2in/5cm of stem. When the leading branch has reached the desired height, cut back to five leaves in summer and one bud in winter.

Propagating

In early to late autumn, take black currant cuttings of 12in/30cm of that year's growth. Trim the tip and remove all the leaves but not the buds. Reduce the cuttings to 9in/22.5cm, trimming just above a bud at the top and just below at the bottom. Plant them in a trench, leaving two buds showing above the soil. Plant out the following autumn.

Growing in containers

All varieties are suitable for container growing, but the best is Ben Sarek because it is a compact grower. For red currants, choose Stanza and Red Lake, and for white currants, White Versailles.

Move newly bought plants into a container 2in/5cm larger in diameter than the root ball. Use loam potting compost. Pot-on in spring every two or three years, as necessary. It is time to pot-on when the roots are visible near the surface of the compost and they have started to grow through the drainage hole of the pot. The

maximum manageable size for a pot is 18in/45cm and after that, instead of potting-on, remove the top 4in/10cm of the compost and replace it with fresh. Take care not to damage the roots near the surface.

Feed with a high potash fertilizer in spring and then monthly with general fertilizer liquid feed. Keep well watered at all times.

Prune as described for plants growing in the ground.

CURRANT PESTS AND DISEASES

Black currant pests
Aphids will cause the most damage if not controlled, stunting the growth of the bushes. Spray with malathion, the more organically acceptable pyrethrum, or one of the new sprays containing fatty-acid soaps.

Caterpillars find the young leaves irresistible. Spray with malathion or derris.

Black currant diseases
Gooseberry mildew can attack, leaving a white deposit on leaves and fruits. Spray regularly with benomyl or dinocap. Alternatively, spray with a solution of washing soda in early spring and then at monthly intervals.

Reversion disease is spread by gall mites in the buds, which then swell and spread the disease. Dig up and burn infected bushes. Take preventive measures by spraying with lime sulphur when the flowers appear.

Botrytis or grey mould leaves grey mould deposits on fruit. Spray with benomyl when bushes are in flower.

Leaf spot is a fungal disease that covers the leaves with brown or black spots. Spray with benomyl, maneb or zineb.

Red and white currant pests
Aphids and caterpillars can attack. Spray with malathion, pyrethrum or a fatty-acid soap spray.

Red and white currant diseases
Leaf spot can attack. See *Black currant diseases*, above, for treatment.

Coral spot can be a problem. Raised red spots cover dead wood mainly, but the disease can affect new wood. Cut out all diseased wood and then burn it.

COOKING AND FREEZING CURRANTS

Raw black currants are packed with vitamin C, but they are usually too tart to eat raw. Strip the currants from the stalks, add sugar, and simmer in just enough water to cover them for about five minutes; longer and they will collapse. Serve with cream.

Currants are an essential part of summer pudding; the black and white currants especially provide colour contrast with the reds of strawberries and raspberries. Line a pudding basin with slices of stale white bread, with the crusts removed. Gently simmer black, red

and white currants in a little water, with sugar. Drain the fruit and keep the juice. Spoon the currants into the basin along with the raspberries and strawberries. Cover with a layer of bread slices, and put a plate on top, holding it down with a heavy weight. Leave the pudding overnight in the refrigerator. Turn it out and pour the juices over the top.

To freeze currants, strip them from the stalks and pack them into rigid containers just as they are. Don't rinse them because if frozen wet they will be mushy when thawed.

RASPBERRY
(Rubus idaeus)

Raspberries may never replace strawberries as the king of soft fruits, but they are making a spirited challenge. They are not now just a brief summer luxury but can be enjoyed the year round. You can now pick fresh raspberries from the garden in autumn from the increasing number of autumn-fruiting varieties, just as you can fresh strawberries from the Remontant varieties. But the great advantage that the raspberry has over the strawberry is that frozen raspberries, once thawed, are hardly distinguishable from berries picked straight from the canes. They keep their shape as well as their delicious fresh taste.

From the gardener's point of view there are several new reasons for growing raspberries. Recent summer-fruiting varieties crop more heavily on more compact plants, and some are even free of spines. Disease resistance has improved with varieties bred to discourage aphids.

Yellow raspberries have been around for years but have never had the popularity of the luscious red berry. They may have a better chance now that an autumn-fruiting variety has been introduced with sweet berries that freeze well.

Varieties

One of the earliest-ripening varieties is Glen Cova, with large tasty berries in early summer. Glen Moy, a heavy cropper ready at about the same time, is one of the spineless varieties and has aphid and virus resistance. Glen Prosen, also spine-free and disease-resistant, ripens in summer, with improved size of fruit and yield. The latest variety, Malling Joy, has even better resistance to various types of raspberry aphids. It has exceptionally heavy crops from summer through to late summer, and the berries freeze very well. Malling Admiral fruits over the same period. It is resistant to some raspberry diseases but is not as reliable as those vareties already listed. Leo fruits until the end of late summer and sometimes into the beginning of early autumn.

Autumn-fruiting varieties include the new Autumn Bliss, the heaviest cropper, starting in late summer and carrying on into autumn, given good weather. It has good disease resistance. Older autumn varieties include September, fruiting in early autumn; Zeva, carrying on until autumn; and Heritage.

Raspberry, Glen Cova variety.

Old-established yellow-fruiting varieties include Golden Everest and Yellow Antwerp. The latest addition is Fallgold, ripening in early autumn. Its heavy crops of sweet berries are very well suited to freezing.

The plant's needs

Choose a sheltered but sunny part of the garden, although a little light shade for part of the day does no harm. The soil should be fertile and well draining, but moisture-retentive. It is especially important that the soil does not dry out quickly during the summer months when the fruit is developing and ripening. Raspberries will grow in most types of soil, preferring one that is somewhat acid, between pH 6 and 6.5. To improve drainage and fertility, dig in plenty of well-rotted manure or compost in autumn. Dig a trench 2ft/60cm wide and 12in/30cm deep along the rows where the raspberries are to be planted. At the bottom put a 4-6in/10-15cm layer of the manure or compost. Fill to the top of the trench with soil, removing any left over to another part of the garden.

Planting

Canes can be planted from autumn to early spring, but the best time is autumn or late autumn so that they have the winter to become established. Plant the canes 18in/45cm apart in rows 5ft/1.5m apart. Canes must not be allowed to fruit in the first year of growth, so cut them down to 9in/22.5cm after planting. Make a slanting cut just above a bud. Autumn-fruiting varieties, which crop on the current year's growth, should be cut down to just above ground level in late winter after planting in autumn. New growth will appear in spring.

In early spring, dress the ground along the rows with sulphate of potash at a rate of 2oz per sq yd/60g per sq m.

As the canes grow they will need support. Drive posts into the ground along the rows at 10ft/3m intervals with 6ft/1.8m of the posts showing above ground. Stretch wires between the posts, the lowest 2½ft/75cm above the level of the soil and the rest with 12in/30cm between

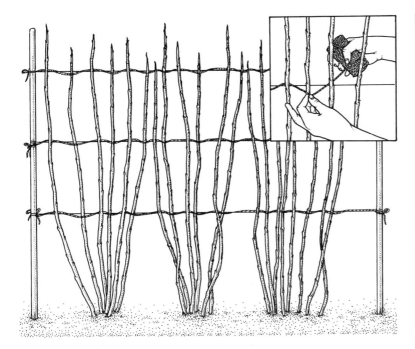

Pests

Aphids are the worst pests, but luckily some of the new raspberry varieties are now resistant to aphids. If they do strike, spray with malathion, the more acceptable derris, or a fatty-acid soap spray.

Raspberry beetles lay eggs in the centre of the flowers and the grubs that emerge burrow into the fruit, ruining it. Spray with malathion or derris as the fruit begins to colour.

Diseases

Viral diseases are the most devastating. As a preventive measure, buy only certified stock. The usual symptoms are stunted growth and yellow-mottled leaves. Affected canes should be burned.

Cane blight causes canes to snap easily, to wither and die. Cut canes and burn. Spray unaffected canes with Bordeaux mixture.

Cane spot causes purple spotting on canes, later with grey-white centres. Cut out affected canes and spray unaffected ones with Bordeaux mixture or benomyl.

Spur blight leaves purple patches around buds in early spring. Cut out affected canes; spray others with benomyl.

Botrytis, or grey mould, is a fungal disease that causes grey deposits on fruit. As a preventive measure, spray with benomyl at flowering time and then at two-week intervals.

them. Tie the canes loosely to the wires with soft string.

In late summer or early autumn during the year after planting, cut down the stumps of the original canes and remove any weak shoots. The following late winter cut off the top 6in/15cm of summer-fruiting canes and cut down all the canes of the autumn-fruiting ones to ground level.

Apply potash in early spring and a mulch of compost, but leave a circle 4in/10cm in diameter clear of the cane itself. Keep plants well watered during the summer months.

Cropping of summer-fruiting varieties starts in early summer and continues until late summer. Autumn-fruiting raspberries start in late summer and carry on until autumn.

When fruiting is over, cut the canes of the summer varieties that have carried fruits down to ground level. Cut out the weakest of the new canes, tying the strongest to the wires at 4in/10cm intervals along the rows. All the canes of autumn-fruiting varieties are cut down to ground level in late winter.

Propagating

Propagation is simple, as raspberries throw up suckers that can be separated from the main canes. In autumn, carefully ease suckers out of the ground with a fork and sever them from the parent canes,

leaving roots on each sucker to support growth. Plant in rows 18in/45cm apart.

Growing in containers

This is not always a great success, so don't be disappointed by poor crops. Try Malling Delight and the autumn-fruiting Zeva. Plant each cane in a container 2in/5cm larger than the root ball, using loam potting compost. Pot-on each year to a pot 2in/5cm larger in diameter until one of 18in/45cm diameter is reached. After that, remove the top 4in/10cm of compost and replace with fresh. Provide a single post as support for the canes of each pot. Apply sulphate of potash each year in early spring. Keep the canes well watered; in warm weather twice daily watering may be needed. Prune the canes as described under *Planting*.

COOKING AND FREEZING RASPBERRIES

The proper way to serve raspberries is to serve them straight from the cane. Serve on their own, with a little sugar if necessary, or with cream or ice-cream.

Raspberries a little past their best can be puréed. Liquidize the berries and mix with cottage cheese, yogurt

and lemon juice. Dissolve gelatine in water and stir in the mixture. Fold in beaten whites of two eggs. Chill .

Freeze raspberries just as they come from the canes. Don't rinse them before freezing; if not totally dry they will be mushy when thawed.

STRAWBERRY
(Fragaria × Ananassa)

The home grower has a decided edge over the supermarket when it comes to strawberries. Today's commercial growers are concerned with a uniform appearance, bright colour and (probably most important of all) the ability to travel well; flavour seems to be of less importance. It is this kind of strawberry that is available on the supermarket shelves, either home-grown in summer or for most of the year imported from Spain, Israel and the United States.

On the other hand, for the home grower there are now plenty of new varieties around with both pleasant flavour and appearance. As well as summer varieties and the few autumn fruiters, there are new varieties which, with a little care can be induced to go on cropping much longer.

These new varieties of strawberry come from the United States. They are 'day neutral' varieties that produce fruit from summer to the first frosts. If planted in pots and kept in a greenhouse with a little heat – 50°F/10°C is the minimum – they will go on producing fruit, regardless of the shorter hours of daylight. Naturally, plants bearing fruit continuously will tail off in yield. This happens after about a year and the plants need replacing, but this regular outlay should pay handsome dividends.

Varieties

Old-established varieties include Cambridge Favourite, probably the most widely grown variety by home and commercial growers. Crops are heavy with a reasonable flavour. Ready from the latter part of early summer to summer. Royal Sovereign is one of the oldest varieties with a reliable flavour, but crops are not heavy. Viral disease used to be a problem, but virus-free plants are now available.

The newest strawberry varieties include Bounty, a Canadian import, with a heavy crop of medium-sized berries of pleasant flavour. Honeoye, from the U.S., has large crops of tasty bright-red fruits. Tantallon and Troubadour have good resistance to red core and mildew, and crop heavily.

Aromel is one of the newer autumn-fruiting varieties that give a brief crop in summer, followed by the main crop from late summer to autumn.

Day-neutral varieties include Selva and Fern, both with pleasant flavour. Tribute and Tristar are varieties yet to prove themselves, but early results are promising.

Baron Solemacher is a well-established Alpine strawberry variety, fruiting on an off from summer to autumn.

The plant's needs

The ideal soil is fertile well-draining loam, but most soils will give worthwhile results if they are adequately manured. In summer before planting, dig in plenty of well-rotted manure and then apply a general fertilizer at 2-3oz per sq yd/60-90g per sq m. Strawberries prefer slightly acid soils with a pH level of 6 to 6.5. Choose a sheltered and – most important – sunny part of the garden.

Growing

Plant summer- and autumn-fruiting varieties in summer or late summer to crop the following year. Day-neutral and alpine varieties are planted in late spring. Space them 15in/37.5cm apart, but if you are planning to replace them every other year to maintain vigorous cropping, plant them at 12in/30cm each way. Make holes in the soil large enough to spread out the roots, and deep enough for the crown of the plants to be at soil level and not buried. Water them well.

The berries hang near the ground on the stems, and it is difficult to keep them clean and to prevent them from rotting in wet weather. There are two ways to do this. The traditional way is to place straw along both sides of the rows when the fruits start to develop. This is not altogether satisfactory because slugs take up residence in the straw. The alternative is to grow the strawberries through black plastic (as practised for potatoes).

Before planting, ridge up the ground a little along the prepared row so that the rain will run off the sheeting, instead of making puddles. Lay the plastic sheeting over the ground and make slits in it at the recommended planting distances, and plant the strawberries through the slits. Weight down the edges of the sheeting.

In late winter, apply a dressing of sulphate of potash at the rate of ½oz per sq yd/15g per sq m. Scatter this between the plants, taking care that it does not touch the plants themselves. Plastic sheeting will have to be lifted a little along the edges to scatter the fertilizer, but weight it down again afterwards. Remove it when the cropping is finished in order to allow runners to develop.

Keep the plants well watered, especially during warm weather. In late spring, remove all blossom that develops on autumn-fruiting varieties, but leave the blossom of other varieties. Scatter slug pellets to protect the fruit and net the plants to keep birds away from the berries.

Summer-fruiting varieties will be ready for picking from early summer to summer. When cropping is over cut off the leaves, leaving only about 3in/7.5cm of stem showing above ground. Take care not to damage the crown of the plant. Burn all old leaves and debris to prevent the spread of pests and diseases.

Autumn-fruiting varieties will be ready from late summer and will go on cropping until the first frosts. Plants are usually good for one season only, so dig up and burn the plants after the last picking. Alpine strawberries will be ready from summer until the first frosts.

The new day-neutral varieties should crop from summer until temperatures drop below 50°F/10°C.

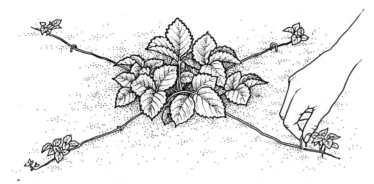

first holes. Push the roots of the plant through the holes into the compost and firm lightly from the inside of the pot. Add more compost until the next layer of holes is reached. Insert plants into these and so on until the whole pot is planted. To finish it off, insert plants in the compost at the top of the pot.

Keep the plants well watered and give

Propagating

The easiest method of propagating summer-fruiting varieties is by layering the runners. Select a few plants from which to propagate and remove all flowers as they develop so that the plants concentrate on producing runners rather than fruit. In summer, pin down the runners into the soil with bent wires, if they have not rooted on their own. By late summer they should have rooted. Sever from the main plant and transplant, spacing them 15in/37.5cm each way.

Some autumn-fruiting varieties can be propagated in the same way. Plants can also be divided if you think it worthwhile, but it is best to buy new plants each year.

Alpine strawberries are usually raised from seed. In early spring, sow seed in a tray of seed compost, but don't cover them. Keep at a temperature of 60°F/16°C. When seedlings can be handled easily prick them out into potting compost, 2in/5cm apart. At the end of late spring plant out 15in/37.5cm apart each way.

Growing in containers

The variety of containers for growing strawberries is endless – straightforward plant pots, growing bags, specially designed strawberry barrels or towers. If planting in ordinary pots, use those 12in/30cm in diameter and in summer or late summer, plant no more than four plants in them, equally spaced to give them room to spread. Growing bags will usually take six to eight plants. Strawberry pots or barrels will take as many plants as there are holes, but don't expect a vast crop from any type of container.

To plant a strawberry pot or barrel, cover the bottom with a layer of crocks, followed by a layer of peat. Then put in loam potting compost to the level of the

them a regular liquid feed. Container-grown plants should be replaced each year.

If you have a greenhouse where a temperature of 50°F/10°C can be maintained, day-neutral varieties can be grown for out-of-season strawberries. Planted in early summer or summer they should be fruiting from autumn onwards. Late-summer or early-autumn plantings should provide a Christmas dessert.

PESTS AND DISEASES: STRAWBERRY

Pests

Aphids can be a nuisance not only because of the damage they do to the plants, but because of viral diseases they carry – the greatest enemies of strawberries. Spray with derris or a fatty-acid soap solution.

Slugs can be kept at bay with slug bait placed between the rows when the fruit is developing. Birds will ruin the fruit unless it is netted.

Diseases

Botrytis, or grey mould, leaves soft grey deposits on fruit. Spray with benomyl as the flowers open and repeat every two weeks.

Mildew will coat the leaves with a white powdery deposit. Spray with benomyl or dinocap.

Viral diseases can best be avoided by buying certified stock and spraying to kill aphids. If the plants are nonetheless affected, lift and burn all of them.

COOKING AND FREEZING STRAWBERRIES

Like raspberries, strawberries are best served as plainly as possible. Serve them with a little sugar if necessary, and cream or ice-cream if liked. Alpine strawberries can be sprinkled with a little sugar and a few drops of white wine vinegar to bring out the flavour. Instead of making strawberry fool with cream try a lighter version with yogurt and

whisked egg whites. Liquidize the strawberries and stir in lemon juice, yogurt and a little sugar. Whisk the eggs whites and fold into the mixture.

Whole strawberries don't freeze well. If you want to freeze strawberries for fools, liquidize them first and then freeze.

TOP FRUITS

Gardeners have often been reluctant to grow top fruit because the trees tend to grow so big that they swamp the average garden. However, now that semi-dwarfing and dwarfing root-stock have been introduced, many more gardeners can grow fruit trees even if there is only limited space. Cordon, espalier- and fan-trained trees grown against walls are especially space-efficient.

The latest space-saver is a columnar tree, so far restricted to apple varieties, and still to prove the quality of its limited varieties. Nevertheless it is suitable for small gardens as the blossom and fruit grow on short spurs from bottom to top of the single main stem, making a most attractive sight.

Inevitably, growing fruit on dwarf root-stock or on drastically, pruned and trained trees will not give the large crops to be gained from large mature trees. But as such crops are often far too large for today's families, smaller crops from a wider range of fruit trees tend to be more popular with the modern gardener.

When starting to grow top fruit, many gardeners become worried by the prospect of pruning. Effective pruning is essential to get the best and largest crops.

To begin with, some mistakes may be made but if you study the way that your trees grow you will realize why they need to be pruned as the experts advise you. After the initial formative training and pruning is completed, annual pruning becomes a relatively simple routine that takes up little time. You can even dodge most of the problem by growing the new columnar trees, which need little or no pruning, but that might mean missing some of the best fruit available.

There is such a wide choice of fruit trees nowadays, with both old-established varieties and new trees with many of the diseases bred out of them, that there has never been a better time to grow top fruit.

Opposite left, *apple,*
James Grieve variety.
Above, *an espalier-trained apple tree*
makes fruit growing possible even in a
limited space.

147

APPLE
(Malus pumila)

You don't need an orchard to grow apples. The new dwarfing rootstocks on which apple varieties are grafted have brought apples out of the orchard into even the smallest of gardens.

Nurseries now sell trees that indicate by a simple root-stock code how big they will grow. For example, the smallest trees are on root-stock M 27 and they will reach about 6ft/1.8m, ideal for container growing. M 9 makes bushy trees of 6-8ft/1.8-2.4m; M 26 grows to 9-12ft/2.7-3.6m and MM 106 from 12-18ft/3.6-5.4m. M 111 is for the largest gardens only.

From MM 106 has been developed the ultimate space-saver – a columnar tree that might well be called the 'telegraph-pole' apple. It does not form lateral branches as apples usually do, but short spurs. The apples look as though they are clinging to the main stem itself and they are produced along its full height.

Now that there are trees of a manageable size there is every reason for growing your own apples so that you can have a better choice than is usually available in the shops. Most of the year there seem to be three: Golden Delicious, juicy but tasteless; Cox's Orange Pippin, tasty but often woolly textured; and Granny Smiths, juicy but acidic. In late summer and early autumn these may be supplemented by the occasional and welcome appearance of Worcester Pearmain and Egremont Russet, but that is usually all. Open a fruit nursery catalogue and you will realize what the apple lover is missing – endless varieties of apples of diverse tastiness. That, if nothing else, should encourage you to grow your own.

Varieties

NOTE The choice of varieties to grow is in part affected by the need to ensure cross pollination, which is essential for a strong crop. In this list the names of the varieties are followed by the letters A B and C. To ensure pollination, plant varieties with the same or adjacent letters. Bramley Seedling and the 'telegraph-pole' varieties have special needs, which are noted in the list.

Dessert apples The earliest-fruiting trees, in late summer, include Discovery (B), an almost entirely red apple, juicy, crisp and sweet with a distinctive flavour, and George Cave (B), green flushed with red, and sweet-flavoured. Following them in autumn are James Grieve (B), greenish-

yellow skin, striped orange and red with creamy-white juicy flesh; Cox's Orange Pippin (B), which can be superb if in good condition; and Egremont Russet (A), which has a distinctive dull-brown skin and yellow-white flesh with a nutty flavour. Redsleeves (B) is a new variety for picking in autumn. It has heavy crops of red fruits and is resistant to scab and mildew. Fiesta (B), yellow skin flushed with red, is ready in early autumn and is said to store well until spring. The dark-red fruits of Spartan (C), exceptionally sweet and juicy, are ready in autumn and store well into winter. Lord Lamborne (A) crops in autumn to late autumn. Its green-yellow skin is flushed with bright red and its sweet-flavoured flesh is crisp and juicy. Laxton Superb (B) crops in late autumn, but can be erratic, with poor yield every other year. The yellow, red-flushed fruits of Tydeman's Late Orange (C) will store well until early spring.

Varieties of 'telegraph-pole' apples include Bolero, green apples flushed with yellow, and Polka, green flushed with red, both ready in early autumn. Waltz is ready in autumn and keeps well into the new year if storage conditions are ideal. Grow any two varieties to ensure pollination. There is also a crab apple called Maypole.

Cooking apples By far the most popular and reliable is Bramley's Seedling. It is ripe for picking in late autumn and stores well until late winter. This apple is a triploid, which means that it is not an efficient pollinator. Grow it along with Spartan, Redsleeves, or Cox's Orange Pippin to ensure satisfactory pollination.

Emneth Early (Early Victoria) (B) is the first-ripening cooker, ready in late summer. Lane's Prince Albert (C) is a late cropper and will store until early spring.

The plant's needs

Choose a part of the garden that is sunny, sheltered, well draining and not usually affected by spring frosts, which kill the blossom. In the early autumn before planting, dig in well-rotted manure or compost. Lime acid soils for a pH level of about 6. Fork in general fertilizer or bone meal at the rate of 2oz per sq yd/60g per sq m.

Plant trees from early winter to early spring; the earlier the better unless there is frost. If it is frosty when the trees are delivered, don't attempt to plant them, but store them in a frost-free place until the weather improves.

Planting distances between trees depend on the type of root-stock.

Root-stock	M 27	5ft/1.5m apart
	M 9	6-7ft/1.8-2.1m apart
	M 26	14ft/4.2m apart
	M 106	14ft/4.2m apart
	M 111	18ft/5.4m apart
Cordons		2½-3ft/75-90cm apart
Espalier-trained		10ft/3m apart
'Telegraph-pole'		3ft/90cm apart

Planting and growing

Make holes for the plants large enough for the roots to be well spread out. All the trees, apart from the 'telegraph-pole' apples, will need supporting with posts to begin with, and trees on M 27 and M 9 root-stocks will need support all their life. For M 27 and M 9 root-stocks, the posts should be 4½ft/135cm long; 7½ft/2.25m for M 26; and 9½ft/2.85m for all others. Drive them 18in/45cm into the ground just off the centre of the hole.

Place the tree in the hole about 3in/7.5cm away from the post on a small mound of soil to support it. Fill in the hole with soil, firming it down. The tree must be planted at the same level as it was in the nursery, and the join between the root-stock and the grafted stem should be above the surface of the soil, otherwise it may root. Secure the tree to the post, which should reach just below the lowest branches, with a rubber strap that has a buffer between the post and the tree to prevent chafing. Apply a mulch of compost of rotted manure around the base of the tree, but leave a small circle of soil round the tree free of mulch.

Cordon apples grown against a wall will need support. Stretch wires at 2ft/60cm intervals, starting 2ft/60cm from the ground, up to a height of 6ft/1.8m and secure them to the wall at both ends. If they are being grown in the open, stretch the wires between posts driven 18in/45cm into the ground and showing 6ft/1.8m above soil level. Secure canes to the wires at an angle of 45°, at 2½-3ft/75-90cm intervals. If only a few cordons are being grown, they can be grown upright.

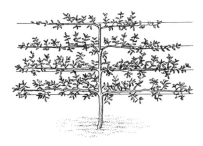

Espaliers are supported in the same way, with 18in/45cm gaps between the wires, along which the tiered branches will be trained.

Each year in late winter, fertilize dessert apples with 1oz of sulphate of potash per sq yd/30g per sq m. For cooking apples, apply sulphate of ammonia, 2oz per sq yd/60g per sq m. In spring, apply a mulch of compost or manure. In periods of very dry weather the trees will benefit from a good soaking, especially from summer to late autumn. Little thinning should be needed on pyramids and cordons. In summer, reduce clusters to two fruits, or to one if there is a large crop.

Apples are ready to pick when they come away in the palm of the hand after a gentle twist. The early-maturing varieties will keep only a few weeks, so they should be eaten straight away. Varieties that will store should be wrapped in newspaper or waxed paper and stored in boxes or stacked in fibre trays used by commercial

growers. Keep the apples in a cool frost-free place around 45°F/7°C. Inspect them regularly to remove any going rotten.

(For pruning, see page 153.)

Growing in containers

The best varieties for container growing are those on M 27 root-stock or the latest 'telegraph-pole' apples. Containers should be at least 12in/30cm deep and the same in diameter. Use quality loam compost. Choose a sunny sheltered spot, not

susceptible to frost, and plant in early winter. Keep pot-grown trees well watered, especially in periods of warm weather. Give a liquid feed every two weeks when the fruit begins to develop. Every other year pot-on after fruiting, increasing the container size by 2in/5cm diameter until an 18in/45cm container is reached. Thereafter remove the top 4in/10cm of the compost each year, replacing it with fresh. Prune and thin as for trees growing in the open ground, as described on page 153.

PESTS AND DISEASES: APPLE

Pests

Aphids can be sprayed with malathion, or more acceptably, a solution of fatty-acid soaps, or in extreme cases, a systemic insecticide.

Codling moth caterpillars bore into the centre of the apple, ruining most of it. Spray in early summer with fenitrothion, before the caterpillars have had time to attack the fruit, and again in summer.

Apple sawfly caterpillars bore into the fruit. To prevent this, spray the flies when all the blossom has fallen

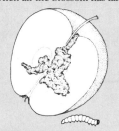

from the trees.

Diseases

Scab is the worst disease to attack apples. It starts on the shoots of trees and spreads to leaves and fruits. The leaves become blotched a darker green and the skin of the fruit bears brownish scabs. Remove diseased areas and all diseased fruit. To take preventive action, spray with benomyl or captan when flower buds first appear, and continue spraying every two weeks until the end of summer.

Mildew, which puts white deposits on leaves and fruit, is controlled in the same way as scab.

Apple canker is a fungal disease that attacks branches and the trunks of trees. The bark is eaten away, exposing new wood underneath. Cut out the rotten area and apply a canker paint to the wound.

COOKING AND FREEZING APPLES

Dessert apples are best eaten raw. They can be cooked, but it is a waste of tasty apples and the vitamin C they contain. Add them raw and chopped to coleslaw salads. Grate white cabbage and carrot and add the chopped apple. Then coat the mixture with mayonnaise. The flavours of chopped apple and celery coated with a mixture of sour cream and yogurt complement well.

Cooking apples make excellent pies. Peel, core, slice and put them in a pie dish or on a plate. Sprinkle them with water, add sugar, cover them with short-crust pastry and bake in a hot oven for about 30 minutes. Or they can be mixed with soft fruits such as blackberries and black currants and baked in pies.

Apples can be cooked before freezing, making them into a purée

that can be used for sauces with meat and poultry, or as pie fillings. Cook with sugar and a little water until soft. Allow to cool, and freeze. Raw apples can also be frozen. Peel, core and slice them. Dip in water with lemon juice to prevent them from turning brown. Pat dry, pack in bags and freeze.

APRICOT
(Prunus armeniaca)

Growing apricots has been largely ignored as a viable proposition in temperate or cool climates. Certainly commercial growers hardly give them a second thought and home gardeners should think hard before considering them. They need warmth and a frost-free environment. Gardeners with warm sheltered gardens and perhaps only an occasional light frost might think it worth the gamble, the only reward might be the joy of picking a single apricot.

For the smaller garden, they can be grown as bush trees – though they still need a fair amount of room – or fan-trained against a warm sunny wall; south- or west-facing are the best prospects. The trouble is that the trees blossom early in the year and the flowers can be wiped out overnight with a single sharp frost.

Varieties

The most popular variety is Moorpark,

Apricots – a challenge to grow.

ripening in late summer with large yellow fruits flushed with red-brown. The fruits of Alfred are ready a little earlier, but they are not as big.

The plant's needs

Grow in well-draining, preferably loamy soil – certainly not in light, quick-draining sandy soil. Acid soils should be well limed for a pH level of about 7. Choose the warmest, sunniest sheltered part of the garden and grow against a west- or south-facing wall, preferably as a fan tree. This will eventually take up about 12ft/3m of wall space; a bush tree will eventually have a similar or larger spread.

Growing

In early autumn, prepare the ground by digging in plenty of well-rotted manure or compost. Planting takes place in autumn. Dig a hole large enough to accommodate the root ball with the roots well spread

out, and plant to the same depth as the tree was growing originally. Position it about 6in/15cm away from the wall. Fix wires horizontally along the wall, starting 12in/30cm from the ground and then at 9in/22.5cm intervals. Tie canes to the wires along which to train the branches.

In late winter of each year, scatter sulphate of potash around the tree at the rate of 1oz per sq yd/30g per sq m. In spring, apply a general fertilizer at the rate of 2oz per sq yd/60g per sq m. Also in spring, spread a mulch of compost or rotted manure around, but not touching the tree.

Trees can blossom early in the year, so protect them from frost with fine nylon netting. As there are few insects about at this time to pollinate the flowers, your help will be needed. Use a soft brush to transfer the yellow pollen grains from the anthers to the stigma of the flowers.

When the fruits reach the size of cherries, start thinning. Remove distorted fruits and thin clusters to doubles, making sure that there are at least 3in/7.5cm between them. Leave the fruits to ripen fully on the tree. By then they will be a rich yellow with red flushing, and should come away easily.

Training a fan tree

In the late winter after planting, prune all the leaders back to about 30in/75cm. By summer these leaders will have produced new shoots. Choose three of the strongest on each leader that are growing where they will best cover the wall. Tie them to the canes. Prune all other shoots back to the leaders.

In the following spring, prune back all the leading branches by a quarter or a third. Rub out between finger and thumb any shoots growing towards the wall or outwards away from the wall. Leave those that will grow flush along the wall.

Prune in this way for the next two springs, by which time the main framework will have developed. In each spring, also rub out the unwanted buds, that is, those growing in the wrong directions. Each summer, pinch back to six leaves any new shoots that would otherwise overcrowd the framework. After cropping is over in late summer, further pinch back these shoots to three leaves.

Every five years or so older fruiting branches should be cut away to allow new vigorous growth to take their place. Make sure that there are enough new shoots before removing too many old branches. Leave the new shoots to develop for two years before pruning them.

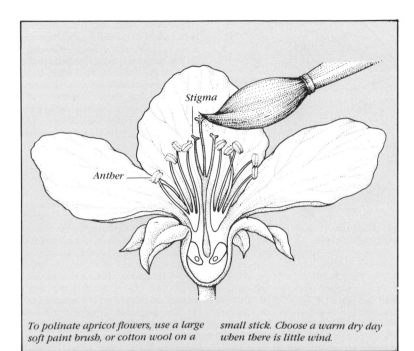

To polinate apricot flowers, use a large soft paint brush, or cotton wool on a small stick. Choose a warm dry day when there is little wind.

PESTS AND DISEASES: APRICOT

Pests

Aphids can be controlled by spraying with malathion, derris or a solution'of fatty-acid soaps.

Red spider mite causes mottling on leaves, yellowing and then leaf fall. In extreme cases, fine webs are found on branches and leaves. Control them in the same way as aphids.

Diseases

Dieback is the major disease. The first sign is wilting blossom, followed by dying spurs. Remove all affected parts and seal the wounds.

COOKING AND FREEZING APRICOTS

Even if apricots are ripe they are not usually at their best eaten raw. Far better to poach them in a little water, with sugar, to bring out the full flavour. No need to go to the trouble of stoning them first because the stones give an added flavour. Cook for no more than five minutes or they will collapse into mush.

Apricots that have gone rather beyond their best can be used as a puree to accompany lamb, pork or poultry. Or make them into a dessert. Cook and then liquidize the apricots. Blend in yogurt and stiffly beaten egg whites.

Before freezing apricots, halve and stone them. Place in boiling water and then in cold water and lemon juice to prevent them from turning brown. Dry and freeze.

PEAR
(Pyrus communis)

Pears used to be sweet, juicy and full of flavour with tender skins and flesh. This is not just nostalgia, for the fact is that 'improvements' to pears in the past few decades have been of greater profit to the growers than to the consumers. The grower's priority is that pears must travel well to the shops, so the skins have been made tougher. And since they travel better before they have ripened (and some never do), what we often buy is an unpleasantly tough-skinned, rather hard pear, with little or no flavour.

So, increasingly, the only way to enjoy really delicious pears is to grow them yourself, pick them when they are ripe but still hardish and eat them when they have softened in storage.

As with apples, commercial growers produce only a limited range of varieties, so home growing opens up new opportunities. You can not only re-experience the flavours of the old varieties but try out the best of the new ones too.

Pears are today raised on quince rootstock, usually referred to as Quince A and Quince C. Those rooted on Quince A will grow to 18ft/5.4m, while Quince C produces dwarf or medium-sized trees – 8-14ft/2.4-4.2m. Variations in size will depend on growing conditions as well as the variety chosen. Varieties are available as trees, cordons, espaliers and the attractive fan-trained trees.

Varieties

The varieties have been grouped to ensure that they pollinate each other. Two varieties from each group must be grown together.

Group A Louise Bonne of Jersey, with green fruits flushed with red, and sweet succulent flesh, is ready in autumn. Packham's Triumph crops at around the same time; yellow skin, flushed with orange-red.

Group B Beurre Superfin is juicy with a superb rich flavour; ready in early autumn. Beurre Hardy, with sweet flesh, crops later in autumn. Durondeau's compact growth makes it an excellent tree for the small garden; crops from late autumn. Home-grown Conference pears should dispel the bad experiences of the often tough and woody commercially grown fruits; ready from autumn to late autumn. Josephine de Malines is another compact tree. Pick its pears in late autumn and store for eating in early winter and winter.

Group C contains the variety Doyenne du Comice, which many people consider to be the best pear. Pick it in autumn to late autumn and, given ideal conditions of storage, it will keep into the New Year. Very juicy, sweet, mouth-watering flesh. Concorde is a new variety developed from Doyenne du Comice and Conference. It crops heavily in autumn, storing until winter. Onward is an early variety, ready in early autumn. Winter Nellis is an old variety with beautifully juicy flesh, ready in late autumn and storing well into the New Year. Eat the fruit while the skin is still yellow. As it turns red, the flesh becomes brown and mealy, the worst pear-eating experience of all.

The plant's needs

Choose a sunny sheltered part of the garden, where frost does not linger; spring frosts can wipe out all the blossom. The best soil is a rich moisture-retentive loam, but pears will grow in most types of soil. Dig in plenty of well-rotted manure or compost in early autumn. This will not only increase fertility but will improve the quality of less than ideal soil, making wet clay soil more free-draining and sandy soild more moisture-retentive. Adding peat also helps.

Planting and growing

Planting can be carried out between late autumn and early spring, but the best time is late autumn or early winter. If there is frost about when the plants arrive from the nursery, store them for a few days until the frost has gone. Before planting, fork in general fertilizer at the rate of 2oz per sq yd/60g per sq m. Plant dwarf pyramids about 6ft/1.8m apart, bush trees 12ft/3.6m apart and cordons 2½-3ft/75-90cm apart.

To plant, dig a hole wide enough to take the root ball with the roots spread out, and deep enough for the soil mark on the stem to be at the same depth as it was originally. Test this by putting the tree in the hole, but before finally planting it drive a post 18in/45cm into the ground a little off-centre in the hole. It must be long enough for the top to reach almost as far as the lowest branches of the tree. Then plant the tree, making sure when filling in the hole that the point where the root-stock and the graft meet is above soil level. Secure the trunk to the post with a rubber strap and buffer between the post and the tree.

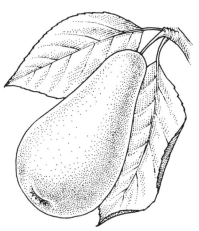

Spread a mulch around the tree, but not touching the trunk.

Cordon apples are supported by lines of wire at 2ft/60cm intervals to an overall height of 6ft/1.8m, the wires being secured to a wall or to posts. Fix canes to the wires at an angle of 45° at 2½-3ft/75-90cm intervals and tie the cordons to them. Support espaliers in the same way, but with only 18in/45cm gaps between the wires.

In late winter each year, apply a dressing of sulphate of potash, 1oz per sq yd/30g per sq m, and in spring a mulch of compost or manure. Keep trees well watered as the fruit develops. If any are overcrowded with fruit, reduce the clusters to two fruits or one.

PESTS AND DISEASES: PEAR

Pests

Aphids will cause the most bother. Spray with malathion, a solution of fatty-acid soaps, or a systemic insecticide for serious infestations.

Caterpillars can be a nuisance, chewing tender new leaves. Pick them off, or if there are too many for that, spray with derris or fenitrothion.

Diseases

Scab is the biggest problem. The shoots first become affected, then the leaves develop darker-green blotches, and unpleasant brown scabs appear on the skin of the fruits. Cut out the diseased areas and destroy affected fruit. As a preventive measure, spray with benomyl or captan every two weeks from the first appearance of flower buds until the end of summer.

Pear flesh softens when the fruit has been picked and stored for a while, but it is easy to pick the fruit before it is ready. To test, place the pear in the palm of the hand and give it a gentle twist. If it is ready, it comes away readily. If it resists, leave it a day or two longer. Store the pears in trays, unwrapped but not touching each other, at a temperature of 40°F/4°C. They should be ready to eat when the flesh softens around the stalk.

Growing in containers

Choose the compact varieties, such as Durondeau and Josephine de Malines, growing on Quince C root-stock. Containers should be at least 12in/30cm deep and 12in/30cm in diameter. Plant trees in early winter using a quality loam compost. Keep the container in a sunny sheltered part of the garden where it is unlikely to be touched by frost. Water well in warm weather and never let the compost dry out. Give a liquid feed every two weeks as the fruits begin to develop.

Pot-on, after fruiting, every other year, increasing the pot size by 2in/5cm until the maximum manageable size of 18in/45cm is reached. After that, remove the top 4in/10cm of compost every year and replace it with fresh. The roots should be disturbed as little as possible.

COOKING AND FREEZING PEARS

Raw pears and cheese, like apples and cheese, are supposed to go well together. But why adulterate the flavour of a sweet juicy pear with anything else? Peel if you must, quarter, then simply enjoy the wonderful taste of a home-grown pear.

Pears cooked in wine and served cold are a classic dessert. Dissolve sugar in a mixture of half red wine and half water. Add some cinnamon and nutmeg. Peel the pears, but don't remove the stalks. Place in the wine mixture and poach gently until soft. For a real designer flourish, cook equal numbers of pears in a red wine mixture and in a white wine mixture. Arrange the red and cream pears together in a dish and serve with the juices.

Pears are not worth freezing as they quickly collapse when defrosted.

PRUNING APPLES AND PEARS

Pruning a dwarf pyramid

Pruning starts immediately after planting, when the main stem is cut back to 20in/50cm to an upward- and outward-facing bud. Cut back any side-shoots to four buds.

In the following winter, reduce the leading stem by 8in/20cm to a bud pointing in the opposite direction to that selected the previous year. Cut back side-shoots to 8in/20cm to a downward- and outward-facing bud. In the later summer of that year, cut back side-shoots to four leaves.

In the third winter, cut back the main stem, leaving about 10in/25cm of new growth to a bud pointing in the opposite direction to that selected the previous year. Cut back main branches by about a third of the new growth.

When the tree has grown to a height of 7ft/2.1m, stop cutting back in winter. In spring, restrict the growth of the main stem to the desired height of the tree. At the same time, cut back any branches at the top of the tree and restrict side-shoots to four leaves.

Pruning for a bush tree

After planting, reduce the main stem to 3ft/90cm above the ground. Select about four side-shoots that are reduced by half to within two or three buds of the main stem. Remove any other shoots completely.

In the following winter, reduce the selected four shoots by half to an outward-facing bud. By the third winter there should be eight main branches that are again reduced by half in length. Any shoots that are crowding the centre of the tree should be removed.

By the fourth year the tree should be well established and start to bear fruit. Pruning is now carried out each winter to keep the shape and open growth.

Pruning a cordon

Most of the pruning of cordons takes place in summer. After planting, reduce side-shoots to four buds but don't touch the leading stem.

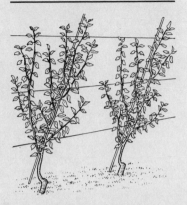

In the following summer, reduce side-shoots to four leaves, ignoring the clusters of leaves growing close to the main stem. Side-shoots should now be no longer than about 9in/22.5cm. Any growths from side-shoots or spurs are cut back to one leaf. In early autumn or autumn, cut

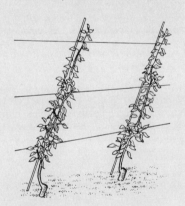

back to one bud any growths that have developed since summer pruning.

Continue pruning in the same way each year. When the leading shoot has grown beyond the top supporting wire, cut it back in late spring so that the cordon is no taller than 7ft/2.1m. In each subsequent summer, cut back all new growth of the leading shoot.

Pruning a cordon

Established espalier trees are pruned in a similar way to cordons. In

summer, cut back any new growth of the leading shoot and the end of the laterals that have been trained along the wires. Also in summer prune side-shoots from the horizontal laterals to four leaves. If further laterals have started to develop from the main stem, cut them back to four leaves.

Trees bought as espaliers usually have two tiers of laterals, but they can be trained beyond that stage. Start in early winter after planting the trees in the usual way. Tie the horizontal laterals to the wires. Prune the main vertical stem to 20in/50cm so that about 2in/5cm of stem is showing above the next horizontal wire. There should be three buds on the main stem just below the wire. One will be trained vertically to grow as the main stem and the other two as horizontal laterals. This training starts in spring.

Fix a cane vertically from the wire just below the top of the main stem to the next higher wire. Tie the shoot from the top bud of the three to the cane. Tie the other two shoots to canes fixed at an angle of 45° between the wires, one to the left and one to the right of the main stem. In early winter, the summer's growth of these two shoots can be carefully lowered and tied horizontally to the wires. Prune back the leading (vertical) shoot to about 2in/5cm above the next wire, in order to train the next layer of laterals.

While training the new layers of the espalier, treat the established horizontal branches in the same way as a mature tree, pruning side-shoots from the horizontal laterals to four leaves. Cut back any further laterals that have developed between the newly trained laterals and those below to four leaves.

Pruning columnar ('telegraph-pole') apples

Columnar apples save not only space but also much of the labour of pruning. You may even get away with no pruning at all, but if any laterals do start to grow, prune them back to two buds in winter.

PEACH
(Prunus persica)

NECTARINE
(Prunus persica var. nectarina)

There was a time when peaches were grown under glass on a large scale in the cooler parts of the northern hemisphere. Then imports from warm Mediterranean countries, where they could be grown cheaply out of doors, meant that commercial peach growing under glass went into decline. Growers tried to make a comeback by growing them outdoors, but this was a dismal failure, mainly because the wrong variety was chosen – Peregrine, which is a fine peach, but needs protection.

The decline was reversed with the introduction of the American variety Rochester. Here was a peach that was less susceptible to disease and a more reliable cropper. Not that the northern growers could compete with the massive imports from the United States in late spring. But at least Rochester and other new varieties mean that home gardeners can now enjoy the satisfaction of growing their own peaches, either in a sufficiently warm and sunny garden or in containers in an unheated greenhouse.

Nectarines are a variety of peach with a smooth polished skin. Think twice before attempting to grow them as they are less hardy than peaches.

Both peaches and nectarines are usually supplied on St Julien A root-stock, producing the smallest trees. They are grown in the same way and need the same kind of growing conditions and pruning. Varieties are self-fertile, so they can be grown as single specimens.

Varieties

Peaches The most reliable choice is Rochester, with medium-sized yellow fruits, flushed with red. This variety is quite hardy, growing well as a fan-trained specimen or a bush. Substantial crops in late summer. Another reliable cropper, Redhaven, is ready from the middle of late summer. The medium-sized fruits are yellow, but largely covered with red. Sweet yellow flesh, which reddens near the stone. Duke of York is one of the earliest-ripening varieties, ready in summer with crimson fruits. Amsden June crops at the same time with greenish-white skins, flushed with red. Bellgarde ripens late in early autumn, yellow-skinned with crimson markings.

Nectarine, less hardy than a peach.

Nectarines Lord Napier is the most reliable and popular variety, ready in late summer with yellow skin flushed with red. For early cropping in summer, John Rivers has yellow-skinned fruit streaked with red. Juicy with a good flavour. Pineapple combines the best of the peach flavour with a slight pineapple after-taste. Good outdoors in sheltered positions or for growing under glass. Elruge crops in late summer, with pale-green fruits.

The plant's needs

Peaches and nectarines will grow in any type of soil as long as it drains well. If drainage is poor, dig a hole 3ft sq/90cm sq to a depth of 2ft/60cm. Cover the bottom with brick rubble followed by chopped turves. Fill the hole with newly bought loam compost, using the soil removed in another part of the garden.

There is no need to do this if the soil is high-quality. Instead fork in general fertilizer and bone meal, both at the rate of 3oz per sq yd/90g per sq m. Lime acid soils to reach a pH level of 6.5 to 7. Choose a sunny, well-sheltered part of the garden that is usually frost-free.

Growing

Fan-trained trees should be planted only against south-, south-west- or west-facing walls. If more than one fan tree is being planted, the distance between the trees should be 12ft/3.6m. Bush trees need even more space, 15ft/4.5m apart.

Planting can be carried out between late autumn, which is the best time, and early spring. Dig a hole big enough to take the root ball with the roots well spread out. Plant to the same depth as the tree was originally grown, and a fan tree should be 6in/15cm away from the wall. Fix horizontal wires to the wall, starting 12in/30cm above the ground and then at 9in/22.5cm intervals. Between the wires attach canes along which the branches will be trained.

Support bush trees with a post driven 18in/45cm into the ground. Immediately after planting, spread a mulch of well-rotted manure or compost round the tree.

Every year in late winter, apply general fertilizer at the rate of 3oz per sq yd/90g per sq m. Protect trees in blossom from frost with fine nylon net or hessian. Pollinate flowers using a soft brush to transfer the yellow pollen from the anthers to the stigma. Keep well watered, especially in periods of warm weather.

Start thinning the fruits when they are the size of peas and stop when they reach the size of golf balls. By that time individual peaches should be 9in/22.5cm apart and nectarines 6in/15cm apart. To harvest the fruits, hold them gently in the palm of the hand and twist. They should come away easily.

Pruning for a fan-trained tree

In late winter after planting, cut back the main stem to 24in/60cm, leaving a lateral branch just below the cut. Immediately below this branch there should be two other laterals, one pointing to the left and the other to the right. Prune these, and any other laterals, back to one bud.

In early summer, start to train the top branch vertically. Choose two others just below the lowest wire to train, one to the left and one to the right. Remove any other shoots completely. In summer or late summer, secure the two side laterals to canes at a 45

ag angle. Then remove the central upright shoot. This is the basic framework for the fan formation, and some nurseries supply trees already pruned to this stage.

In the second year, in late winter, cut back the two laterals to a bud about 15in/37.5cm from the main stem. By summer new branches will have grown from the pruned lateral and that too will have lengthened with new growth. Choose two shoots above this lateral and one below, securing them to canes attached to the wires. Cut all other shoots back to one leaf. The tree will now have eight shoots, four trained on each side of the main stem.

In the third year, in late winter, shorten each of the eight shoots by a third to a downward-pointing bud. During summer new growth will have developed. Select three new shoots from each of the main ones and tie those in to cover the wall. Cut back any other shoots to one leaf. In late summer, pinch back the selected shoots to 18in/45cm. The framework should now be complete and the tree ready to fruit.

From then on there should be regular annual pruning of old fruiting stems and selection of new ones to take their place. In late spring each year, remove any shoots not growing flush with the wall. In summer, select new shoots to replace those that will fruit in the current year. Pinch back all other new shoots to two leaves. When the selected shoots are 18in/45cm long, pinch out the growing tips. When all the fruit has been picked, cut back the stems that have fruited, leaving the new ones to fruit the next year.

Pruning for a bush tree

After planting reduce the main stem to 3ft/90cm. Choose four side-shoots, reducing them by half to within two or three buds of the main stem. Remove all other shoots.

In the following spring, prune those four shoots by half to an outward-facing bud. By the third spring there should be eight main branches. Prune them by half. The tree should be well established by the fourth year. From then on prune to keep the tree's shape, and remove a few of the centre branches for open growth.

Growing in containers

Containers should be at least 12in/30cm deep and 12in/30cm in diameter. Plant the tree in late autumn using a quality loam compost. Place the container in a sunny sheltered part of the garden and keep it well watered, especially in warm weather. Apply a liquid feed every two weeks once the fruit begins to develop. Pot-on every other year, after fruiting, increasing the diameter of the pot by 2in/5cm until an 18in/45cm pot is reached. After that re-move the top 4in/10cm of compost and re-place with fresh. Prune and thin as for trees growing in the open ground, as described above.

PESTS AND DISEASES: PEACH AND NECTARINE

Pests
Red spider mite can be a nuisance in warm weather. Spray with malathion, derris or a solution of fatty-acid soaps.

Aphids can be a problem. Control them in the same way as the mites.

Diseases
Peach leaf curl is a fungal disease, the worst disease to affect peaches and nectarines. It causes red blistering of leaves, which eventually brown and fall. Take the preventive measure of spraying with Bordeaux mixture or copper fungicide when the leaves fall in autumn and again in late winter.

Stones of fruit may split and the fruit be forced open near the stalk. To avoid this, keep the trees well watered and fed. Maintain a pH level of 6.5 to 7. Hand pollinate the flowers.

COOKING AND FREEZING PEACHES AND NECTARINES

As with many fruits peaches and nectarines are best eaten ripe and raw, straight from the tree. They can be sliced and mixed with other fruits to make a fruit salad or, better, served just with raspberries, the ideal combination. Peel and slice the peaches, add to raspberries. Cover with a little sugar and a spicy wine, such as Gewürtztraminer, to bring out the full flavour.

If peaches and nectarines are not properly ripe, poach them gently with sugar and water or wine. First remove the skin by dropping the fruit in boiling water for about a minute. Peel, halve, remove the stone and poach.

To freeze peaches and nectarines, peel, halve and stone and brush with a mixture of lemon juice and water to prevent discolouring. Dry, pack in a rigid container and freeze.

CHERRY
(Prunus avium)

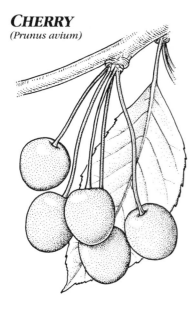

In the past cherry trees have been too big for an average-sized garden, growing fast and furiously to 30ft/9m. Now even a small garden can sport a cherry tree on the space-saving Colt root-stock. They are not dwarf, as apples can be, but it is possible to keep them to a manageable 10ft/3m as small pyramid bushes or fan-trained against a wall to a height of 8ft/2.4m. Some new varieties are even claimed to be self-pollinating, making a single cherry tree possible.

There have been many other improvements in breeding. Trees crop earlier in the year, and the fruit is of higher quality. Above all, new varieties are not as afflicted by the diseases the old ones were prone to – viral diseases and bacterial canker.

There are three types of cherry: the sweet cherry; the acid cherry, of which Morello is the most familiar variety; and, in between, the Duke cherry with a sweet and sour taste. Both Duke and acid cherry trees are less vigorous than the sweet cherry.

Varieties

Merton Glory has emerged as one of the most popular varieties. The large yellow-white cherries, flushed with crimson, crop early in summer. Pollinate with Morello or Merton Biggareau; the latter has large black cherries ripening in summer. Early Rivers, a dark-red, almost black, variety is the earliest to ripen in early summer. Pollinate with Merton Glory. Of the self-fer-

tile varieties there is Stella, with dark-red fruits ready to pick in summer, and the latest variety Sunburst, with black fruits at the beginning of summer. Two new varieties that have high resistance to bacterial canker are Mermat, with crops of black cherries, early summer to summer Merchant, with summer crops of black cherries. Pollinate both with Early Rivers.

May Duke is a Duke cherry variety and the usual acid cherry variety is Morello. The fruits of Morello are large, juicy and dark-red, ready for picking in late summer to early autumn. Both are self-pollinating.

The plant's needs

To protect the blossom early in the year from damage by frost, and from poor crops, trees must be grown in a sunny sheltered part of the garden where frost is unlikely. Grow fan trees against a south-, south-west- or west-facing wall for best results. Acid cherries will tolerate a certain amount of shade and will even grow on a north-facing wall.

Cherries are not fussy about the type of soil, but it must be fertile and well draining. Prepare the ground in early autumn by digging over an area 3ft sq/90cm sq to a depth of 2ft/60cm. If the ground is not very fertile, dig in plenty of well-rotted manure or compost, and apply a general fertilizer at the rate of 4oz per sq yd/120g per sq m. Lime acid soils for a pH level of 6.5 to 7.5.

Planting and growing

Plant all types of cherry tree between early winter and early spring, but preferably in early winter so that the tree has time to settle down before new growth starts in

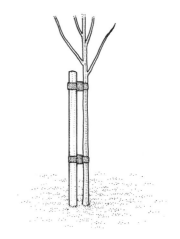

spring. Dig a hole large enough to take the root ball with the roots well spread out. Bush trees will need support, so drive a post 18in/45cm deep just off the centre of the hole. The post should be long enough to reach the lowest branches. Place the tree in the hole, fill in and firm down the soil. Secure the tree to the post by a rubber strap with a rubber buffer between the post and the tree to prevent chafing and possible damage. With more than one tree, plant them 15ft/4.5m apart.

Fan-trained trees will need support against a wall. Secure wires to the wall, the lowest 12in/30cm above the ground and the rest at intervals of 9in/22.5cm. Apply a mulch of well-rotted manure around the base of the tree.

Each year in late winter, apply a general fertilizer – 4oz per sq yd/120g per sq m, and a mulch of compost or manure. Once the fruits have started to develop, water the trees frequently to keep the soil moist at all times. This is especially important for fan-trained trees grown near walls where the soil dries out more quickly than in the open ground. Net trees to protect the fruit from birds. Harvest the cherries by cutting away clusters complete with the stalk, rather than by pulling them away.

Pruning for fan-trained sweet and Duke cherries

In spring after planting, cut back the main stem to 18in/45cm above the ground, leaving two laterals – one branching to the left and the other to the right. Make the cut just above the uppermost lateral. Tie the laterals to canes fixed to the wires at an angle of 40°.

In the spring of the second year, reduce

the length of the laterals to 12in/30cm, pruning to a healthy bud. During the summer new growth will appear that will form the framework of the fan.

In the third year, in spring, train the shoots that have emerged from each of the laterals so that they are spread over the wall in a fan shape. Tie the shoots to canes secured to the wires. Cut back all the shoots to about 18in/45cm.

In the fourth year in spring, remove shoots that are not growing flush along the wall. In summer, cut back to six leaves any shoots that are overcrowding the framework. When the tree has reached the height you want, prune back the shoots or tie them horizontally to the top wire. In early autumn, reduce to three leaves those shoots that were restricted to six leaves in summer; this encourages fruiting shoots for the next year. This is the pruning system to carry out in all following years.

Pruning fan-trained acid cherries

In late spring, cut back the main stem to 24in/60cm and any laterals back to one bud. In early summer, train the top branch vertically, one lateral to the right and one to the left just below the bottom wire. Remove all other shoots. In late summer, secure the two laterals to canes at a 45° angle to the wires and remove the central upright shoot.

In the following late winter, cut back the two laterals to 15in/37.5cm. In summer, choose four or five branches that have grown from the laterals to form the fan, securing them to canes attached to the wires. Cut back all other shoots to one leaf.

In late winter in the third year, reduce

all shoots by a third to a downward-facing bud. From the new growth that has appeared in summer, select three new shoots from each main stem and tie them in. Cut back the other shoots to one leaf. In late summer, pinch back the chosen shoots to 18in/45cm.

As acid cherries fruit on the previous year's growth, new shoots must be selected in early summer each year. Choose those growing near the base of fruit-bearing shoots and reduce all others to 6in/15cm. When fruiting is over, cut back shoots that have fruited, leaving the new ones to take their place.

Pruning for dwarf pyramids – all cherries

In early spring, cut back the main stem to 4ft/1.2m, to an upward- and outward-facing bud. Remove any laterals growing within 18in/45cm of the ground and cut back the remaining laterals by a half. In summer, reduce all new growth of the

main laterals to 8in/20cm – always to downward-facing buds.

In the following spring, reduce the main stem by a half of the new growth to a bud pointing in the opposite direction to that selected the previous year. In summer, cut back the current year's growth of laterals to eight leaves, and reduce any shoots growing from the laterals to six leaves. Remove altogether any strong-growing shoots near the top of the tree that would spoil its shape if left to grow.

Continue with this pruning each year until the tree has reached the desired height – 8ft/2.4m is a reasonable size. Then cut back the main stem each year in late spring to restrict growth.

As acid cherries fruit on the previous season's wood, select some of the other shoots each year to be cut back to stimulate new growth.

Growing in containers

Containers should be at least 12in/30cm deep and a similar diameter. Plant in late autumn, using loam compost, and place in a sunny sheltered spot. Frequent watering will be needed in warm weather, possibly twice a day. When the fruit begins to develop, give a liquid feed every two weeks. Pot-on every other year after fruiting to a container 2in/5cm larger in diameter until the largest convenient size of 18in/45cm is reached. Each year after that remove the top 4in/10cm of compost and replace it with fresh. Container-grown cherries are best trained as dwarf pyramids, restricting growth to about 7ft/2.1m. Follow the pruning instructions given under *Pruning for dwarf pyramids*.

PESTS AND DISEASES: CHERRY

Pests

Cherry blackfly These aphids distort the growth of new shoots and leaves, causing them to curl. They also secrete honeydew, making leaves and shoots sticky. As a preventive measure spray with a tar-oil wash in winter. To cope with an attack, spray with malathion, derris, a solution of fatty-acid soaps, or a systemic insecticide, dimethoate.

Caterpillars adore new foliage and they may appear in spring. Pick them off or spray with fenitrothion, but not when the tree is in blossom.

Diseases

Bacterial canker is the most serious disease. It forms open wounds often surrounded by gummy secretions. Cut out the infected shoots and spray with Bordeaux mixture monthly between late summer and autumn, and again in spring.

Silver leaf may also be a problem, recognized by silvering of the leaf surface. Cut away all affected branches and burn them.

COOKING AND FREEZING CHERRIES

Sweet and Duke cherries should be eaten as they come off the trees; just wash them. Gently poach morello cherries in sugar and water for about five minutes, until tender but before the skins become wrinkled. If you can bear the fiddle, remove the stones with a cherry stoner – it takes out the stones without mangling the cherries.

As a change from water, cook cherries in red wine or madeira, sugar and a little cinnamon.

To freeze cherries, wash and dry them and remove the stones. Pack in rigid containers and freeze.

DAMSON
(Prunus damascena)

Damsons have never been as popular as plums. Because they have been largely ignored by commercial growers, plant breeders have spent little time on developing new varieties. The few varieties available have been around for decades; indeed some are more than a century old. However, there have been advances in the root-stocks on which the varieties have been grafted. For smaller gardens, it is now possible to grow semi-dwarfing trees, raised on St Julien A root-stock and the latest introduction, Pixy, is a real space-saver. The trees grow – much more slowly than on a St Julien root-stock – to 8ft/2.4m, with a more compact head. They can even be grown in containers.

One of the great virtues of damsons is their hardiness; indeed, they are often planted as windbreaks to protect more tender fruit trees. So where you may not succeed with such exotic fruits as peaches and apricots, there should be no problem with damsons. Most varieties are self-fertile, so only one tree needs to be grown, but crops will be heavier if it is planted with another variety of damson or with a plum blossoming at the same time.

Varieties

The oldest-established variety is Farleigh Damson, over 160 years old with almost black fruits ripening in early autumn. Grow this one with another variety for the best results. There are three self-fertile varieties that don't need pollinators. Bradley's King, ready for picking in early autumn, has the sweetest purple fruits. The smallest variety is Shropshire Damson, also called Prune Damson. The blue-black fruits ripen from early autumn to autumn. Merryweather has large sweet fruits that crop early in its life.

The plant's needs

Damsons will grow in any type of soil as long as it is fertile and moisture-retentive. Prepare the soil in late summer before planting by digging in plenty of well-rotted manure or compost. The addition of peat will also make the soil both free-draining and water-retentive; this is most important for varieties grown on Pixy root-stock. Lime acid soils for a pH level of 6.5 to 7. Just before planting rake in general fertilizer at the rate of 3oz per sq yd/90g per sq m. Trees can be planted in

Damson, Merryweather variety.

the open as single specimens or as a windbreak. If more than one tree is planted, they should be 8-10ft/2.4-3m apart for Pixy root-stock and 10-12ft/3-3.6m for St Julien A root-stock.

Damsons can also be fan-trained against a wall. Secure horizontal wires to the wall against which the fan can be trained, starting 12in/30cm from the ground and then at 9in/22.5cm intervals.

Planting and growing

Plant trees between early winter and early spring, and preferably at the beginning of this period. Dig a hole large enough to take the root ball with the roots well spread out. If planting a tree to train as a pyramid or bush, drive a post 18in/45cm deep into the ground, just off the centre of

the hole. The top of the post should reach just below the lowest branches of the tree.

Plant the tree at the same level as it was growing originally, as shown by the soil mark on the main stem. Fan-trained trees should be planted about 6in/15cm away from the wall. Spread a mulch of well-rotted manure or compost round the base.

In late winter each year, apply a general fertilizer at the rate of 3oz per sq yd/90g per sq m and apply a mulch in spring. Plums blossom early, so any protection in the form of fine nylon netting or hessian is welcome. Assist pollination of the flowers by transferring the yellow pollen from anthers to stigma with a soft brush. Net trees against birds when the fruits are developing. Thin them when they are the size of peas so that clusters are well spaced with no more than two fruits. Pick damsons when they are tender, breaking them off complete with the stalk.

Pruning for a pyramid tree

In early spring, cut back the main stem to 4ft/1.2m to an upward- and outward-facing bud. Remove any laterals within 18in/45cm of the ground and reduce the remaining laterals by half. All new growth of main laterals is reduced by 8in/20cm in summer to downward-facing buds.

In spring of the following year, reduce the main stem by a half of the new growth to a bud pointing in the opposite direction to that selected the previous year. Then in summer cut back the current year's growth of laterals to eight leaves, and six leaves for shoots growing from laterals.

Continue with this system of pruning each year until the tree has grown to a height of about 8ft/2.4m. Thereafter, each year in spring cut back the main stem to restrict growth. Damsons fruit on old and new wood, so restrict pruning to removing a few shoots every year in order to stimulate new growth and to keep the pyramid shape.

Pruning for a fan

After planting in early spring, cut back the main stem to 18in/45cm, leaving a lateral immediately below the cut. Below this there should be at least two other laterals – one pointing to the left, the other to the right. Prune those, and any other laterals to one bud.

In early summer, train the top branch vertically and select two of the strongest to train, one to the left and the other to the right. Prune all other shoots to the main stem. In summer, tie the laterals to canes secured to the wires at an angle of 45°.

In late winter the following year, reduce the length of the laterals to 18in/45cm, cutting back to a healthy bud. In summer train the shoots growing from the two laterals to form the fan shape, tying them to the canes. Choose two above and one below each lateral. Reduce all other shoots by a third of new growth to a downward-pointing bud. In summer select three new shoots from each of the branches and tie them in, covering the wall. Prune all other shoots to one leaf.

In spring the following year, remove any shoots not growing flush with the wall. In summer, reduce to six leaves shoots that may be overcrowding the framework. Prune back shoots when the tree has reached the height wanted. Shoots reduced to six leaves in summer should be further reduced to three leaves in early autumn to stimulate growth of new fruiting shoots.

Container growing

Choose those varieties that have been grafted on to Pixy root-stock. Containers should be a minimum of 12in/30cm deep with a similar diameter. Plant in late autumn using quality loam compost. Place in a sunny sheltered position. Keep trees well watered at all times, especially in periods of warm weather. Apply a liquid feed every two weeks when fruit has formed a stone. After fruiting, pot-on every other year to a container 2in/5cm larger until the largest manageable size of 18in/45cm is reached. After that remove the top 4in/10cm of compost each year and replace with fresh. Train the tree as a dwarf pyramid for shape and restrict the growth when it gets to 7-8ft/2.1-2.4m. The fact that it is being grown in a container will help to check vigorous growth.

Pests and diseases: damson

See under *Damson, plum and greengage pests and diseases*, page 161.

COOKING AND FREEZING DAMSONS

Damsons are too tart to eat raw and are usually cooked. The simplest way of serving them is poached in water with a little sugar. Cook for about five minutes so that the skins remain intact and the fruit does not turn to mush. Serve with cream. Damson cheese is the ideal way to get rid of a glut of fruit. The end result is a thick concentration of fruit. Simmer 3lb/1.5kg of fruit in half a pint of water until it is tender. Sieve the mixture to remove the skins and boil with ¾1lb/375g of sugar to each 1lb/500g of sieved pulp until nearly solid. Delicious on freshly baked bread.

Damsons can be frozen. Wash, halve and stone them. Leave to dry and pack in rigid containers.

PLUMS
(Prunus domestica)

GREENGAGES
(Prunus italica)

Plum jam and tinned plums are no longer as popular as they once were, but the fruit itself has not lost its appeal. The commercial decline has meant that few new varieties have arrived on the scene. However, as with damsons, the improvement has been in the use of different root-stocks that produce smaller trees to the benefit of those with smaller gardens.

St Julien A is now the most usual root-stock on which plums are grafted. These trees are semi-dwarfing, growing to 15ft/4.5m, but they can be restricted to a more manageable 10ft/3m if trained as a pyramid tree. Where space is very limited choose Pixy root-stock. By careful pruning and training to a pyramid shape the tree will grow to no more than 8ft/2.4m, keeping a compact shape that is easy to care for.

Few varieties are grown commercially and these are not always the best flavoured. By growing plums yourself you can choose those that crop reliably with consistently good flavour.

Greengages are now an increasingly rare sight in the shops. To taste and enjoy the distinctive sweetness of these fruits, there is often no choice but to grow them yourself.

Both plums and greengages have suffered over the years from pests and diseases and none has been eliminated for good. But buy stock certified as pest- and disease-free. It will be when you buy it although there is no guarantee that it will not be attacked in the future.

Varieties

Plums For dessert eating, there is nothing to beat Victoria with pale-red, sweet juicy fruits ripening in late summer and early autumn. It is self-fertile, so no pollinators are needed. Kirke's Blue, another dessert plum with purple colouring, is ready in early autumn. Grow with Victoria as a pollinator. Yellow-fleshed Early Laxton is the earliest plum to ripen in the later part of summer. Pollinate with Kirke's Blue or Victoria. Plums best suited to cooking include Marjorie's Seedling, which is yellow-fleshed with purple-blue skins, ready from early autumn to autumn and self-fertile. The earliest cooking plum is Rivers' Early Prolific, ripening in summer

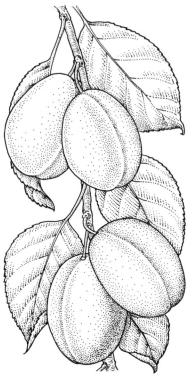

and late summer. This plant has yellow-fleshed juicy fruits. Pollinate it with Victoria. Czar is self-fertile with purple fruits ready to pick in late summer. Edwards is one of the few new varieties with purple-blue skins and yellow flesh. It is ready in early autumn and should be pollinated with Victoria.

Greengages Early Transparent Gage is a self-fertile variety with pale-yellow juicy fruits, ripening in late summer. Oulin's Golden Gage is also self-fertile, fruiting at the same time. Denniston's Superb produces heavy crops of yellow-green fruits in late summer.

The plant's needs

Plums and gages are not fussy about the type of soil they grow in, but it must be both well draining and moisture-retentive. Less fertile soils should be prepared in late summer by digging in plenty of well-rotted manure or compost. To make soils more water-retentive and free-draining, dig in peat. Acid soils should be limed to a pH level of 6.5 to 7.

Choose a sunny sheltered spot to ensure fruits ripen properly with a sweet juicy flavour. Take particular care with greengages, growing them against a

south- or west-facing wall. If more than one tree is planted in the open, space varieties on St Julien A root-stock 10-12ft/3.6m apart, and those on Pixy root-stock 8-10ft/2.4-3m apart.

If trees are to be fan-trained against a wall, fix horizontal wires to the wall, starting 12in/30cm above the ground and then at 9in/22.5cm intervals.

Growing

Immediately before planting trees, apply a general fertilizer at the rate of 3oz per sq yd/90g per sq m. The usual planting period is between early winter and early spring, the earlier the better to allow trees to settle down before new growth starts in spring. Dig a hole large enough to take the root ball with the roots well spaced out. Drive a post 18in/45cm into the ground just off the centre of the hole for trees to be grown as pyramids or bushes. The top of the post should reach to just below the lowest branches. Secure the tree to the post with a rubber strap that has a buffer to prevent chafing of the stem. Plant trees for fan training about 6in/15cm away from the wall. Apply a mulch of well-rotted manure or compost round the base of the tree, leaving a gap of about 3in/7.5cm between the mulch and the tree.

Apply a general fertilizer at the rate of 3oz per sq yd/90g per sq m each year in late winter. Each spring apply a mulch round the tree but not touching the trunk. If there is a chance of frost at blossom time, protect the trees with fine nylon netting or hessian. As the trees blossom early in the year, when there are not many insects about, assist pollination by transferring the yellow pollen from anthers to stigma with a soft brush.

Protect the fruit from birds with netting. Thin plums and greengages once the stones have formed so that they are about 2in/5cm apart. Gather the fruits by cutting them away complete with the stalk. They will ripen in stages, so look at the tree regularly as soon as the first fruits have ripened.

Pruning for a pyramid tree

Cut back the main stem to 5ft/1.5m in early spring to an upward- and outward-facing bud. Remove any laterals that are within 18in/45cm of the ground and prune the remaining laterals by half. In summer, prune the new growth of the laterals by 8in/20cm to downward-facing buds.

In the following year in spring, prune the main stem by half of the new growth to

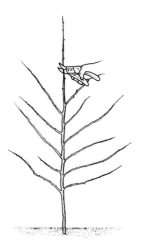

a bud pointing in the opposite direction to that selected the previous year. In summer, cut back the current year's growth of laterals to eight leaves, and to six leaves for any shoots growing from laterals. Carry on with this sequence of pruning each year until the overall height is about 8ft/2.4m.

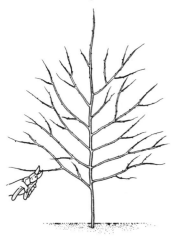

Then in spring each year, cut back the main stem to check any further growth. Plums, like damsons, fruit on old and new wood, so prune each year, removing a few shoots to encourage new growth and to retain the pyramid shape.

Pruning for a fan

In early spring after planting, cut back the main stem to 18in/45cm, leaving one lateral below the cut. Below this there should be at least two other laterals, one to the left and one to the right. Prune them and all other laterals to one bud.

In early summer, train the top branch

vertically and choose two of the strongest below for training to left and right. Cut out all other shoots. In summer, secure canes at a 40° angle to the wires and tie the laterals to them.

In late winter the following year, reduce the length of the laterals to 18in/45cm. During summer new growth will appear from the two pruned laterals. Tie in two new shoots above and one below each lateral to form the fan shape, securing them to canes. Cut back all other shoots to one leaf.

In the following years in spring, pinch out all the shoots that are not growing flush with the wall. Any shoots not needed for the framework should be reduced to six leaves. When the shoots have reached the top of the wall, cut them back. In autumn, reduce to three leaves shoots that were pruned to six leaves in summer. Plums fruit on old and new wood, so don't be too savage with annual pruning. Cut out very old and bare branches to stimulate new growth.

Container growing

Varieties grown on Pixy root-stock are those to choose for container growing. Containers should be a minimum of 12in/30cm deep with a similar diameter. Use quality loam compost and plant in autumn. Place the container in a sunny sheltered spot. Frequent watering will be necessary in periods of warm weather, often twice a day. As the fruit starts to form apply a liquid feed once every two weeks.

When fruiting is over, pot-on to a container 2in/5cm larger every other year until an 18in/45cm container is reached. Then remove the top 4in/10cm of compost each year, replacing with fresh. For compact growth, prune to a dwarf pyramid shape and restrict growth when the tree is 7-8ft/2.1-2.4m high.

COOKING AND FREEZING PLUMS AND GREENGAGES

The simplest way to enjoy plums and greengages is to stew them. Sprinkle with sugar, just cover with water and poach gently for about five minutes. The aim is to prevent the skins from splitting and the fruit disintegrating. Cook plums in a mixture of water and red wine or madeira, and greengages in water and white wine.

For a quick dessert, halve the fruit, remove the stones and chop the flesh. Mix equal parts of double and sour cream and stir in the fruit with sugar and lemon juice. Pour into a dish and cover with a thin layer of soft brown sugar. Place under a grill and cook until the sugar has melted. Leave to cool before serving.

Before freezing, wash, halve and stone the fruit. Dry. Pack into rigid containers and freeze.

MELON
(Cucumis melo)

It is now quite possible to cultivate melons in temperate or cool climates. They do need to be cultivated under glass, but it is not necessary to have a greenhouse – a garden frame or cloche will do. The other important element is sun – so if you give them a try, pray for a sunny summer.

Since melons have not been commercially viable in cool climates, there has been little incentive to raise new varieties that will grow there. However, increased interest by the home grower has now led to the appearance of one F_1 hybrid that is quick to mature and will grow well in cooler areas in a frame or under cloches. Cantaloupe and musk melons have the best flavour; cantaloupes may have a ridged, smooth or scaly skin, and musk melons have a netted skin. While cantaloupes can be grown in a frame or under cloches, musk melons do better in a greenhouse.

Varieties

Sweetheart is the latest variety, an F_1 hybrid with a pale-green smooth skin and orange-pink flesh. Romeo is another F_1 hybrid with a netted skin and dark-orange flesh. Charentais, the staple melon of France, has sweet orange flesh. Ogen melons were developed in Israel and they are exported from there in vast quantities. The small fruits have pale greenish-yellow flesh.

Musk melon varieties include Emerald Gem, with green flesh, and Blenheim Orange, with orange-red flesh. Both have netted skins.

The plant's needs

The soil for cantaloupe melons grown in a frame must be fertile, free-draining but moisture-retentive; this is most important since they are very thirsty plants. Dig in plenty of well-rotted manure or compost. If the ground does not hold moisture well, also dig in well-moistened peat.

For plants raised in containers in a greenhouse, choose quality loam compost. Growing bags can also be used. Melons grown in this way need plenty of water and feeding when the fruits begin to develop.

Sowing and growing

In late winter or early spring, sow seed in 3in/7.5cm pots of loam seed compost – one seed to a pot and the seed must be pushed in sideways. Keep at a temperature of 65-75°F/18-24°C. Either place them in a heated propagator or enclose each pot in a plastic bag and put it somewhere warm, such as an airing cupboard,

Melon, Charantais variety.

until the seed has germinated. Move on to larger pots if the original ones become filled with roots. Plant out to a frame or under cloches in late spring, spacing them 2½-3ft/75-90cm apart.

When five true leaves have developed (after the seed leaves), pinch out the growing tip and side-shoots will develop. If the melon is being grown in a frame, choose four shoots with the sturdiest growth and train them to the corners of the frame. Remove any other shoots altogether.

If under cloches, train two shoots in each direction. When the shoots have grown to 18in/45cm pinch them out to encourage further growth, which will eventually bear the fruit. When the plants come into flower, they will need help with pollination. Plants produce both male and female flowers; the female can be recognized by a tiny lump behind the flower – the melon-to-be. Push the stamens on the male flower into the centre of the female flower. Pollinate all the flowers at the same time if possible, to ensure even development of the melons.

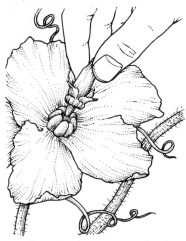

As the melons begin to grow, thin them out, removing all but four fruits on each plant. Pinch out shoots two leaves beyond the fruit. Pinch out any other laterals to four leaves. Any new shoots that develop should be removed completely.

Give a liquid feed every week as the melons begin to swell. Keep them well watered at this stage, but as the fruits start to ripen stop watering and keep them almost dry so that the skins don't split. Cut the melons from the plants before they are fully ripe but when they have a distinct melon smell and when the base of the fruit feels soft. Leave to ripen fully in a cool place indoors.

Growing melons in a greenhouse

Sow seed as described under *Sowing and growing*. About a month after germination plants can be transferred to the greenhouse and their final growing position. Plants will need support, so stretch wires horizontally 12in/30cm apart along one wall of the greenhouse and then attach canes to the wires, vertically, to support the stems.

Transplant each plant to a 9in/22.5cm pot, setting the pots 2½-3ft/75-90cm apart. Or place three plants at equal distances in a growing bag.

When the plants are 6in/15cm tall, with four or five true leaves, pinch out the growing tip. Select two of the new vigorous shoots that develop, tying each to a cane. When the stems are 6ft/1.8m tall, pinch out the growing tips. Tie laterals to the wires as they develop, following pinching out.

When the laterals have five leaves, pinch them out and pollinate any flowers that appear on the new growth that follows this pinching out. Remove any other flowers.

Remove all but four melons from each plant and pinch out the shoots to two leaves beyond the fruit. Any other laterals

PESTS AND DISEASES: MELON

Pests

Aphids can be kept under control by spraying with malathion, the more acceptable derris, or a solution of fatty-acid soaps.

Red spider mites often plague melons grown in greenhouses. Foliage becomes mottled, yellows and dies. Fine threads can be seen on leaves and stems in severe infestations. Treat in the same way as aphids. In serious cases, the systemic insecticide dimethoate can be used.

Whiteflies lurk under leaves excreting honeydew, sapping plants of vitality. Spray with malathion or pyrethrum, or introduce the parasitic *Encarsia formosa*.

Diseases

Cucumber mosaic virus may attack. Leaves are mottled yellow, shrivel and die. Fruits are misshapen and never develop properly. Remove and burn all affected plants and fruits. In future years, take the preventive measure of keeping aphids at bay – the carriers of the disease.

COOKING AND FREEZING MELONS

Melons are mostly water and though sweet don't have a high sugar content. Slice a melon in half or quarters, remove the seeds, and it is ready to eat just as it is, or sprinkled with a little Cointreau to enhance the flavour. Forget about chilling before serving; that only masks or destroys the flavour. The flesh can also be cut into cubes and added to fresh fruit salads.

There are unlikely to be any melons left over for freezing, but if so they can be cubed and then frozen.

should be pinched out to four leaves. New shoots that appear should be cut altogether. Keep well watered and apply a weekly feed. As the fruit swells support each with a net secured to wires, canes and the framework of the greenhouse.

GRAPE
(Vitis viniferis)

For anyone living in a reliably mild climate and able to provide the necessary sheltered and sunny space, grape vines can provide fascinating gardening and delicious crops.

The important element, of course, is the weather, but even in bad years the lush decorative foliage of the vine is some compensation for a poor crop.

The chances of success will be greater if the vines are grown under glass. But they do take up a lot of room and if they are trained across the roof, there is a poor outlook for anything growing underneath them. It is better to try your luck at growing them outside.

Varieties

Make sure when choosing a variety that you select a dessert variety and not one for winemaking. The best dessert grape is Black Hamburgh – black sweet and juicy – but it is usually grown under glass and is worth trying outdoors only in very mild areas. Brant is probably the most reliable outdoor variety, producing crops of small dark-blue grapes ready for picking in autumn. Its vigorous growth quickly covers a wall and the foliage colours magnificently in autumn. Fragola, or strawberry grape, produces small bunches of black grapes with a hint of strawberry flavour; another variety with attractive autumn colouring. Madeleine Angevine

has white grapes suitable for both dessert use and for winemaking. This variety is usually fairly successful in cooler areas.

The plant's needs

There are certain essentials for grape growing and if you cannot provide them you will not get any grapes worth eating. The vine should be planted against a south-facing wall where it will be sheltered and get the sun. Soil should be fertile, but not too rich or there will be lush foliage growth at the expense of the fruit.

The type of soil is not particularly important, but if it is acid, lime it for a pH level of 6.5 to 7. Efficient drainage is essential. To deal with waterlogged soil, dig a

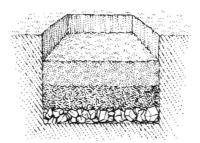

hole 18in/45cm deep and 2ft sq/60cm sq. Fill the bottom with a layer of stones or rubble. Follow this with a layer of compost or well-rotted manure and cover it with soil to bring the depth of the hole to within 6in/15cm of the surface of the soil. The hole is now ready to receive the vine.

Planting and growing

Planting time is usually between autumn and early spring. It is best to plant in autumn to give the plant time to settle down before new growth begins in spring. Place the vine in the prepared hole, 6-9in/15-22.5cm away from the wall, and spread out the roots. Fill in the hole and firm down. If more than one vine is being planted, space them 4ft/1.2m apart.

Support the plants by stretching wires between posts sunk 18in/45cm into the ground, with 5ft/1.5m showing above ground. The first wire is fixed 18in/45cm above ground, followed by two others at 12in/30cm intervals. Attach a cane to the wire to support each plant.

In spring each year, apply a general fertilizer at the rate of 3oz per sq yd/90g per sq m, followed by a mulch around the base of the vine to keep the soil moist. Water well in warm weather, but stop once the fruit begins to swell.

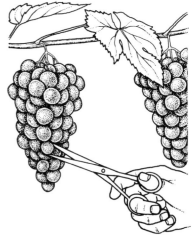

When the largest grapes are the size of peas, start thinning, removing the smaller ones and those in the centre of the bunch with fine-pointed scissors. The aim is to leave a gap of ¼in/0.6cm between each grape. By early autumn the grapes should have their full colour and look ready to pick. Pick one or two grapes and try them. If they are not properly ripe (and they will probably not be), leave them for a further three to four weeks. They should be ready for picking in autumn.

Cut the branch with secateurs, removing a little of the lateral branch on each side of the main stem holding the grapes. This will give you something to hold the bunch by so that the bloom is not brushed off the grapes.

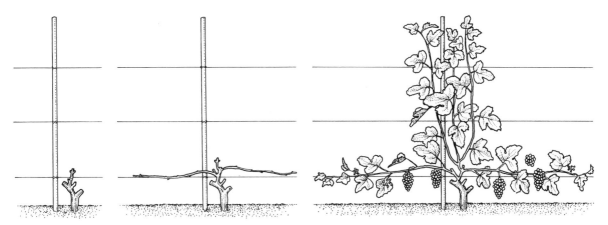

Training and pruning

Immediately after planting cut back the cane, leaving three buds. In the following spring or late spring, these buds should burst, producing three shoots. Remove the weakest, leaving the other two to grow on, and tie them to the cane as they grow. When side-shoots develop from the two stems, cut them back to one or two buds. In early winter, cut down the canes to three buds. During the following summer leave three of the sturdiest shoots to develop, cutting back any others that may appear. Pinch out any lateral shoots and remove flowers. In early winter, train one shoot to the left and one to the right along the bottom wire and cut back the third shoot to three buds. The two shoots should produce fruiting laterals the following year, while the cut-back shoot will provide replacement shoots for fruiting.

As the fruiting laterals grow during the next summer train them vertically, attaching them to the wires. When they reach the topmost wire, cut them back and remove any shoots growing from them.

For a few years, three or four bunches of grapes should be allowed to grow each year; all others should be removed. In later years it may be possible to leave one bunch per fruiting lateral. The replacement laterals that have grown during the summer are tied to the cane vertically and any shoots that grow from them are pinched back to one leaf. In early winter, cut back the laterals that fruited in the autumn and replace them with two of the three new shoots that have grown. Train one to the left along the wire, and the other to the right. Cut these two back to 2½ft/75cm. Cut the remaining lateral back to three buds.

This is the training and pruning system to be followed each year in the future.

Growing in containers

Grapes can be grown in containers, one vine to a pot or tub, at least 12in/30cm deep and 12in/30cm wide. Place the container against a warm, sunny south-facing wall so that the vine can be trained against it. Plant in autumn, using quality loam compost. Water well in warm weather, but keep drier when the grapes begin to swell. Apply a liquid feed every two weeks after the fruit begins to form. Pot-on after fruiting when necessary – that is, when the roots have filled the container. Move the plant to a pot 2in/5cm larger each time until an 18in/45cm pot is reached. After that remove the top 4in/10cm of compost each year and replace with fresh.

Train and prune the vine as described.

PESTS AND DISEASES: GRAPE

Pests

Vines grown out of doors usually stay free from attacks by insects, but:

Wasps can be a nuisance when the grapes begin to ripen. Entice them away from the fruit by sinking jars of sugared water or beer in the ground round the base of the vine.

Birds The only way to keep birds off the precious grapes is to net the vine.

Diseases

Pests may not be troublesome but fungal diseases are.

Downy mildew leaves white deposits on leaves – usually the undersides – and stems. Don't let the vine get too dry or the fungus will strike, and there is no cure. Preventive measures can be taken. Spray with Bordeaux mixture, benomyl or dinocap after flowering is over, and every two weeks until early autumn.

Powdery mildew is a grey mould fungus that covers leaves, shoots and, worst of all, the fruit itself. Remove all infected fruit and leaves. Take preventive measures in early summer by dusting with sulphur or Bordeaux powder before flowering begins. Stop when the vine is in flower and dust again when flowering is over.

COOKING AND FREEZING GRAPES

Grapes should be eaten just as they come off the vine. Even washing ruins some of the pleasure by removing the bloom on the skin. Peeling them takes a long time and sacrifices one of the pleasures of eating grapes – breaking the skin and filling your mouth with the sweet juice.

It is unlikely that any grapes will be left over for freezing. Any that are should have the pips removed first, so it is best simply to eat them fresh.

NUTS

*I*f you are the sort of gardener that likes a challenge, you might well consider growing your own nut trees. However, it is important to choose the right variety. A walnut, for example, will eventually grow into a tree 25ft/7.5cm tall. Almonds cannot be relied on to produce nuts unless they have perfect weather – no frost to damage the blossom and warm summers to ripen the nuts. If you want to grow almonds, it is better to grow them on a bush in a sunny sheltered position than on a tree.

Hazels and filberts are easier to handle. Both can be pruned to stay about 6ft/1.8m tall, though the spread can be twice that. Moreover, they usually produce reliable crops of nuts.

HAZEL or COB NUT
(Corylus avellana)
FILBERT
(Corylus maxima)

Commercial production of hazels has dwindled to almost nothing, with more profitably produced crops such as apples, pears and cherries taking their place. Major nut production is now in the hands of Italy and Spain. This decline in the market has brought the development of new varieties to a standstill. However, the older varieties – many over a century old – are quite reliable.

Varieties

Size and shape are the main differences between cobs and filberts: filberts are larger and have an elongated oval shape while cobs are a dumpy oval. Both cob nuts and filberts are self-fertile, so only one tree need be planted. However, results are often better when two varieties are planted. Cosford is a cob nut bearing large, sweet-flavoured nuts in autumn and late autumn. Many catkins are produced, making this a good pollinator. So is Pearson's Prolific, a cob with medium to small nuts, ready in autumn.

Kentish Cob is the best-known and most popular variety of filbert nuts. Red Filbert, with bright-red catkins, produces a nut generally considered to have the best flavour. This variety must be grown with a pollinator for strong crops. Filberts ripen in autumn to late autumn.

The plant's needs

Hazels will grow in any type of soil, but it must not be too rich, which encourages lush foliage instead of nuts. Acid soils should be limed for a pH of about 6.5. Choose a sheltered sunny site for the tree so that the flowers have the maximum protection when they open early in the year. Avoid planting in frost pockets.

Growing

Prepare the soil in advance of planting by digging in well-rotted manure or compost. Dig a hole 3ft sq/90cm sq and 2ft/60cm deep, and mix compost or manure with the soil removed from the hole. Put the excess soil in another part of the garden.

Plant the tree in autumn or late autumn. Spread the roots out in the hole and plant to the same depth as the tree was originally growing. The soil mark on the stem will show the correct level. If more than one tree is planted, space at 12ft/3m.

In spring each year, apply a mulch of well-rotted manure or compost round the base of the tree, making sure that the mulch does not touch the main stem.

Nuts should be ready to pick when their shells have turned brown and hard. After picking, leave them to dry out for a few days in a warm place and then keep them in cool storage. Eat within two to three months.

Pruning

Trees are usually supplied on short stems, 15-18in/37.5-45cm tall, with a strong cup-shaped growth of branches above. The aim is to keep that shape and restrict growth to a manageable 6ft/1.8m. After planting, cut back the leading stems by half of that year's growth to an outward-facing bud.

Continue with this pruning each year until the tree starts to flower. The trees usually supplied are three years old, so they should start to flower after two years. At that stage pruning should take place in late winter or early spring when flowering is nearly over, and when pollen from the catkins has fertilized the female flowers. After the tree has started bearing nuts, pruning should be confined to those shoots that have borne nuts the previous year. These are cut back to three buds. Don't touch shoots bearing flowers as these will later produce the nuts.

In late summer, remove any shoots that spoil the cup shape of the bush and over-crowd the centre; growth should always be open in the centre of the bush.

Pests and diseases

Seldom give trouble.

Sweet almond blossom.

SWEET ALMOND
(Prunus dulcis)

Expect a crop of almonds only in the mildest, frost-free areas with sunny summers. Elsewhere, be content to grow them simply for the beautiful blossom. Even that is often short-lived, destroyed by the slightest frost.

Varieties

The tree usually offered is *Prunus dulcis*.

The plant's needs

Almonds will grow in any type of well-draining soil. To improve poor drainage where the tree is to be planted, dig a hole 3ft sq/90cm sq and 2ft/60cm deep. Place a layer of rubble at the bottom of the hole and chopped turves on top. Fill the hole with fresh loam compost. If the soil is already of reasonable quality, merely fork in general fertilizer at the rate of 3oz per sq yd/90g per sq m. Acid soil should be limed to a pH level of 6.5 to 7. Most important of all, choose a sunny sheltered site with no frost pockets.

Almonds are not fully self-fertile, so crops will not be large unless the tree is pollinated by another *Prunus* variety.

Growing

Plant trees in late autumn either in the specially prepared areas described under *The plant's needs*, or in straightforward holes big enough to take the root balls with the roots well spread out. Plant at the level at which the tree was originally growing, and support the tree with a post driven 18in/45cm into the ground along-side it. After planting, and every year afterwards in spring, spread a mulch of well-rotted manure or compost round the base of the tree but not touching the stem.

The nuts should be ready in autumn when the husks start to split. Remove the almonds and dry them well spread out in the sun. When dried out, store them in a cool place.

Pruning for a bush tree

After planting, reduce the main stem to 3ft/90cm. Choose four strong laterals, reducing them by half to within two or three buds of the main stem. Remove all other shoots.

In the following spring, prune the four shoots by half to an outward-facing bud. By the third spring there should be eight branches, each to be pruned by half. By the fourth year the tree should be well established. From then on prune lightly to keep open growth in the centre of the tree and to keep the height in check.

PESTS AND DISEASES: SWEET ALMOND

Pests are seldom a problem.

Diseases
Peach leaf curl may be troublesome. This disease covers leaves with red blisters, until they eventually brown and fall. Take preventive measures, spraying with Bordeaux or copper fungicide when the leaves fall in autumn and winter.

A

A Coeur Plein (dandelion) 21
Abundance (tomato) 102
Achilles (gooseberry) 138
acidity, soil 8
Acme (swede) 88
adzuki bean *see* bean
Ailsa Crag (onion) 92
Ailsa Crag (tomato) 102
alfalfa sprouts **32**
Alfred (apricot) 150
Alfresco (tomato) 102
Alicante (tomato) 102
alkalinity, soil 9
All the Year Round (lettuce) 26
almond, sweet 166, **167**
Alpha (cauliflower) 39
Ambassador (courgette) 97
American Green Greensnap (celery) 52
Amsden June (peach) 154
Amsterdam Forcing (carrot) 76, 77
angelica **118**, 125, 126
anise **119**
Annie Oakley (okra) 68
anthracnose (disease) 69
aphids 11, *see also* individual plant pests
apple 33, 38, 75, 137, **148-9**, 153
apple mint **127**
apricot 125, **150-1**, 158
April Cross (radish) 82
Aquadulce Claudia (broad bean) 62
Aramis (French bean) 66
Aromel (strawberry) 144
artichoke,
    Chinese 70, **71**
    globe 46, **50-1**, 54, 55
    Jerusalem **70-1**
Ashton Cross (blackberry) 136
asparagus 16, 46, **48-9**
Atlantic Giant (pumpkin) 100
aubergine 94, **95**
Autoro (cabbage) 37
Autumn Bliss (raspberry) 142
Autumn King's (carrot) 76
Autumn Mammoth Argenta (leek) 90
Autumn Mammoth Snowstar (leek) 90
Avon Resister (turnip) 80
Avoncrisp (lettuce) 27, 29
Aztec (sweet corn) 59

B

balm **119-20**
Balstora (onion) 92
barley sprouts **32**
Baron Solemacher (strawberry) 144
Barrier Reef (cauliflower) 39, 40
basil **120**
Batavian Broad-Leaved (endive) 24
Batavian Green (endive) 24
bay, sweet **131**
bean 16
    broad 58, **62-3**
    flageolet 68

French 58, 63, **66-7**, 69
    haricot 63, **68**
    runner 58, **64-5**, 69
bean sprouts 31, 32, 33, 109, 114
Bedford Giant (blackberry) 136
Bedfordshire Champion (onion) 92
beds, raised garden 16
beet,
    seakale *see* chard, Swiss
    spinach *see* spinach
beetle, (pest) 41, 49, 83, 87, 89, 107, 112, 117, 137, 143
beetroot 17, **74, 75**
Bellgarde (peach) 154
Ben Lomond (black currant) 140
Ben More (black currant) 140
Ben Sarek (black currant) 140, 141
benomyl (fungicide) 29, 41, 69, 87, 89,
    93, 101, 103, 112, 139, 141, 143,
    145, 149, 152, 165
Berkley (blueberry) 135
Berlicum Berjo (carrot) 76
Berliner (Hamburg parsley) 79
Best of All (swede) 88
Best of All (tomato) 102
Beurre Hardy (pear) 151
Beurre Superfin (pear) 151
Bianca di Milano (sugar loaf chicory) 22
Big Boy (tomato) 102
birds as pests 61, 145, 165
birds/pets and pesticides 42
Black Hamburgh (grape) 164
Black Prince (aubergine) 95
Black Spanish Round (radish) 82
Black Velvet (gooseberry) 138
blackberry 134, **136-7**
Blackdown (black currant) 140
blackfly (pest) 63, 69, *see also* fly
blanching 21, 22, 23, 24, 43, 52-3, 54, 55, 91
Blauwgroene Winter Kajak (leek) 90
Blenheim Orange (melon) 162
blight (disease) 44, 69, 73, 103, 143
block planting 16-17, 20, 35, 40, 63, 66, 75, 78
Blue Crop (blueberry) 135
Blue Lake (French bean) 66
blueberry **135**
Bokki (runner bean 64, 65
Bolero (apple) 148
Bolthardy (beetroot) 75
Bonica (aubergine) 95
borage **120**
borax solution 89
Bordeaux mixture (fungicide) 53, 61,
    69, 73, 87, 93, 143, 155, 157, 165, 167
Boskoop Giant (black currant) 140
botrytis *see* mould, grey
Bounty (strawberry) 144
Bowles variety (mint) 127
Bradley's King (damson) 158
Bramley's Seedling (apple) 148
Brant (grape) 164
brassicas 16, 17, **34-41**
broccoli 16, 34, **36-7**

Chinese (Chinese kale/spinach
  mustard) 106, **112**
bromophos (insecticide) 41, 69, 73, 77,
  78, 93, 107, 117
Brussels sprout 16, 17, **34-5**, 51
buckwheat sprouts **32**
burdock **108-9**
burning to destroy pests and diseases 1, 11, 29, 41, 44,
  49, 53, 57, 69, 73, 77, 78, 87, 89, 93, 101, 117
Burpee Hybrid (cucumber) 98
Burpees Golden (beetroot) 74
Burpless Tasty Green (cucumber) 98
Bush Champion (cucumber) 98
Bush Crop (cucumber) 98, 99
butterflies (pests) 41, 107, 112, 117

C
cabbage 16, 17, 34, **37-8**, 75, 84, 107, 149
  Chinese 37, 106, **107**, 115
calabrese 34, **36**
Californian Golden Wonder (sweet pepper) 96
calomel (fungicide) 41, 87, 89, 93, 107, 112, 117, 124
Cambridge Favourite (strawberry) 144
Camus (carrot) 76
Canape (sweet pepper) 96
Canberra (cauliflower) 39, 40
canes for staking/supporting 63, 64, 67, 98, 99, 102,
  103
canker,
  (disease) 80, 81, 149, 156, 157
  paint 149
capsicum 94
captan (fungicide) 41, 69, 149, 152
Cara (potato) 72
caraway **121**
carbaryl (pesticide) 61
Cardinal (carrot) 76
cardoon 46, 54, **55**
carrot 17, 33, 38, 74, **76-7**, 84, 87, 107, 109, 133, 149
catch cropping 17
caterpillars 41, 107, 112, 117, 139, 141, 149, 152, 157
cauliflower 16, 17, 34, **39-41**
Cavallo (corn salad) 20
Celebrity (celery) 52
celeriac 16, 74, **78**
celery 16, 18, 32, 46, 51, **52-3**, 68, 75, 78, 87, 115, 149
Celtic (cabbage) 37
celtuce 18, **19**
Champagne Early (rhubarb) 56
Chantenay Red Cored (carrot) 76
chard,
  ruby (rhubarb chard) 42
  Swiss (seakale beet) **42-3**
Charentais (melon) 162
Cheltenham Green Top (beetroot) 75
Cheltenham Mono (beetroot) 75
chemical sprays 11
cherry **156-7**
Cherry Bella (radish) 82
chervil 83, **121**
Chevrier Vert (haricot bean) 68
chick pea *see* pea

chicory 18, **22-3**, 28
  Grumolo 22, 23
  sugar loaf 22
  Witloof (Belgian) 22, 23
China Rose (radish) 82
Chinese Long Green (cucumber) 98
Chinese tsai shim (pak choi) 117
chives 83, 106, **121-2**
  Chinese (garlic chives) 106, **113**, 114, 117
chop suey greens (shungiku/garland chrysanthemum)
  106, **114**, 117
cinnamon 118
Citadel (Brussels sprout) 34
Citation (calabrese) 36
Clairon (carrot) 76
Clemson's Spineless (okra) 68
cloche, use **12**, 19, 20, 28, 29, 44, 45, 47, 66, 69, 76, 93,
  95, 96, 97, 100, 103, 109, 116
club-root (disease) 16, 41, 87, 88, 89, 107, 112, 117
cob nut *see* hazel nut
Cobham Improved Marrow (turnip) 80
columnar tree growing 147, 148, 153
compost, manufacture and use 9, 10, **11**, 14, 16, *see also*
  individual plant species
Concorde (pear) 152
Concorde (potato) 72
Conference (pear) 151, 152
Connovers Colossal (asparagus) 48
container cultivation 7, 14-15, *see also* individual
  species
cooking *see* individual species
copper fungicide 155, 167
cordon tree growing 138-9, 140, 141, 146, 148-9, 153
coriander 118, **122**
corn, sweet 58, **59**
corn salad 17, 18, **20**
Cornet de Bordeaux (endive) 24
Cosford (hazel nut) 166
courgette 33, 94, 96, **97**, 100, 101, 127
Coville (blueberry) 135
Cox's Orange Pippin (apple) 148
crab apple 148
cress **25**, *see also* mustard; watercress
  American (land cress) **18-19**
crop management 16-17
Crystal Head (sugar loaf chicory) 22
cucumber 28, 33, 94, **98-9**, 101
curl, leaf (disease) 155
Curlina (parsley) 128
currants **140-1**
  black currant 134, **140**, **141**
  red currant **140**, **141**
  white currants 140, 141
Custard White (squash) 100
Custard Yellow (squash) 100
cut-and-grow again technique 18, 19, 20, 22, 23, 24, 26,
  28, 42, 44, 45, 86, 87, 106, 110-11, 114, 116
cutworm (pest) 29
Cylindra (beetroot) 74
Czar (plum) 160

D

damping off (disease) 41
damson **158-9**
dandelion 18, **21**
Dandie (lettuce) 28
Danny (tomato) 102
Darlington's Grain Spawn (mushroom) 104
Denniston's Superb (greengage) 160
derris (pesticide) 10, *see also* individual plant pests
Desire (potato) 72
Desire (runner bean) 64
Desire (potato) 72
Detroit Little Ball (beetroot) 75
Detroit New Globe (beetroot) 75
dieback (disease) 151
digging 11, 16, *see also* individual plant species
dill 99, **123**
dimethoate (insecticide) 61, 131, 157, 163
dinocap (fungicide) 139, 141, 145, 165
Discovery (apple) 148
diseases,
    resistance to 7
    see also individual plant diseases
Dixi (blueberry) 135
Dok Elgon (cauliflower) 39
Dombito (tomato) 102
Dominant (cauliflower) 39
Doyenne du Comice (pear) 152
drying herbs/vegetables 114, 127, 133, *see also* individual species
Duke of York (peach) 154
Durondeau (pear) 151
Dutch Yellow (shallot) 92
Dwarf Green Curled (kale) 38
Dwarf Sweet Green (pea) 60

E

Earlibelle (sweet corn) 59
Early Extra Sweet (sweet corn) 59
Early French Frame (carrot) 76
Early Gem (courgette/marrow) 97, 100
Early Laxton (plum) 160
Early Nantes (carrot) 76
Early Prolific (sweet pepper) 96
Early Rivers (cherry) 156
Early Transparent Gage (greengage) 160
Early White Stone (turnip) 86
Easter Egg (Egg Plant) 95
Edwards (plum) 160
eel-worm (pest) 16, 73, 93, 124
Egg Plant, Oriental 95
Egremont Russet (apple) 148
Elruge (nectarine) 154
Emerald Gem (melon) 162
Emneth Early (Early Victoria) (apple) 148
Emperor (calabrese) 36
endive 18, **24**, 28
Enorma (runner bean) 64, 65
espalier trees 146, 149, 153
Express (broad bean) 62
Express Yellow 0-X (onion) 92
Extra Early Kaizuka (onion) 92

F

Fallgold (raspberry) 142
fan-training of trees 150-1, 154-5, 158-65 *passim*
Farleigh Damson 158
Fedora (carrot) 76
Feligreen (broad bean) 62
Feltham First (pea) 60
'Fem' varieties (cucumber) 99
Femspot (cucumber) 99
fenitrothion (pesticide) 61, 149, 152, 157
fennel **123-4**
fennel, Florence 46, **47**
fenugreek sprouts **32**
Fern (strawberry) 144
fertilizer 9-10, 16, *see also* compost; individual plant species; manure
Fiesta (apple) 148
filbert **166-7**
Fine Maraîchré (endive) 24
fish, ornamental 11
Flora Blanca (cauliflower) 39
Florence fennel *see* fennel
fluid seed sowing 15
fly (pest) 41, 53, 69, 76, 78, 81, 93, 105, 107, 117
forcing 21, 22, 23, 54, 56-7
Fordham Giant (Swiss chard) 42
Foremost (potato) 72
Forono (beetroot) 74
Fortress (Brussels sprout) 34
Fragola (grape) 164
frame, the garden 13, 35, 63, 91, 92, 116, 128, 162
freezing,
    fruit and vegetables *see* individual plant species
    fruit and vegetables unsuited 28, 47, 54, 71, 73, 75, 79, 84, 85, 89, 93, 95, 101, 105, 114, 117
    herbs unsuited 122, 129
French Breakfast (radish) 82
Fribor (kale) 38
Frosty (kale) 38
fruits,
    soft **134-45**
    top 16, **146-65**
    use raw 137, 139, 143, 145, 149, 151, 152, 155, 157, 163, 165
fungicides 30, *see also* individual fungicides; individual plant diseases
Fuseau (Jerusalem artichoke) 71

G

Garant (cauliflower) 39
garden beds, raised 16
Gardener's Delight (tomato) 102
garlic 31, 32, 33, 111, 113, **124**
garlic chives *see* chives, Chinese
Gennevilliers Splendid (leek) 90
George Cave (apple) 148
Giant Pink Trench (celery) 52
Giant Red (shallot) 92
Giant Red Trench (celery) 52
Giant (salsify) 84
Giant White Trench (celery) 52
Giant Winter Catalina (leek) 90

Gigante di Romagna (cardoon) 55
Gladiator (turnip) 80
Glaskins Perpetual (rhubarb) 56
glass,
    growing under 12-13, 26, 28, 35, 44, 63, 68, 94, 96,
        99, 102, 103, 163, 164
    see also cloche; frame, garden; greenhouse
Glen Cova (raspberry) 142
Glen Moy (raspberry) 142
Glen Prosen (raspberry) 142
Globus (celeriac) 78
Gold Rush (courgette) 97
Golda (endive) 24
Golden Ball (turnip) 86
Golden Bell (sweet pepper) 96
Golden Delicious (apple) 148
Golden Everest (raspberry) 142
Golden Self-blanching (celery) 52
Golden Sunrise (tomato) 102
Good King Henry **43**
gooseberry 134, **138-9**
Granny Smith (apple) 148
grape 28, **164-5**
Great Lakes (lettuce) 27, 29
Green Bush (marrow) 100
Green Comet (calabrese) 36
Green Curled (endive) 24
Green Globe (globe artichoke) 50
Green Lance (Chinese broccoli) 112
Green Pagoda (Chinese cabbage) 107
Green Rocket (Chinese cabbage) 107
Green in (the) Snow (Chinese mustard) 109
Green Top Stone (turnip) 86
Green Velvet (okra) 68
greenfly (pest) 44, 101, *see also* fly
greengage **160-1**
greenhouse, using 12-13, 55, 59, 63, 68, 94, 95, 98, 99,
        102-03, 104, 116, 120, 128, 162
greens,
    chop suey *see* chop suey greens
    Japanese *see* mizuna
Grover (blueberry) 135
Grumolo Verde (Grumolo chicory) 23

H
Habil (scorzonera) 85
Hamburg Turnip-rooted (Hamburg parsley) 79
hardening seedlings 15, 49, 55, 59, 63, 66, 68-9, 78, 91,
        92, 95, 97, 103
hazel nut (cob nut) **166-7**
Heerma 1 (blueberry) 135
Herbert (blueberry) 135
herbs 16, **118-33**
    drying, *see* individual herb species
    preservation **133**
Heritage (raspberry) 142
Hilde (lettuce) 27
Himalayan Giant (blackberry) 136
Hispi (cabbage) 37
hon tsai tai (pak choi) 117
Honeoye (strawberry) 144
horse-radish **124-5**

Hurst Beagle (pea) 60
Hurst Green Shaft (pea) 60
hygiene, garden 11
Hygro (onion) 91
Hylon (broad bean) 62
Hyper (onion) 91
hyssop **125**

I
Ice Queen (Savoy cabbage) 37
Iceberg (lettuce) 26
Imai Early Yellow (onion) 92
Improved Hollow Crowned (turnip) 80
insecticides 11, 30, 149, 152, 157, 163, *see also*
        individual insecticides and pesticides
insects, scale (pest) 11, 131
intercropping 17
Invicta (gooseberry) 138
Iran (celeriac) 78
Ivory Tower (celery) 52
Ivory White (cardoon) 55

J
Jackpot (pumpkin) 100
James Grieve (apple) 148
January King (cabbage) 37
Japro (pak choi) 116
Jersey (blueberry) 135
Jersey Royal (potato) 72, 73
John Rivers (nectarine) 154
Joi Choi (pak choi) 116
Jos (celeriac) 78
Josephine de Malines (pear) 151
Jubilee (gooseberry) 138
Jubilee Hysor (broad bean) 62
Jupiter (cabbage) 37

K
kale 16, **38-9**
    Chinese *see* broccoli, Chinese
Kasumi (Chinese cabbage) 107
Kelvedon Sweetheart (sweet corn) 59
Kelvedon Wonder (pea) 60
Kentish Cob (filbert) 166
King of Denmark (spinach) 44
King Edward (potato) 72
King Richard (leek) 90
King of the Ridge (cucumber) 98
Kinghorn Wax (French bean) 66
Kirke's Blue (plum) 160
Kirsty (potato) 72
kohlrabi 74, **79**
Kondor (potato) 72
Kwiek (lettuce) 27, 28
Kyoto (cucumber) 98

L
Lakeland (lettuce) 27
Lancashire Lad (gooseberry) 138
Lane's Prince Albert (apple) 148
Lange Jan (scorzonera) 85
Lanro (kohlrabi) 79

Large Fruited Slice-Rite (aubergine) 95
Large-Leaved Italian (corn salad) 20
Largo (French bean) 66
Lathom Self-blanching (celery) 52
Laxton No 1 (red currant) 140
Laxton Superb (apple) 148
leaf vegetables **42-5**
leek 16, **90-1**
Lei-Choi (pak choi) 116
lentil sprouts **32**
Leo (raspberry) 142
lettuce 17, 18, **26-8**
Leveller (gooseberry) 138
Lily White (seakale) 54
lime soil, liming soil 16, 41, 73, 81, 84, 87, 88, 89, 107,
    117
lime sulphur (pesticide) 141
Little Gem (lettuce) 26, 27, 28, 29
Little Marvel (pea) 60
Lobjoits Green (lettuce) 27, 28
Loch Ness (French bean) 66
loganberry **136-7**
Lola (potato) 72
Lolla/Lollo Rossa (lettuce) 26, 27
Long Green (okra) 68
Long Green Trailing (marrow) 100
Long Purple (aubergine) 95
Long Standing Round (spinach) 44
Long White Icicle (radish) 82
Long White Trailing (marrow) 100
Lord Lamborne (apple) 148
Lord Napier (nectarine) 154
Louise Bonne of Jersey (pear) 151
lovage **125-6**
Lucullus (asparagus) 48
Luteus (sweet pepper) 96
LY59 (loganberry) 136
LY654 (loganberry) 136

M
M adeleine Angevin (grape) 164
malathion (pesticide) 29, 53, 78, 81, 95, 101, 103, 105,
    131, 137, 139, 141, 143, 149, 151, 152, 155, 157, 163
Malika (lettuce) 27, 28
Mallard (Brussels sprout) 34, 35
Malling Admiral (raspberry) 142
Malling Jet (black currant) 140
Malling Joy (raspberry) 142
Mammoth (pumpkin) 100
Mammoth Sandwich Island (salsify) 84
Manchester Market (turnip) 86
maneb (fungicide) 73, 103, 141
manure, use 10, 16, *see also* individual plant species
Marble Ball (celeriac) 78
Marfona (potato) 72
Marian (swede) 88
Maris Bard (potato) 72
Maris Piper (potato) 72
marjoram **126-7**, 131
Marjorie's Seedling (plum) 160
Marmande (tomato) 102
Marmer (lettuce) 27

marrow 94, 97, **100-1**
Martha Washington (asparagus) 48
Masterpiece (French bean) 66
May Duke (cherry) 156
May Duke (gooseberry) 138
May Queen (lettuce) 27, 28
Maypole (crab apple) 148
mealybugs (pest) 11
Medana Tayberry 136
Medania (spinach) 44
Mei Quing Choi (pak choi) 116
melon **162-3**
Mercedes (calabrese) 36
Merchant (cherry) 156
Mermat (cherry) 156
Merryweather (damson) 158
Merton Biggareau (cherry) 156
Merton Glory (cherry) 156
Merton Thornless (blackberry) 136
metaldehyde (pesticide) 49
Meteor (pea) 60
methiocarb (pesticide) 49, 101
Michihili (Chinese cabbage) 107
Milan White (turnip) 86
mildew,
    (disease) 26, 29, 101, 138, 139, 140, 141, 144, 145,
        149
    downy (disease) 41, 44, 60, 61, 93, 112, 165
    powdery (disease) 41, 87, 88, 89, 112, 139, 165
Minibel (tomato) 102
Minicole (cabbage) 37
Mino Early (radish) 82
Minowase Summer (radish) 82
mint 99, **127**
mite, red spider (pest) 95, 151, 155,
mitsuba *see* parsley, Japanese
mizuna (Japanese greens) 106, **110-11**, 117
Mokum (carrot) 76
Moneymaker (tomato) 102
Monopoly (beetroot) 75
Mont d'Or (French bean) 66
mooli *see* radish, Japanese
Moorpark (apricot) 150
Morello (cherry) 156
mosaic virus (disease) 26, 29, 44, 101,
    102, 103, 163
Moss Curled (endive) 24
Moss Curled (parsley) 128
moth, (pest) 41, 60, 61, 149
mould,
    grey (botrytis) (disease) 29, 101, 103, 141, 143, 145
    leaf (disease) 102, 103
mulching 11, *see also* individual plant species
Multistar (pea) 60
Munchen Bier (radish) 82
mung bean *see* bean
Musette (lettuce) 26
mushroom 33, 93, **104-5**, 109, 116
mustard 25
    Chinese 106, **109**
    Japanese white celery *see* pak choi
mustard spinach 106

N

Nagaoka (Chinese cabbage) 107
Nandor (carrot) 76
Nantes Tiptop (carrot) 76, 77
nectarine **154-5**
netting 61, 145, 165
New Ace (sweet pepper) 96
New Zealand spinach *see* spinach, New Zealand
Nine Star Perennial (broccoli) 36
Noisette (Brussels sprout) 34
Normato (Witloof chicory) 22
North Holland Blood Red (onion) 92
Norvak (spinach) 44
nuts **166-7**

O

Offenham 1 – Myatts Offenham Compacta (cabbage) 37
Ogen (melon) 162
okra **68-9**
onion 16, 31, 32, 33, 68, 69, 75, 77, **90-3**, 95, 96, 99, 105, 107, 117, 129, 130, 133
    sets 91, 92
    spring and salad 17, 21, 109, 111, 114, 117
Onward (pea) 60, 61
oregano (wild marjoram) 126
Oregon Sugar (pea) 60, 61
Oregon Thornless (blackberry) 136
organic gardening 9-10
Oulin's Golden Gage (greengage) 160
Outdoor Girl (tomato) 102
oyster plant *see* salsify

P

Packham's Triumph (pear) 151
pak choi,
    flowering and flowering purple **117**
    Japanese white celery mustard/Chinese pak choi 106, **116**
Parisian Rondo (carrot) 76
Parmex (carrot) 76
parsley 83, 97, 99, 115, **127-8**, 131
    Hamburg 74, **79**
    Japanese (mitsuba) **115**, 117
parsnip 16, 71, **80-1**, 82, 133
Patriot (blueberry) 135
pea 16, **60-1**, 63
pea sprouts, chick **32**
peach **154-5**, 158
pear **151-3**
Pearson's Prolific (hazel nut) 166
peat pot/block, seed sowing use 15, 63, 66, 68
Peer Gynt (Brussels sprout) 34, 35
pepper, sweet 33, 59, 68, **96**, 109, 127
Peregrine (peach) 154
Perfection (Florence fennel) 47
Perpinex 69 (cucumber) 99
pesticide, organic 11, 49, 53, 73, 101, 107, *see also* individual pesticides
pests,
    control 11
    resistance 7
    see also individual plant pests

Petita (cucumber) 99
pets, birds, and pesticides 49
Pickwick (runner bean) 64
pineapple mint 127
Pineapple (nectarine) 154
Pink Fir Apple (potato) 72
Pissenlit (dandelion) 21
Pixie (cabbage) 37
Pixie (tomato) 102
Pixy (damson) 158, 159
Pixy (plum) 160
Plain-leaved parsley 128
plastic/polythene, garden use 11, 12, 13, 14, 19, 72, 73, 99, 102, 103, 104
plum 158, **160-1**
pods and seeds **58-69**
Polestar (runner bean) 64
Polka (apple) 148
pollination 101, 148, 151, 152, 155, 156, 158, 160
potato 16, 30, 70, **72-3**, 80, 87, 91, 127, 130
pots, garden use 15, *see also* individual species
preservation,
    herbs 119, **133**
    see also drying; freezing
pricking out seed 15
Prince, The (French bean) 66
propagation 139, 141, 143, 145
propagator, the seed 13, 15, 66, 69, 91, 92, 96
Pros Gitana (French bean) 66
pruning 138-9, 140-1, 147, 150-1, **153**, 155, 156-7, 159, 160-1, 165, 167
Prunus dulcis (almond) 167
pumpkin 94, **100-1**
Purple Globe (globe artichoke) 50
Purple Queen (French bean) 66
Purple Top Milan (turnip) 86
Purple Vienna (kohlrabi) 79
Purple-Podded (French bean) 66
pyrethrum (pesticide) 11, *see also* individual plant pests

Q

quintozene (fungicide) 41

R

radicchio (Italian chicory) 18, 22 *see also* chicory
radish 74, **82-3**
    Chinese 74, 82
    Japanese (mooli) 74, 82, 83
radish sprouts **33**
Rampart (Brussels sprout) 34, 35
raspberry 134, 136, **142-3**, 155
recipes,
    apple, baked 149
    apricot dessert 151
    artichoke, stuffed 51
    beouf bourguignon 92, 93, 131
    bortsch 75
    bouquet garni 131, 133
    breakfast cereal 167
    cake, plain 119
    candying 119, 125, 126

cassoulet 68
cheese straws 126
cheesecake 135
chicken with tarragon 132
claret cup 129
coleslaw 37, 38, 77, 84, 107, 149
curry 32
damson cheese 159
fish with fennel 124
fruit, stewed 125, 132, 135, 137
fruit salad 155, 163
gooseberry fool 139
gravlax 123
gumbo 68
horse-radish sauce 125
Italian dishes 127
mint sauce 127
moussaka 95
muesli 33, 167
omelettes 120, 122
pak choi and mushrooms 116
pasta sauce 103, 120
pie 101, 135, 137, 149
plum/greengage dessert 161
potato 122, 127, 128
raspberry pure 143
ratatouille 96, 97
rhubarb crumble 57
rosemary sweet dish 129
sage and onion stuffing 129
salad, *see* individual fruits, herbs, and vegetables
sauce 120, 123, 125, 127, 129, 139
sorrel pure 130
soup 19, 25, 28, 32, 33, 53, 71, 77, 78, 87, 91, 99, 105, 109, 120, 121, 126, 130, 133
sponge, Victoria 121
stir-fry *see* individual herbs and vegetables
strawberry fool 145
summer pudding 141
tarragon vinegar 132
Red Alert (tomato) 102
Red Filbert 166
Red Knight (runner bean) 64
Red Lake (red currant) 140, 141
Red Salad Bowl (lettuce) 27
Red Treviso (chicory) 22
Red Verona (chicory) 22
Redhaven (peach) 154
Redskin (sweet pepper) 96
Redsleeves (apple) 148
Regala (beetroot) 75
Remontant (strawberry) 142
reversion disease 141
Revlon (broad bean) 62
rhubarb 16, 46, **56-7**, 119
rhubarb chard *see* chard
Ribella (radish) 82
Riccia Panacalieri (endive) 24
Rijnsburger (onion) 91-2
Rivers' Early Prolific (plum) 160
Rochester (peach) 154

Roger (Brussels sprout) 34, 35
Romanesco (calabrese) 36
Romano (potato) 72
Romeo (melon) 162
Ronaclave (tomato) 102
roots 16, **74-89**
    disease 69
rosemary 118, **128-9**
rot (disease) 49, 57, 77, 89, 93, 124
rotation of crops 16, 41, 107, 112, 117
Rowel (kohlrabi) 79
Royal Sovereign (strawberry) 144
Ruby Ball (cabbage) 37
ruby chard *see* chard
Russian Giant (scorzonera) 85
rust (disease) 11, 127
rye sprouts **33**

S

sage **129**
Salad Bowl (lettuce) 27
salad burnet **129**
salad plants 16, 17, **18-29**
Saladin (lettuce) 27
salsify (vegetable oyster/oyster plant) 16, 84
Sandwich Island (salsify) **84**
savory **130**
sawfly (pest) 149
Saxerre Robino (radish) 82
scab (disease) 73, 149, 152
Scallopini (squash) 100
Scarlet Globe (radish) 82
Scarlet Intermediate (carrot) 76
scorzonera 16, 74, **85**
seakale **54**
seakale beet *see* chard, Swiss
seed, seed sowing 15, 17, *see also* individual species
seed sprouts, sprouting techniques 31
seeds and pods **58-69**
Selva (strawberry) 144
Senator (pea) 60
Senshyu Semi-Globe Yellow (onion) 92
September (raspberry) 142
shallot **92**
Shirley (tomato) 102
Shogun (calabrese) 36
shoots and stalks **46-57**
Short Tom (aubergine) 95
Shropshire (Prune) Damson 158
shungiku *see* chop suey greens
Sigmaleaf (spinach) 44
silver leaf (disease) 157
Silver Skinned (Jerusalem artichoke) 71
Sirio (fennel, Florence) 47
Sleaford Abundance (tomato) 102
slugs,
    bait/pellets (pesticide) 29, 42, 49, 51, 53, 73, 99, 107, 117, 145
    pest 29, 42, 49, 51, 53, 73, 100, 101, 107, 117, 145
Smoothstem (blackberry) 136
snail (pest) 29, 49, 51, 53
Snow White (celeriac) 78

Snowball (cauliflower) 39
Snowball/Early Snowball (turnip) 86
soap solutions (pesticide) 11, 29, 41, 44, 95, 101, 103,
    112, 114, 119, 120, 131, 139, 141, 143, 145, 149, 151,
    152, 155, 157, 163
soda solution, washing (fungicide) 139, 141
soil(s) 8-11
Soraya (lettuce) 27
sorrel **130**
Southport Red Globe (onion) 92
soya bean *see* bean
Spartan (apple) 148
spearmint **127**
spinach 16, 42, **44**
    beet (perpetual spinach) 42, **45**
    mustard *see* broccoli, Chinese
    New Zealand 42, **45**
Spirit (pumpkin) 100
Spitfire (cabbage) 37
Spivoy (cabbage) 37
spot (disease) 41, 53, 69, 141, 143
Spring Hero (cabbage) 37
sprouting seeds **30-3**
squash 94, **100-1**
St Julien (damson) 158
St Julien (plum) 160
St Valery (carrot) 76
stalks and shoots **46-57**
Stanza (red currant) 140, 141
Stella (cherry) 156
Stonehead (cabbage) 37
straw, garden use 19, 20, 45, 50, 83
strawberry 134, 142, **144-5**
Sturon (onion) 92
Stuttgarter Giant (onion) 92
Sugar Ann (pea) 60
Sugar Snap (pea) 60, 61
sulphur powder (fungicide) 165
Sunburst (cherry) 156
Sunburst (squash) 100
Sundance (sweet corn) 59
sunflower sprouts **33**
Sunrise (sweet corn) 59
Sutton, The (broad bean) 62
swede 16, **88-9**
Sweet 77 (sweet corn) 59
sweet cicely **132**
sweet corn *see* corn
Sweetheart (melon) 162
Swiss chard *see* chard

T
Table Ace (squash) 100
Table Dainty (marrow) 100
Takinogawa Long (burdock) 108
Tall Green Curled (kale) 38
Tantallon (strawberry) 144
tar-oil wash (pesticide) 157
tarragon **132**
Tayberry 136, 137
Telegraph (cucumber) 98
Telegraph Improved (cucumber) 98

Tellus (celeriac) 78
Tender and True (turnip) 80
Tendergreen (French bean) 66
Tendergreen (mustard, Chinese) 109
thiram (fungicide) 41, 53
Thornfree (blackberry) 136
thrips (pest) 61
thyme 97, 105, 131, **132-3**
Timperley (rhubarb) 56
Tiny Tim (tomato) 102
Tip Top (Chinese cabbage) 107
tipburn 27
Tokyo Cross (turnip) 86
Tokyo Slicer (cucumber) 98
Tom Thumb (lettuce) 27
tomato 28, 30, 32, 33, 69, 75, 94, 95, 96, **102-3**, 113,
    115, 119, 120, 122, 127
Totem (tomato) 102
Tours (cardoon) 55
trace elements/minerals in soil 8, 16, 44
transplanting 17, *see also* individual species
trays, seed 12, 13, 68, 78
trenches, celery 52
Tribute (strawberry) 144
Tristar (pea) 60
Tristar (strawberry) 144
triticale sprouts **33**
Troika (Brussels sprout) 34
Troubadour (strawberry) 144
tubers **70-3**
tubs, garden use 14
turnip 16, **86-7**, 109
Tydeman's Late Orange (apple) 148

U
Vanessa (potato) 72
Variegated Chioggia (chicory) 22
vegetable fruits **94-105**
Vegetable spaghetti (squash) 100
vegetables,
    Oriental 7, 16, 17, **106-17**
    use raw 18, *see also* individual species
Vert de Cambrai (corn salad) 20
Vert de Laon (globe artichoke) 50
Victora (rhubarb) 56
Victoria (plum) 160
virus diseases 29, 41, 103, 138, 139, 142, 143, 144, 145,
    156

W
Walcheren Winter (cauliflower) 40
Waltz (apple) 148
wasp,
    parasitic (pest control) 101, 103, 163
    (pest) 165
Watanabe (burdock) 108
watercress 18, **25**, 28
watering 14, *see also* individual plant species
Waverex (pea) 60
Webbs Wonderful (lettuce) 27
weeding, weeds 10, 16, 17, *see also* individual plant
    species

Index

Western Perfection (swede) 88
Westland Autumn (kale) 38
wheat sprouts **33**
Whinhams Industry (gooseberry) 138
White Bush (marrow) 100
White Gem (turnip) 80
White Grape (white currant) 140
White Lisbon (onion, spring) 93
white mustard **25**
White Versailles (white currant) 140
White Vienna (kohlrabi) 79
whitefly (pest) 11, 101, 103, 163, *see also* fly
Whitesmith (gooseberry) 138
Widgeon (Brussels sprout) 34
Wiltja (potato) 72
window-box, planting 14
Winter Density (lettuce) 27, 28
Winter Nellis (pear) 152
wire stem (disease) 41

wireworm (pest) 73
Wirosa (Savoy cabbage) 37
Wong Bok (Chinese cabbage) 107
Worcester Pearmain (apple) 148

Y
Yellow Antwerp (raspberry) 142
Yellow Bell (sweet pepper) 96
Yellow Long Keeping (shallot) 92
Yellow Perfection (tomato) 102

Z
Zefa Fino (Florence fennel) 47
Zeva (raspberry) 142
zineb (fungicide) 29, 41, 44, 61, 69, 73, 93, 103, 112, 141
Zoom (chicory) 22
Zucchini (courgette) 97

ACKNOWLEDGEMENTS

Editorial
Editorial Director
Andrew Duncan
Editors
Stella Maidment, Laura Harper, Fiona Hardwick
Editorial assistance and index
Rosemary Dawe

Design
Art Director
Mel Petersen
Design Assistants
Beverley Stewart, Rozelle Bentheim
Line drawings
Will Giles, Sandra Pond
Photographs
Harry Smith Horticultural Photographic collection